Florida A&M University, Tallahassee
Florida Atlantic University, Boca Raton
Florida Gulf Coast University, Ft. Myers
Florida International University, Miami
Florida State University, Tallahassee
University of Central Florida, Orlando
University of Florida, Gainesville
University of North Florida, Jacksonville
University of South Florida, Tampa
University of West Florida, Pensacola

Public Benefits
of Archaeology

Edited by Barbara J. Little

University Press of Florida
Gainesville · Tallahassee · Tampa · Boca Raton
Pensacola · Orlando · Miami · Jacksonville · Ft. Myers

First cloth printing, 2002
First paperback printing, 2005

Library of Congress Cataloging-in-Publication Data
Public benefits of archaeology / edited by Barbara J. Little.
p. cm.
Includes bibliographical references and index.
ISBN 0-8130-2455-2 (cloth); ISBN 0-8130-2921-X (pbk.)
1. Archaeology and history—United States. 2. Archaeology—Social aspects—
United States. 3. Public history—United States. 4. Community life—United
States. 5. United States—Antiquities—Collection and preservation. 6. His-
toric sites—Conservation and restoration—United States. I. Little, Barbara J.
CC77.H5 P83   2002
973—dc21   2001043730

The University Press of Florida is the scholarly publishing agency for the
State University System of Florida, comprising Florida A&M University,
Florida Atlantic University, Florida Gulf Coast University, Florida Interna-
tional University, Florida State University, University of Central Florida,
University of Florida, University of North Florida, University of South Flor-
ida, and University of West Florida.

University Press of Florida
15 Northwest 15th Street
Gainesville, FL 32611–2079
http://www.upf.com

This volume is dedicated to every reader who has ever thought about the past or visited an archaeological site or museum and has been changed by that experience of touching another time and place.

The spirit and direction of the Nation are founded upon and reflected in its historic heritage; . . . the historical and cultural foundations of the Nation should be preserved as a living part of our community life and development in order to give a sense of orientation to the American people.

National Historic Preservation Act

(16 U.S.C. 470 et seq.)

Contents

Figures and Tables

Foreword

The Value of Archaeology

My subject is the relationship of archaeologists to the work of knitting together the American community and enlarging America's sense of its own continuities.

Archaeologists speak for the silent people. They take objects that in themselves would be mute and permit these objects to have voices. Their particular gift is linking the craftsmanship, the focused caring, and the experience of the past to the present. That is done in archaeology because it is grounded in the specific object and in the particular place. In this way archaeologists can make it possible for those who have no tongues to become articulate for and to us and to our descendants. This is serious business.

All this can be done, and it is being done by some but not all archaeologists. It is not yet a convention of the profession to assume public discourse to be an essential aspect of the work. This is not strange. Archaeologists, like curators, are very "thingy" people. They have highly developed fingertips. Some have good noses, too, but it's the fingertips that matter. In general, thingy people frequently have difficulty in relating one thing to another thing in a narrative style. They—we—like touching things. We don't mind holding something up and showing it to others, to tell where we got it, to offer hypotheses as to who made it, and even why, but we less easily include in our discourse two objects—two paintings, two pots, two shards. Narration begins with juxtaposition, and we do not find it easy to extend our gaze to very many objects at once. Yet because many archaeologists have their bases in museums, they have been learning from their colleagues how crucial to their role as citizens it is to make the shift from the curatorial to the narrative.

In the museum world, for a generation curators have felt emboldened to press beyond custody and description toward narration, commencing with the juxtaposition of objects in telling ways upon walls. This has offended some critics, who discourse ponderously and snobbishly about connoisseurship and wish ordinary mortals would go away, but the process has become irreversible.

Archaeologists have had a more difficult transition toward narrative. Their most powerful teaching tools are composites of objects in place. The sites that make sense of their work are not portable. They cannot be racked up on the walls of museums. Specificity of place is at once the burden and the glory of archaeology. Fortunately, there is no mystery in this to another set of persons with whom archaeologists frequently work—park personnel. The significance of place is the core of their work, too, especially in the case of the National Park Service. Its people, like curators and archaeologists, are drawn to their work not so much by theoretical or general enthusiasms but by the specific. They too have had to exert themselves to move beyond analysis and description of the places in their care toward narratives uniting many places in larger patterns.

The significance of any one place—how it feels, how it smells—the specific causes of its present condition, and the signs of its changing toward something else—is often almost as mute as an object in isolation. To be fully understood, the place must be linked to other places in narrative form.

There are few experiences more delightful than being at a dig with an archaeologist working there and participating in the process. When that participation is wholehearted, the observer becomes a part of the observed. That is, I think, the magic of archaeology.

That magic does not transmit readily, however. Its glow declines like the light of a lamp running out of kerosene—remember those?—when reduced to writing. The problem is that "thinginess" is not magical. Narration is magical. Precise description is not. I have often enjoyed the thought of Victor Borge reading an article from the average archaeological journal, with a *bloop* for each parenthesis. Furthermore, there is a remarkable disposition on the part of many archaeologists to write about other archaeologists rather than about archaeology. Historians do that too much as well, but they have a grand narrative tradition to shame them away from too much back-fence gossip.

It has been my experience that field archaeologists are more often than not friendly people. Non-archaeologists—even historians—are often made welcome on sites by people working there. This is a good lesson for the profession as a whole. As curators have learned to link objects in museums, and the park services—state and national—have learned to link their sites by "themes," these professions have not abandoned their roots. They have built upon the specific toward the general, extending an invitation to non-specialists to join in their own delights. In the National Park Service the story begins with the place and proceeds to examine how humans have affected that place and have been affected by it. Biologists have helped us learn that ecosystems can be watersheds for human experience as well as for water. There are equivalent lessons to be gained from archaeologists.

I do not suggest less rigor but, instead, more effort. Rigor is sometimes taken to mean narrowness, but that is a pernicious notion. Effort in enlarging the audience of informed and conscientious citizens is required now more than at any previous time because the pressure of human population is engulfing and destroying the evidence of the human and prehuman past. Archaeology has an immense opportunity to inform us in the gritty, specific ways that are most compelling to people deadened by too much diffuse and lazy discourse.

The occasion is upon us to educate through objects connected by narrative. Otherwise we will have failed in our role as custodians, as curators, as park servants, as archaeologists, and as citizens. To reiterate: archaeologists are the people who make it possible for those who have no tongues to speak to us and to our descendants. This is serious business.

Roger G. Kennedy
Director, National Park Service, 1993–1997

Acknowledgments

This book was originally conceived at the "Public Benefits of Archaeology" conference held in Santa Fe, New Mexico, November 5–8, 1995, to discuss the value of archaeology to the broader public. More than 150 participants exchanged innovative and exciting ideas and made the conference a success. Sponsors of the conference were the Department of Interior, National Park Service (National Register of Historic Places, Archeology and Ethnography Program, Southwest System Support Office, Pecos National Historical Park); Society for American Archaeology; Society for Historical Archaeology; National Conference of State Historic Preservation Officers; National Trust for Historic Preservation; New Mexico State Historic Preservation Office; National Association of State Archaeologists; and Advisory Council on Historic Preservation.

An immediate follow-up to the conference was a brochure entitled *25 Simple Things You Can Do to Promote the Public Benefits of Archaeology*. Many of the action items printed in the brochure came from the concluding discussion at the conference. The brochure was produced by the National Register, the Society for Historical Archaeology, and the Society for American Archaeology under a cooperative agreement with the National Conference of State Historic Preservation Officers. It is available from the National Park Service, National Register of Historic Places, and on the Internet at <http://www.cr.nps.gov/nr/publications/bulletins/archaeol.htm>.

The conference was organized by the National Park Service (NPS) through the office of the National Register of Historic Places with assistance from several of the cosponsors. It was the brainchild of National Register archaeologist Jan Townsend, who later joined the Bureau of Land Management, and Carol Shull, keeper of the National Register. They and Frank McManamon, chief of the NPS Archeology and Ethnography Program, and Donna Seifert and John Sprinkle, both serving short-term appointments as archaeologists for the National Register, organized the structure of the conference and identified many of the speakers.

Thanks are due to those who presented papers and acted as moderators and to all those who came to listen and contribute through discussion. Roger Kennedy, then NPS director, gave an inspiring keynote address on the value of archaeology. New Mexico's Senator Jeff Bingaman kindly sent a representative to address the gathering. In addition to those represented in this volume, excellent presentations were given by Ricky Lightfoot of the Crow Canyon Archaeological Center; William Whatley and Lieutenant Governor Vincent Toya of the Pueblo of Jemez; Mark Michel, president of the Archaeological Conservancy; Senator Bingaman's representative, Ricardo Zuniga; Robert Bush, former executive director of the Advisory Council on Historic Preservation; and Hester Davis of the Arkansas Archeological Survey.

Participants enjoyed a visit to Pecos National Historical Park, guided by Judy Reed, Ann Rasor, John Loleit, and Courtney White, and a tour of the collections at the Museum of Indian Arts and Culture arranged by Sarah Schlanger.

Special thanks are extended to those who acted as moderators for sessions focused on particular audiences or "users" of archaeology: Sarah Schlanger, acting assistant director of the Laboratory of Archaeology at the Museum of Indian Arts and Culture (moderating the session on visitors to sites and museums); George Smith of the Southeast Archeological Center, NPS (teachers and students); Eric Blinman, assistant director of the Museum of New Mexico's Office of Archaeological Studies (Native Americans); Francis McManamon, NPS chief archaeologist (local communities and identity); Brona Simon, then president of the National Association of State Archaeologists (community planners and decision makers); Donna Seifert, then president of the Society for Historical Archaeology (avocational archaeologists); William Lipe, then president of the Society for American Archaeology (sciences and humanities); Carol Shull, keeper of the National Register of Historic Places, NPS (heritage tourism); Donald Craib, manager of government affairs and counsel for the Society for American Archaeology (political leaders); and William Rathje, director of the Garbage Project (getting the word out). William Lipe, Donna Seifert, Francis McManamon, and Robert Bush directed the closing discussion.

Appreciation goes also to those who agreed to contribute to the volume although they were not formal speakers at the conference. Their work has added greatly to the scope of the work.

I am grateful to Mark Warner and Paul Mullins for their helpful comments and suggestions. As always, I thank Paul Shackel for his support and good ideas.

For further information on archaeology and public outreach, contact the Departmental Consulting Archeologist, NPS Archeology and Ethnography Program, 1849 C Street NW, Room NC310, Washington, D.C. 20240, <www.cr.nps.gov>; the Society for American Archaeology <www.saa.org>; or the Society for Historical Archaeology <www.sha.org>. Royalties from the sale of this volume are contributed to the Public Education Endowment fund of the Society for American Archaeology.

Thanks as well to Carol Shull, Francis McManamon, and Jerry Buckbinder at the National Park Service for helping to make sure this book got off the ground. I would especially like to thank the good people at the University Press of Florida, Meredith Morris-Babb and Judy Goffman, for their cheerful efficiency and professionalism, and our copyeditor, Sally Antrobus, and indexer, Lynda Stannard. It has been a pleasure.

I

Finding Common Ground

p. 2 is blank

Archaeology as a Shared Vision

Barbara J. Little

Why do archaeology? That simple question can render an archaeologist speechless, not because there is no answer but because there are many valid answers. One straightforward response is that we do archaeology—and spend public money on it—because archaeology provides benefits not only for professional archaeological research but also for the many participants and publics who use and value it.

While the research values of archaeology are not the focus of this book, those values underlie and support the greater public benefits. Research values support the authenticity that is basic to public benefits (Lipe, this volume). The complexity of the research process, however, may be lost in translation. Discussing the controversial Kennewick case, David Hurst Thomas (2000:xxxviii) points to the power of the media to refocus and sensationalize research results, sometimes with unfortunate and unintended effects. There is no question that archaeologists need to do a better job at identifying and communicating the public benefits of archaeology. One aim of this book is to invite more dialogue among archaeologists and the many publics interested in the field.

The authors of this book illustrate some of the public benefits that extend beyond archaeological research, using sites and artifacts for such purposes as education, community cohesion, entertainment, and economic development. Archaeological research finds its way into textbooks, trade books, other sciences and humanities, museum exhibits, site tours, television shows, magazines, computer games, Internet sites, and school curricula.

The purpose of this volume is to illustrate, promote, and enhance the public benefits of archaeology. Involvement of a diverse and committed public is one important theme. A substantial percentage of the authors consists of people from outside the discipline, and fewer than a third write from academic institutions. Readers will find a variety of writing styles conveying a range of viewpoints. Even such a variety of authors can only begin to suggest the complexity and variety of the intersection between archaeology and the public.

Archaeologists have long suspected a widespread interest and support among the American public for their work. A national telephone survey by Harris Interactive in the summer of 1999 provided data to support that suspicion. The report summarizes the knowledge that Americans have about archaeology and archaeological sites (Ramos and Duganne 2000). In general, Americans believe that archaeology is important and is valuable and are interested in learning about the past. They believe that archaeology is important because we improve the future by learning about the past and because archaeology helps us understand the modern world. Almost all Americans believe that archaeological objects and sites have educational value. The majority view is that archaeological objects and sites also have aesthetic or artistic value, express personal heritage, and have spiritual value. The research shows that the majority of the public believes that there are and should be laws to protect archaeological resources regardless of where they are found.

Asking the question "What are the public benefits of archaeology?" invites further questions. What are the public benefits of heritage, knowledge of the past, inquiries into the human condition? How do we, here and now, fit into the expansive course of history? These are not questions only relevant in a remote Ivory Tower; they are questions for each of us. These are questions for citizens to address in pondering their relationship with the land and the insights it contains.

Author Jean Auel (1991) sees the value of archaeology in defining our common humanity as defined by compassion, curiosity, art, and invention. She is convinced that ancient lifeways, relevant to all people around the globe, can convince us of our common needs and desires. Indeed, communities all over the country have found that archaeology can bring them together by providing a sense of continuity (see McManamon 1991 and this volume). This benefit of archaeological sites—and of buildings and other historic resources—is partly due to "the universal role that the material culture environment plays in providing cultural continuity and perspective, and hence in linking past, present and future within the experience of any given human generation" (Lipe 1984:2).

The question of "who owns the past" has been raised time and again in the context of the modern preservation movement. Some dismiss this question as a paradox that cannot be resolved (e.g., Chamberlin 1979). Others are far more emphatic in affirming that the past belongs to everyone (see Fagan, this volume). The United Nations Educational, Scientific and Cultural Organization, for example, is clear that civilization is made up of contributions from all peoples and that all humanity shares a common heritage (UNESCO 1970). Federico Mayor, former director general of UNESCO, wrote in 1989: "One of the most recent concepts to emerge in our time [is] that of the cultural heritage of mankind as a whole: through its realization that it shares a common destiny, mankind is finding out that it has a shared past, and the history of each country belongs to everyone" (quoted in Timken 1993:93). Lowenthal (1981:236) writes that "the past belongs to everyone: the need to return home, to recall the view, to refresh a memory, to retrace a heritage, is universal and essential." Ernestene Green (1984:270) acknowledges that "archaeologists have become used to the idea that archaeological resources on public lands belong to all Americans and are held in public trust."

Explicitly discussing the public trust, Ruthann Knudson and Bennie Keel (1995) write that the common history of a nation is recognized as the common property of the group. Archaeology contributes to the "grand enterprise of creating knowledge about the undeniable common thread of our humanness" (Keel 1995:8). They also recognize, however, that there is some opposition by native peoples to archaeology, in spite of the belief common among archaeologists that their discipline truly is in the public interest.

It is part of the ethical code of professional archaeologists that the past belongs to everyone, but ethics and values often differ between tribes and professional archaeologists (Society for American Archaeology 1996). If the past indeed belongs to everyone, it is also true that not all parts of the past may be freely shared. The Zuni in New Mexico, for example, wish to guard religious information (Ferguson 1984; see Swidler et al. 1997). There is a classic conflict between the "archaeological ethic of freedom of inquiry into all categories of data without hindrance and the Native American ethics that remains of Indian culture belong to Indians, that it is tribal prerogative to decide what investigations are undertaken on tribal land, and that certain classes of objects are so sacred that their study would diminish their religious power" (Adams 1984:236). Many tribes, of course, have a great interest in archaeology and support their own archaeology programs (Echo-Hawk 1993; Swidler et al. 1997; Dongoske et al. 2000; Kuwanwisiwma, this volume).

Archaeologists and indigenous groups are likely to have quite different interests in the events of the past, but there is universal concern for the past (Layton 1994). Mark Leone and Robert Preucel (1992:132) recognize multiple interests in the past, joining many archaeologists in their call for more dialogue: "making the past belongs not to scientists, nor to specific ethnic groups, but to all of us by virtue of our common humanity. However, we do not hold with the hyperrelativist view that all positions are equally valid, but rather we argue that all positions deserve a voice in the context of arriving at archaeological conclusions. Archaeologists have rarely, if ever, seriously asked what are Native Americans' views of their past. The active engagement of such groups, not their exclusion, may be an effective strategy for democratizing the past."

Alison Wylie (1994:10) writes of the dual capacity of archaeology to "incorporate and reproduce racist, nationalist, and other agendas, *and* its democratising power, its capacity to counter 'mythologies' . . . and to support decisive critical reexamination of the assumptions that both inform and are promoted by these agendas." With such capacities, archaeology is profoundly political, and archaeologists have responsibility to other scholars and to the public interested in what archaeologists sometimes consider their own material (Wylie 1994:13). There are many interested publics besides Native Americans, but Native Americans and the archaeologists who study their past have an inescapable and problematic relationship (Swidler et al. 1997).

The use and abuse of science is a long and disturbing story. Scientific racism has left a bitter legacy. As Thomas Crist (this volume) explains, the major source of conflict between archaeologists and Native Americans is the treatment of Native American human remains. In his recent *Skull Wars: Kennewick Man, Archaeology, and the Battle for Native American Identity*, Thomas (2000) describes the history of that conflict. The ongoing tension between archaeology and the people whose past is studied concerns the ownership of the past and the worldwide issue of intellectual property rights (see also Kuwanwisiwma, this volume). Thomas is tentatively hopeful for the future (2000:260): "Once the fundamental dilemma has been defined—that archaeologists no longer exercise sole control over the ancient American past—perhaps the two sides will be freed to form new partnerships and build new bridges."

The poet Gary Snyder has written that for Americans, the "real work" is becoming native to North America. He means that each of us "non-native" Americans must accept citizenship in the continent and come to understand that our loyalties are to the place where we live (Moyers 1995:66). Without an embracing of a common history of the land, it is difficult to imagine resolving the uneasiness of a diverse immigrant nation cohabiting with impoverished indigenous nations. Archaeology is one of the paths that can help us find our way to the elusive connections between all Americans and America.

Many Publics, Many Benefits

There is no single public and no single past. "If we are to develop a new understanding of the past, one that appreciates the complexity of its messages, then we must recognize and learn to deal with a public that is equally diverse" (Molyneaux 1994:6). Members of the public are increasingly aware of the benefits of archaeology, and they are actively involved in guarding those benefits. The many publics who value and use archaeology do so in many ways. Archaeologists and non-archaeologists have entered into a dialogue about respecting all of the varied values of the archaeological heritage.

There is a further tension between national and local heritage. National heritage building tends to lean toward more homogeneous versions of heritage. Celebrations of local identity, on the other hand, often instigated by tourism concerns, tend toward creating heterogeneous heritage (see Molyneaux 1994; Tunbridge and Ashworth 1996). In considering the relationship between their discipline and nationalism, some archaeologists are quite hopeful that a critical self-awareness can make archaeology a positive force (e.g., Atkinson et al. 1996; Bond and Gilliam 1994; Kohl and Fawcett 1995; Rowlands 1994). Brian Molyneaux (1994:12) is confident of the goodwill of archaeologists, writing that a goal of the contributors to *The Presented Past*—and, by extension, of other archaeologists working to promote the public benefits of archaeology—is "to achieve a greater measure of social justice in the study of the past in their own countries and situations. They are all motivated by the belief that, if there is going to be a shared vision of the future, there must be a recognition of the multiple pasts that have determined the present in which we stand."

Archaeologists need to be aware of the social and political roles of their discipline if archaeology is truly to be of benefit to the public. Archaeology can empower local groups by supporting local identities and cultural heritage, but it can also fuel ethnic nationalism and distort the past to serve dangerous political goals (e.g., Molyneaux 1994; Rowlands 1994; Wylie 1994). Michael Rowlands (1994) cautions that the promotion of local identity and "heritage" may divert engagement from national politics, thereby effectively omitting local communities from broader political dialogue. Molyneaux (1994:9) notes that "this problem, that the past is an essential, but dangerous, social need, is a conundrum" and suggests that the challenge is to make people aware of and respectful of the past but not so burdened by it that they cannot adapt to changing conditions.

Communities of many types find that archaeology benefits them in various ways. Francis McManamon (this volume) highlights two types of benefits: those heritage benefits that derive from connections with people in the past; and those research or "history" benefits that derive from archaeological study in the present. Sharing his personal perspective as the Hopi tribal preservation officer, Leigh Kuwanwisiwma (this volume) emphasizes the need for true collaboration between living descendants and archaeologists. Adrian Praetzellis (this volume) describes some of the practical public benefits to the Chinese-American community in Sacramento and the African-American community in Oakland. Crist (this volume) addresses benefits accruing to African-American communities in New York and Philadelphia.

In addition to a large public avidly interested in knowing about archaeological research, there is a large and active avocational community. People who make a living in a wide range of professions find that archaeology offers a satisfying avocation or even a second career. The rewards of patient, often painstaking, sometimes difficult work include the satisfaction of making real contributions to our understanding of the past, the thrill of discovery, and the joy of learning new skills. Lynn Harris (this volume) describes innovative cooperation between sports divers and professional archaeologists in South Carolina, South Africa, and Namibia.

Earthwatch, Elderhostel, Crow Canyon, the Center for American Archaeology, and formal field schools through colleges and universities provide some of the growing opportunities for individuals to participate in archaeology. The Boy Scouts of America recently introduced an Archaeology Merit Badge with carefully designed requirements, and the Girl Scouts are incorporating archaeology into the specifications for several of their badges. Federal agencies such as the National Park Service, the Bureau of Land Management, and the United States Forest Service also offer opportunities. Many participants in such programs find themselves "bitten by the archaeology bug." They join the avocational societies in their state and become active contributors to research.

The Forest Service has run the popular Passport in Time (PIT) project since 1991 as part of its Windows on the Past initiative. An average of 2,000 volunteers a year work with archaeologists and historians on such things as excavating archaeological sites, recording oral history, and restoring historic structures (USDA-USFS 1995).

In addition to serving local communities through research and promotion of heritage, and in addition to engaging a large and dedicated avocational community, archaeology also serves other disciplines. Archaeology is truly an interdisciplinary science. It has borrowed from every scientific and humanistic discipline. Physics has given us radiocarbon dating; botany and zoology allow us to analyze past environments and the use of plants and animals; cultural anthropology leads us to living societies to help interpret past cultures; history offers us to the rich documentation of the recent past. The list could go on and on: geology, soil science, art history, geography, materials science, engineering, astronomy. From the perspective of a historian, James Whittenburg (this volume) describes the contribution of archaeology in changing the way historians think about early English life in the Chesapeake colonies. It is not surprising that the tools of archaeology are expansive; after all, it is the whole of human history that archaeologists study.

Similarly, archaeology can contribute to nearly every discipline from which it borrows. For example, archaeology reveals information on environmental stability and change. People have contributed to the success and failure of ecosystems for thousands of years, and they have coped with varying degrees of success. In coping with current environmental trends, archaeology can help in surprising ways. William Rathje (this volume) demonstrates the importance of "garbology," which has made direct contributions to solid waste management and environmental policy.

Archaeology provides important perspectives for other branches of anthropology, including physical anthropology, and forensic anthropologists are trained on excavations. Archaeology has also been of service to law enforcement agencies, particularly in the exacting investigation of crime scenes and the identification of illicit burials. Thomas Crist (this volume) demonstrates the relevance of skeletal analysis to current events, from the prosecution of war crimes to the fight against racism. Crist promotes the excavation of historic cemeteries as a tool to educate people about science and to dispel racist ideas based on misunderstandings of biology.

Learning from an Authentic Past

Anyone reading the literature on public archaeology will find that much of archaeologists' interest in public outreach stems from the need to protect and preserve archaeological resources. Site preservation was not always a widespread concern. However, rapidly increasing threats to sites have caught the attention of both the profession and the public. Archaeologists have come to recognize their responsibilities to the record of human heritage and, importantly, to the peoples whose heritage is chronicled in archaeological sites (Vitella 1996).

It should not be surprising, therefore, that the benefits of preserving sites often are couched in terms of benefit to archaeology through the creation of a public interested in and supportive of archaeology (e.g., Binks et al. 1988; Davis 1989, 1991). Preserving sites is essential if we are to preserve the public benefits of archaeology. George Smith and John Ehrenhard (this volume) recognize the remains of the past not only as our national patrimony but also as humanity's lifeline.

The issue of authenticity surfaces many times in the chapters of this volume. Authenticity certainly requires the preservation of places and objects. It also requires appreciating a great diversity and complexity in the past. If we are fortunate, such appreciation translates into a better understanding and celebration of diversity today.

We are familiar with the common statement that we can learn from the past to improve the future. In the Harris Interactive survey of public perceptions of archaeology in the United States, respondents answered the question "How important do you feel archaeology is in today's society?" Ramos and Duganne (2000), in analyzing the response, generalize that the public's view about the importance of archaeology is influenced by interest in the past and seeing the value of archaeology as learning about the past to improve the future.

Whether learning about the past takes place at historic places or in the classroom, one of the pervasive ironies of our time is that we insist on editing our understanding of the past, often focusing nearly exclusively on what is judged good or patriotically appropriate (see Metcalf, this volume).

But, indeed, how can we expect to learn from the past if we don't see it complete with mistakes and disgraces as well as actions we judge as heroic?

Thomas (this volume) observes that museums, in common with archaeology, retain great public appeal because they offer authenticity. Things that can be trusted as real are highly valued, particularly in a cynical world. Esther White (this volume) describes the experience of integrating archaeology into the programs at Mount Vernon. Archaeology enhances the visitor experience and makes historic house museums even more compelling destinations than they already are.

In a broad view of museums, surely national parks are some of our most visited national museums. Visitors to many national parks see the results of archaeology. Parks in the Southwest, such as Mesa Verde and Chaco Canyon, come to mind most readily because the spectacular ruins have been well publicized, but nearly all parks have archaeological resources. Often the archaeology is less visible than at the two parks mentioned but is nevertheless fundamental to the park's purpose. Reconstructions based on archaeological research are centerpieces at several national parks. Some of these are Saugus Iron Works in Massachusetts, Fort Stanwix in New York, Grand Portage in Minnesota, the Outer Line Cabins at Valley Forge in Pennsylvania, Bent's Old Fort in Colorado, Fort Union Trading Post in North Dakota, Arkansas Post in Arkansas, and parts of Fort Larned and Fort Scott in Kansas.

Many parks offer a variety of ways for visitors to learn about archaeology: tours, pamphlets, interpretive trails and roadside displays, films, and book sales in the visitor center. In most national parks archaeologists are not directly involved with the public but provide essential information to the interpretive staff, who then convey it to visitors. Less frequently, visitors see actual excavation in progress and get to talk to archaeologists. Paul Shackel (this volume) underscores that it is crucial to share with visitors the intellectual content of archaeological interpretations rather than simply the mechanics of excavation. He argues for making national presentations about the past more inclusive by telling stories about all classes and all time periods.

One of the public benefits of archaeology is the same as that of history and science: an educated citizenry. Understanding, or at least awareness, of the methodological and theoretical tools that are used to make interpretations equips people to think critically and to make judgments about the information with which we are bombarded every day. Because stories about the past are used for many purposes—both noble and nefarious—citizens must be in a position to judge those stories for themselves. Learning the methods, logic, important questions, and some of the results of scientific inquiry helps us all to sort the truth from lies and misrepresentations.

The National Standards for History set out the significance of history for the educated citizen. One of the primary qualities history conveys is competence in a multicultural world.

> Today's students, more than ever before, need also a comprehensive understanding of the history of the world, and of the peoples of many different cultures and civilizations who have developed ideas, institutions, and ways of life different from the students' own. From a balanced and inclusive world history students may gain an appreciation both of the world's many cultures and of their shared humanity and common problems. . . . Especially important, an understanding of the history of the world's many cultures can contribute to fostering the kind of mutual patience, respect, and civic courage required in our increasingly pluralistic society and our increasingly interdependent world. (National Center for History in the Schools 1996:1)

Although post-contact history is clearly the focus of the national history standards in the United States, the writers recognize that all American citizens need some understanding of indigenous societies. Three of eight standards for kindergarten through fourth grade include some understanding of early native peoples. Standard 3A, for example, reads: "The student understands the history of indigenous peoples who first lived in his or her state or region." The first standard for United States history for grades five through twelve reads: "Comparative characteristics of societies in the Americas, Western Europe, and Western Africa that increasingly interacted after 1450. Standard 1A expects that "the student understands the patterns of change in indigenous societies in the Americas up to the Columbian voyages" and that the student can draw upon data from archaeology and geology as well as upon Native American beliefs.

The national history standards provide a wedge—the need for competence in a multicultural world—that opens the possibility of archaeology and Native American traditional knowledge becoming integral to the curriculum. This goal has not yet been achieved. What is excluded from most public education curricula around the world is the prehistoric past and the past of many indigenous, minority, or oppressed groups. The step between contempt for prehistoric people as primitive and contempt for contemporary nonagricultural or nonindustrial groups may be far too easy (MacKenzie and Stone 1994). For example, Shirley Blancke and John Peters Slow Turtle (1994) connect native children's well-being and the teaching of their culture and history in the schools.

Educators know that children need to learn how to live in a multicultural society within a multicultural world. Each of the three education chapters here—by Moe, Metcalf, and Jones and Longstreth—address this concern. The authors are convinced that archaeology can teach some of the essential skills for coping with an increasingly complex world. Fay Metcalf stresses that archaeology is one source of authenticity that can set the record straight by dismantling many of the myths and lies believed by so many children and adults. Jeanne Moe describes Project Archaeology, one of the aims of which is to allow children to learn about other cultures and other times and to understand current diversity better. Jones and Longstreth tell us about the ZiNj Education Project, where science becomes fun and challenging, creating a basis for lifelong learning. The approach of the ZiNj program fits in well with current advances in environmental education. Kindling excitement and appreciation is much more effective as a tool for learning and lifelong interest than is delivering messages of loss, fear, and doom (see Sobel 1996).

Many states and professional archaeological organizations have flourishing educational programs for children, as do several private archaeological consulting companies (see Smardz and Smith 2000). Several federal agencies, charged with the stewardship of our national historic places, design and contribute to educational programs. Two outgrowths of the Utah Interagency Task Force on Cultural Resources are discussed here by Moe and by Jones and Longstreth. Archaeologists employed in the public sector frequently give public talks; construct traveling exhibits; create school programs, tours, traveling trunks, curriculum guides, and lesson plans; and participate in archaeology week or month celebrations organized by states. For example, the National Park Service in the U.S. Department of Interior has a Public Education Initiative (see Jameson 1997) as well as the active involvement of many parks.

Promoting the Public Benefits of Archaeology

Archaeological sites and the thousands of years of heritage they contain are enshrined in the public memory in several ways. Archaeological sites become part of the nation's sense of itself through tourism at the sites themselves; virtual tours on the Internet and via other electronic media; promotion in magazines, books, and movies and on television; education in museums; local exhibits seen in daily life; and in the official state and national registers of important historic places (Little 1999). Carol Shull (this volume) states that for much of the public, the National Register of Historic Places is the most accessible source of information about archaeological sites. Nominations summarize conclusions from technical reports otherwise unavailable to most of us.

Promoting public benefits of archaeology requires a wide range of tools. Formal commemoration is one tool. Local ordinances are another. Mary Grzeskowiak Ragins (this volume) explains the balancing of interests that makes such an ordinance work in the city of Santa Fe. Grassroots pride in local heritage is clear in Santa Fe, but it is not always evident elsewhere. Writing of the importance of visible reminders of the past to create a place in time, Laszio Agosthazi notes that even tiny details can suggest the past and enrich the townscape. In an ICOMOS collection on archaeological heritage management, he writes (Agosthazi 1993:2): "Areas where historic remains are shown have a strong influence with their rich contents on transforming human cons[c]iousness. I believe that every possibility of apprehending the past—literally each available scrap that remained— should be seized and utilized. These may include the presentation of fragments of reliefs standing in parks or fixed on walls with appropriate explanatory text added. I should call these marks of the past as small lamps helping people to dispel the obscurity of the past."

The vision of surrounding people with visible clues to the past is shared by Terry Goddard (this volume). The city of Phoenix, Arizona, is surrounded and underlain by archaeological sites, but public appreciation of this fact was not a foregone conclusion. Goddard urges archaeologists to make archaeology politically relevant, especially through the mechanism of public art, which has great power to convey a sense of community and continuity.

Whether one lives in a community with visible reminders of the past or chooses to travel to historic tourist destinations, there is nothing quite so compelling as personal experience of a place to begin to understand its significance. Sightseers, tourists, and locals all visit such places and there is clear economic benefit to capturing the tourist trade. Communities and the managers of travel destinations also see tourism's drawbacks of short- and long-term damage to both resources and community privacy. We need a careful balance between providing opportunities and hospitality for visitors and protecting often fragile resources. Katherine Slick's how-to guide (this volume) encourages archaeologists to take an "activist" approach to promoting tourism, while understanding that tourism is not an unmixed blessing.

Satisfying interpretation may require a balance among a realistic variety of perspectives in presentations about the past. Interpreters in many locations have become more sensitive to Native American culture, particularly since the passage of the Native American Graves Protection and Repatriation Act (NAGPRA). They have reassessed exhibits, removing offensive displays such as human skeletons. For example, at Aztec Ruins National Monument, a temporary exhibit label from the early 1990s read: "We used to think nothing was wrong with showing objects from the so-called 'Warrior Burial.' But after consulting with the Hopi Tribe, we learned that exhibiting those burial items was highly insensitive. The Hopis were deeply disturbed about their separation from the person accompanying them as well as their display. We have removed the items, and will develop an appropriate replacement exhibit."

Peter Stone (1994:16) critiques static views of the past and offers archaeology as a way to challenge and change interpretation constantly: "While many (?most) museums and historic sites seem to be concerned with the presentation of a frequently static, well-understood past that reflects the achievements of a specific period—and frequently a particular section of society—as part of a national inheritance . . . modern archaeology is more concerned with questioning the validity of any interpretations or presentations of the past."

In sharing the excitement and value of their ever-changing discipline, archaeologists are using media beyond public schools and museums. For the "virtual visitor," the World Wide Web offers nearly unlimited opportunities in the wide world of archaeology. Terry Childs (this volume) demonstrates how that electronic medium provides ways to promote heritage, educational, and economic as well as research benefits of archaeology.

Unfortunately, it is almost a truism that archaeologists write in a jargon-laden, obfuscating way. Jargon in any specialized discipline develops as a shorthand to make communication more efficient, but to the uninitiated, such language is obscure and confusing. Writing for public audiences is a daunting prospect for most archaeologists. Peter Young and Mitch Allen offer a compelling pair of chapters in this volume about different aspects of the writing process. There is a large audience for archaeology, and people deserve the very best efforts of archaeologists to write well. Clear writing is needed whether one is writing magazine articles, books, Internet pages, or television scripts. Brian Fagan (this volume) reminds archaeologists of their identity as storytellers and of the responsibilities that come with the profession.

The Power of Archaeology

Following are a few of the many uses and benefits of archaeology that are illustrated by the chapters in this volume. Tourism councils, museums, and parks have learned that authentic archaeological projects and findings bring people in and keep them coming back. Community leaders find that archaeology can build community links in the present as well as the past. Planners and citizens find that archaeology can contribute to a sustainable community where cultural heritage is valued and nurtured.

Cultural groups find that archaeology can contribute to the preservation of their history and tradition. Avocational archaeologists find the opportunity to make a direct contribution to research about the past. Historians find that archaeology provides both new information to complement the written record and important new questions about the past. Writers, newspaper reporters, and television producers find that archaeology is educational entertainment that sells. Teachers and students find that archaeology can help teach principles of math, science, geography, and logic as well as history and human diversity.

As M. P. Pearson (1993:227) has noted, "through archaeology we visit different times and different cultures, with some aspects similar to our own lives and others very different. In this exploration of sameness/difference we may come to see just how arbitrary and historically rooted are our own "universal truths."

. . .

The turn of the millennium has encouraged a great deal of stocktaking around the world: looking to the future and looking back to gain perspective and lessons from the past. The interest in heritage that has been growing over the past few decades is currently booming, and it is not likely to be a passing fad. Archaeological sites and collections are part of our heritage, both globally and locally. The study of archaeology has the potential to teach about the contingency of all human endeavor. As we expand our view of the past to include the struggles, successes, and failures of all peoples from all times and situations, our wisdom—and compassion— ought also to expand.

References

Adams, E. C. 1984. Archaeology and the Native American: A Case at Hopi. In *Ethics and Values in Archaeology,* ed. E. L. Green, 236–42. New York: Free Press.

Agosthazi, L. 1993. Monuments as Managing Factors in Forming Townscape. In *Archaeological Heritage Management,* ICOMOS International Scientific Symposium, 10th General Assembly, Sri Lanka, 1–3. Colombo, Sri Lanka: ICOMOS.

Atkinson, J. A., I. Banks, and J. O'Sullivan (eds.). 1996. *Nationalism and Archaeology: Scottish Archaeological Forum.* Glasgow: Cruithne Press.

Auel, J. 1991. Romancing the Public. In *Protecting the Past,* ed. G. S. Smith and J. E. Ehrenhard, 123–27. Boca Raton, Fla.: CRC Press.

Binks, G., J. Dyke, and P. Dagnall. 1988. *Visitors Welcome: A Manual on the Presentation and Interpretation of Archaeological Excavations.* London: English Heritage.

Blancke, S., and C.J.P. Slow Turtle. 1994. The Teaching of the Past of the Native Peoples of North America in U.S. Schools. In *The Excluded Past: Archaeology in Education,* ed. P. G. Stone and R. MacKenzie, 109–33. London: Routledge.

Bond, G. C., and A. Gilliam. 1994. Introduction. In *Social Construction of the Past: Representation as Power,* ed. G. C. Bond and A. Gilliam, 1–22. London: Routledge.

Chamberlin, E. R. 1979. *Preserving the Past.* London: J. M. Dent and Sons.

Davis, H. A. 1989. Learning by Doing: This Is No Way to Treat Archaeological Resources. In *Archaeological Heritage Management in the Modern World,* ed. H. Cleere, 275–79. London: Unwin Hyman.

———. 1991. Avocational Archaeology Groups: A Secret Weapon for Site Protection. In *Protecting the Past,* ed. G. S. Smith and J. E. Ehrenhard, 175–80. Boca Raton, Fla.: CRC Press.

Dongoske, K. E., M. Aldenderfer, and K. Doehner (eds.). 2000. *Working Together: Native Americans and Archaeologists.* Washington, D.C.: Society for American Archaeology.

Echo-Hawk, R. 1993. Working Together: Exploring Ancient Worlds. *SAA Bulletin* 11(4): 5–6.

Ferguson, T. J. 1984. Archaeological Ethics and Values in a Tribal Cultural Resource Management Program at the Pueblo of Zuni. In *Ethics and Values in Archaeology,* ed. E. L. Green, 224–35. New York: Free Press.

Green, E. L. 1984. Concluding Remarks. In *Ethics and Values in Archaeology,* ed. E. L. Green, 264–72. New York: Free Press.

Jameson, J. H., Jr. (ed.). 1997. *Presenting Archaeology to the Public: Digging for Truths.* Walnut Creek, Calif.: AltaMira Press.

Keel, B. C. 1995. The Public Trust. In *The Public Trust and the First Americans,* ed. R. Knudson and B. C. Keel, 7–8. Corvallis: Oregon State University Press for Center for the Study of the First Americans.

Knudson, R., and B. C. Keel (eds.). 1995. *The Public Trust and the First Americans.*

Corvallis: Oregon State University Press for Center for the Study of the First Americans.

Kohl, P. L., and C. Fawcett. 1995. *Nationalism, Politics, and the Practice of Archaeology.* Cambridge: Cambridge University Press.

Layton, R. (ed.). 1994. *Who Needs the Past? Indigenous Values and Archaeology.* London: Routledge.

Leone, M. P., and R. W. Preucel. 1992. Archaeology in a Democratic Society: A Critical Theory Perspective. In *Quandaries and Quests: Visions of Archaeology's Future,* ed. L. Wandsnider, 115–34. Center for Archaeological Investigations, Occasional Paper no. 20. Carbondale: Southern Illinois University.

Lipe, W. D. 1984. Value and Meaning in Cultural Resources. In *Approaches to the Archaeological Heritage,* ed. Henry Cleere, 1–11. Cambridge: Cambridge University Press.

Little, B. J. 1999. Nominating Archaeological Sites to the National Register of Historic Places: What's the Point? *SAA Bulletin* 17(4): 19.

Lowenthal, D. 1981. Conclusion: Dilemmas of Preservation. In *Our Past before Us: Why Do We Save It?* ed. D. Lowenthal and M. Binney, 213–37. London: Temple Smith.

MacKenzie, R., and P. G. Stone. 1994. Introduction: The Concept of the Excluded Past. In *The Excluded Past: Archaeology in Education,* ed. P. G. Stone and R. MacKenzie, 1–14. London: Routledge.

McManamon, F. P. 1991. The Many Publics for Archaeology. *American Antiquity* 56(1): 121–30.

Molyneaux, B. L. 1994. Introduction: The Represented Past. In *The Presented Past: Heritage, Museums and Education,* ed. Peter G. Stone and Brian L. Molyneaux, 1–13. London: Routledge.

Moyers, B. 1995. *The Language of Life: A Festival of Poets.* New York: Doubleday.

National Center for History in the Schools. 1996. *National Standards for History.* Basic edition. Los Angeles: University of California Press.

Pearson, M. P. 1993. Visitors Welcome. In *Archaeological Resource Management in the UK: An Introduction,* ed. J. Hunter and I. Ralston, 225–31. Dover, N.H.: Alan Sutton, Inc.

Ramos, M., and D. Duganne. 2000. *Exploring Public Perceptions and Attitudes about Archaeology.* Prepared by Harris Interactive for the Society for American Archaeology. <http://www.saa.org>

Rowlands, M. 1994. The Politics of Identity in Archaeology. In *Social Construction of the Past: Representation as Power,* ed. G. C. Bond and A. Gilliam, 129–43. London: Routledge.

Smardz, K., and S. J. Smith (eds.). 2000. *The Archaeological Education Handbook: Sharing the Past with Kids.* Walnut Creek, Calif.: AltaMira Press.

Sobel, D. 1996. *Beyond Ecophobia: Reclaiming the Heart in Nature Education.* Great Barrington, Mass.: Orion Society.

Society for American Archaeology (SAA). 1996. Society for American Archaeology Principles of Archaeological Ethics. *American Antiquity* 61(3): 451–52.

Stone, P. G. 1994. Introduction: A Framework for Discussion. In *The Presented Past: Heritage, Museums and Education,* ed. P. G. Stone and B. L. Molyneaux, 15–28. London: Routledge.

Swidler, N., K. E. Dongoske, R. Anyon, and A. S. Downer (eds.). 1997. *Native Americans and Archaeologists: Stepping Stones to Common Ground.* Walnut Creek, Calif.: AltaMira Press.

Thomas, D. H. 2000. *Skull Wars: Kennewick Man, Archaeology, and the Battle for Native American Identity.* New York: Basic Books.

Timken, B. C. 1993. World Heritage Education: A Prototype for Teaching Young People. In *Archaeological Heritage Management,* ICOMOS International Scientific Symposium, 10th General Assembly, Sri Lanka, 92–99. Colombo, Sri Lanka: ICOMOS.

Tunbridge, J. E., and G. J. Ashworth. 1996. *Dissonant Heritage: The Management of the Past as a Resource in Conflict.* New York: John Wiley and Sons.

UNESCO. 1970. *Protection of Mankind's Cultural Heritage: Sites and Monuments.* Paris: United Nations Educational, Scientific and Cultural Organization.

USDA-USFS. 1995. *Passport in Time Accomplishments,* Region 6. United States Department of Agriculture, United States Forest Service. Tucson, Arizona.

Vitella, K. D. (ed.). 1996. *Archaeological Ethics.* Walnut Creek, Calif.: AltaMira Press.

Wylie, A. 1994. Facts and Fictions: Writing Archaeology in a Different Voice. Reprinted in *Archaeological Theory: Progress or Posture?* ed. I. M. Mackenzie, 3–18. Brookfield, Vt.: Avebury/Ashgate Publishing Company.

2

Public Benefits of Archaeological Research

William D. Lipe

The benefits of archaeological research are often not directly accessible to the public because the work is highly technical, and research results are generally published in books and articles written primarily for other archaeologists. Many of the papers in this volume are devoted to examining ways in which research results can be made available to the public more readily and rapidly as well as ways for students and other members of the general public to take part in the research process itself. I applaud such efforts to improve public access to archaeological research. In this chapter, I argue, however, that the public benefits of archaeology depend in a very basic way on the success of archaeology as a research field. If archaeological research does not continue to produce improved understandings of the human past, or if archaeological research loses its scientific and scholarly credibility, the public's attention to and interest in things archaeological will diminish. At worst, it can erode into an antiquarian interest in artifacts merely because they are old or into seeking occasional titillation from archaeological fantasies of the usual "lost tribes and sunken continents" sort (Wauchope 1962; also see Williams 1991).

There are at least two ways in which research serves as an essential basis for public understanding of the human past and public interest in how that past can be studied. First, archaeology enables the public to confront the actual material evidence of the past—the structures, artifacts, and other remains that have survived through the ages. Archaeological research not only discovers such things but authenticates them and provides a context in which they can be understood. Second, archaeological research produces credible accounts of what happened in the past. It is the principal way of gaining knowledge about the very distant past, and it stands with oral histories and historical scholarship as a source of evidence about more recent times as well.

Authenticating the Things of the Past

The archaeological record consists of those objects, structures, deposits, and other remains and traces that were intentionally or unintentionally created by past cultures and that have survived—sometimes almost miraculously—into the present. An artifact or structure that was made and used by people who lived a thousand years ago can also be part of our lives today. The people of the past are gone, as are the words they spoke and the things they did, but the artifact that helped shape their lives is still here and stands as a direct, physical, tangible link between past and present. This is the value of authenticity—it is only the real things of the past that can provide such direct links between greatly different times because they actually participate in both. Contact with the authentic things of the past can spark in the general public an empathy with the past that enhances reflection on the meaning of history and on the connections between now and then. The public understands this and hence values authenticity.

When I take groups of laypeople to Mesa Verde National Park, they commonly want to know whether a particular wall or building is "real" or whether it has been restored. Most of the time, I know enough about the structure in question to be able to point out what has been done to stabilize or protect it and also to show them that much of what they are viewing is unequivocally original. Knowing that they are looking at the original fabric of an ancient building makes a difference in how they experience it. This is not to say that accurate restorations or "virtual" representations cannot be effective in helping visitors learn about and reflect on the past. It is just that authenticity is in a class by itself.

Research plays a vital role in authenticating the things of the past. First, whether something really is old and whether it comes from a particular time and place in the past are central questions. Research by archaeologists, often in conjunction with practitioners from other disciplines, can provide this kind of information. The visitor to a site in Britain may recognize a stone wall as a stone wall, but it makes a huge difference for that person to know that the wall was once part of a Roman fort in the third century A.D. And for many kinds of archaeological material, making a connection with the past depends almost entirely on the associated information acquired through research. The earliest stone tools made by human ancestors are mere lumps of rough stone from which a few flakes have been struck. But knowing that they are in fact over two million years old and that they represent the beginning stages of humanity's conquest of the environment through technology makes quite a difference in the viewer's experience. That kind of authenticating information is seldom self-evident to the viewer of an archaeological artifact or structure; conveying it depends on the credibility of the associated research.

Second, conserving the authentic surviving archaeological remains of the past depends on increasingly sophisticated research into the nature of various materials and on technologies developed in association with materials research. Much of this research and technology development is not strictly archaeological, but it often requires input from archaeological research regarding the condition of artifacts or structures when they were found and how they might have looked originally.

Third, while restorations, reproductions, and virtual representations of the things of the past are not a substitute for authenticity, they can provide an effective way to help the public "connect" with the past in a tangible way. They will be effective to the extent that people believe them to be credible representations of the original. This credibility can be provided by archaeological research, often supplemented by other types of study. Paradoxically, public confidence in the accuracy of a reproduction seems to be enhanced if there also is confidence that reproductions are labeled for what they are.

Fourth, and most important, research can provide authentication not only in the narrow sense of verifying age and cultural provenance but by establishing connections to a larger historical context. Thus, interpreters can use the appeal of authenticity to promote a truly historical, rather than a narrowly antiquarian, interest on the part of the visitor to a site or museum display. The "things of the past" can serve as a tangible bridge between the visitor's experience and a past world reconstructed from numerous lines of evidence, including but not limited to evidence from the particular artifact, site, or monument that provides a focal point for attention. Relatively few artifacts or sites can be displayed in order to focus public attention, but many aspects of the archaeological record and numerous lines of research can be brought to bear in placing those particular sites or artifacts in larger historical, cultural, and environmental contexts. Developing those larger contexts is the subject of my next set of comments.

Telling Stories about the Past

There are several sources of evidence about the human past, including but not necessarily limited to written texts; oral traditions; the geographic patterning of cultural, linguistic, and genetic traits; and the archaeological record. Archaeology is the only discipline that can offer accounts of what happened in the human past that are based on systematic study of this last type of evidence—the archaeological record. This is a peculiar kind of record and one that archaeologists and affiliated scientists and scholars have only begun to learn how to read. Yet in the relatively short time since formal archaeological studies began, remarkable progress has been made. One need only consider the understandings of the distant human past that were current seventy-five or a hundred years ago compared with those available today.

Having said this, I must admit that constructing credible human histories on the basis of studies of the archaeological record is a daunting task. The strength of archaeological research is that the accounts of the past it provides are anchored in the physical reality of the remains and traces left by real people in a real past. Its weakness is that multiple interpretations of that record are generally possible, and the ambiguity of interpretation increases as one moves away from technology, the economy, and settlement patterns into the more abstract aspects of culture and human cognition. Nevertheless, for much of human history, the archaeological record is the primary or the only record left by the peoples of the past, and the methods of investigation developed by archaeologists are the primary means by which we can begin to understand that record.

As already noted, when members of the public seek an encounter with the past, they often visit sites, parks, monuments, or museums devoted to displaying authentic archaeological remains. In addition, however, there seems to be a never-ending public appetite for classes, lectures, articles, books, films, and video productions devoted to the archaeological history of particular times and places or to particular archaeological questions and issues. These often are not focused on particular artifacts or sites but are the result of assembling archaeological evidence and interpretations from a variety of sources.

Of course, the individuals who make up the public bring to these various encounters with "public archaeology" their own expectations and preconceptions about what the past was like and what various aspects of the archaeological record might mean. Most, however, are also receptive to being exposed to new information and perspectives based on the work and insights of others. Hence most serious attempts to display archaeological artifacts and sites, or to present information about particular archaeological topics, rely on a broad base of information and perspectives to establish contexts. This base necessarily includes research in archaeology, history, and related fields and is increasingly likely to incorporate traditional interpretations from Native Americans or members of other ethnic groups with connections to the archaeological material being interpreted. The goal of interpretation becomes persuading members of the public to consider these broader perspectives as they pursue their interests in the past. The stories about the past that archaeologists tell based on their research not only help enrich the public's encounters with the authentic things of the past but can become a public interest in and of themselves.

Archaeological research is of necessity a contentious and dynamic endeavor. Hence the stories of the past that emerge from it change as new evidence and ideas are introduced. Consensus among researchers about particular issues is often difficult to achieve or is short lived when it does emerge. The dynamic character of archaeological research has the potential to help make archaeology more interesting to the public. New findings, new ideas, and new controversies based in research can reinvigorate and renew public interpretation in museums and parks, in the classroom, and in media treatments of archaeological materials, questions, and issues. The *process* of seeking knowledge through research can be as interesting as the provisional stories that result from that process. Through immersion in the research process—either as spectators or as volunteer participants— members of the public can gain a deeper, more reflective, and often more skeptical understanding of how accounts of the past are constructed through study of the archaeological record.

If interpreters of archaeology make poor or clumsy use of the dynamic and contentious aspects of research, however, the public may be left with little more than confusion—or with the notion that because archaeologists disagree about some things, "anything goes" in interpreting the archaeological record. The latest New Age theory may thus gain the same standing as interpretation anchored in systematic study of physical evidence from the archaeological record. Alternatively, public interpretation of archaeology may display a "research lag"—that is, it may be based on research results abandoned or modified years or decades earlier. Such lags are sure indicators of poor communication between researchers and those engaged in public interpretation. Stagnant interpretations in archaeological parks, museums, and media treatments contribute to the false perception that the archaeological past is a known quantity and that there is no room for further questioning or research.

The interface between archaeological research and public encounters with archaeology is thus an important and often complex one. Research archaeologists are sometimes directly involved in making archaeology accessible to the public, through roles as lecturers, popular writers, exhibit designers, and so forth. But for the most part, the interface between research archaeologists and the public is occupied by specialists in interpretation—journalists, television producers, museum exhibitors, schoolteachers, park interpreters, etc. There is much work to be done to improve the amount, kind, and quality of interaction between research archaeologists and these various kinds of interpretive specialists. Much is in fact being done to improve this interface—for example, the Public Education Committee of the Society for American Archaeology has developed a number of effective programs for kindergarten through twelfth grade teachers, and the SAA Media Relations Committee works to bring research archaeologists together with members of the press.

This is not the place for a lengthy discourse on ways to strengthen the interface between researchers and interpretive specialists. I offer just three comments. First, research archaeologists need to understand that they can get help in making their research results more accessible to the general public. Some researchers are good at communicating directly with the public, and more power to them. But the primary job of a researcher is to put his or her specialized knowledge and experience to good use in learning about the past through systematic study of the archaeological record. On the other hand, there are numerous professional specialists in various interpretive fields who make a living by helping laypeople understand what is happening in technical areas, including archaeology. By spending relatively brief amounts of time with professional writers, video producers, educators, or the like, researchers can greatly multiply their ability to disseminate research results to the general public.

Second, the profession of archaeology must assign greater credit and status to successful efforts by archaeological researchers to engage with the general public, whether directly or by collaborating with interpretive specialists. It is ultimately the members of the general public who pay the bill for archaeological research. As our part of the bargain, archaeologists must not only do a good job of learning from the archaeological record; we must take at least part of the responsibility for ensuring that significant research results become available to the public. In doing so, research archaeologists must take care to focus on the aspects of their work that have general—as opposed to narrowly technical—relevance. And we must be prepared to explain the importance and relevance of our results in general terms, either to members of the public directly or to professional interpreters. (This exercise in itself may have healthy consequences for the archaeologist's decisions regarding what topics are important in future research.)

Finally, research archaeologists need to do a better job of helping the public (or the interpreters with whom they work) understand the research process. Likewise, interpretive specialists who take on archaeological topics also need to educate themselves about how research gets done. Lack of good communication about the nature of research often results in missed opportunities to provide the public with a deeper understanding of what archaeologists have learned and how that knowledge has been obtained. For example, popular accounts often overemphasize unresolved controversies or mysteries left by archaeological questions that remain unanswered. On the first point, it is too little recognized that controversy is an essential part of the research process—not evidence of its failure. Like other scientifically oriented inquiries, archaeology has as its driving force the attempt to replace existing interpretations with new ones that better account for the available evidence or that reflect new evidence. As part of that process, the evidence itself may be questioned, as may the interpretive models and the arguments that link the evidence with the models. Eventually, some evidence and interpretations come to be accepted by the relevant community of researchers, and some are discarded. But that often fragile consensus then becomes the target for the next round of questioning and revision. It is a messy process but one that works better than any of the alternatives. It would be good to see more public discussions of archaeological research that show how controversy can productively focus and drive inquiry, rather than presenting it as some kind of anomalous breakdown in a presumably monolithic consensus of experts.

The other point—the emphasis on what remains mysterious instead of on what has been learned—is also related to a lack of understanding of the process of scientific research in general and of archaeological research in particular. Mathematics and logic often permit problems to be definitively solved, and religious faith is said to induce certainty, but empirical research of the sort that archaeologists do seldom results in the final, unconditional resolution of questions. Instead, conclusions are always provisional and ordinarily probabilistic, based on the best evidence to date and the best ideas thought up so far as to what that evidence might mean. In some fields of physical science, law-like certainties can be assigned to a few relation-ships among real-world phenomena. In truly complex areas such as ecology and human history, however, the best we can ordinarily do is to recognize some of the recurring processes that account for an essentially endless variety of outcomes, and to infer how a particular outcome came about, in terms of the probabilistic effects of both events and processes. Despite these limitations, the application of scientific modes of inquiry to empirical questions has resulted in an enormous expansion of knowledge about how aspects of the world work and about how they got to be the way they are today. The field of archaeology is no exception.

Therefore, to say that some historical problem has not been "solved" in some definitive way, and therefore remains a "mystery," sets up a false dichotomy between "answered" and "unanswered" questions and ensures that most of the really interesting issues will be glossed over or misunderstood. In fact, our understanding of most historical problems resides in the very large middle ground—where some aspects of the question are well understood, some are partially understood, and some remain intractable.

For example, the question of why there was a series of rapid, large-scale migrations of Pueblo peoples out of the Four Corners area of the southwestern United States in the late 1200s has not been "solved" in some simple, ultimate, final-cause way, and it probably never will be. This is a typically large, complex historical issue, in that the migrations must have involved decisions made by thousands of people from many culturally variable communities during several decades in an environmentally complex area covering thousands of square miles. Because of an enormous amount of archaeological and paleoenvironmental research, we now know a tremendous amount about *how* this demographic and cultural change happened, and we can eliminate a number of the plausible hypotheses about various aspects of why it happened. Chances are good that further study of the archaeological and paleoenvironmental record, as well as of the oral histories of present-day Pueblo people, will continue to improve our understanding of this interesting and historically important event. But there is unlikely ever to be a smoking gun—a single piece of definitive evidence pointing to a single "culprit" that "caused" the migrations.

If, as a result, we continue to treat this problem as a mystery because it has not been conclusively resolved to the satisfaction of all researchers, we are implicitly adopting simplistic and unrealistic models of historical causation and explanation. If this kind of thinking underlies public interpretation of research on complex phenomena, it will continue to inhibit public engagement with what *has* in fact been learned. It will also inhibit intelligent reflection on complex historical processes—both those that took place in the past and those even less well understood ones that are affecting our lives today.

In conclusion, the temporal scale and physical reality of the archaeological record forces us to recognize that our current lives are linked with the lives of others both past and present, as part of a deep and wide river of human experience moving through time. The archaeological record is made up of real things left by real people in a real past. Systematic archaeological study of that record is the primary avenue to gaining an understanding—however imperfect—of much of the human past. The story of the human past, as revealed by archaeological research, is a marvelously complex tale, yet one that returns—often in surprising ways—to a few basic themes. Fantasy and fiction are poor substitutes for the real thing, however dimly that real past might be perceived. Archaeological research is usually a major source, and often the primary source, of the contexts on which the public must rely to arrive at some understanding of particular archaeological sites and artifacts or, more generally, to understand some particular era or episode of the distant past. Hence archaeological research—as well as archaeological things—can and should play essential roles in helping connect us with that deep human history that underlies and can provide perspective on our lives today.

References

Wauchope, Robert. 1962. *Lost Tribes and Sunken Continents: Myth and Method in the Study of American Indians.* Chicago: University of Chicago Press.

Williams, Stephen. 1991. *Fantastic Archaeology: The Wild Side of North American Prehistory.* Philadelphia: University of Pennsylvania Press.

II

Many Publics, Many Benefits

3

Heritage, History, and Archaeological Educators

Francis P. McManamon

Two major kinds of benefits derive from archaeology. These are the commemorative or associative benefits of heritage and the knowledge benefits of history. Historian David Lowenthal (1996: x–xiii) distinguishes between the personal and community associations with places that commemorate the past and historical or archaeological knowledge about the past. He uses the term *heritage* to describe the former and *history* for the latter. His distinction is important because it illuminates how individuals and communities actually use the past, both places that commemorate it and information about it. "In domesticating the past we enlist it for present purposes. Legends of origin and endurance, of victory or calamity, project the present back, the past forward; they align us with forebears whose virtues we share and whose vices we shun. We are apt to call such communion history, but it actually is heritage. The distinction is vital. History [and archaeology] explore and explain pasts grown ever more opaque over time; heritage clarifies pasts so as to infuse them with present purposes" (Lowenthal 1996: xi).

It is important to recognize that many people may have views of the past and of places associated with it that differ substantially from those held by archaeologists or historians with their research-based knowledge. Effectively using such public perceptions about heritage may be crucial for site preservation and obviously must be dealt with in order to ensure accurate interpretation programs (McManamon 2000a: 11–13).

The Heritage Benefit of Archaeology

Like other kinds of historic properties, archaeological sites are places associated with past people, events, and historical processes. Archaeological sites are real places where real events took place. Knowing about these places and having a sense of what happened at them provide an important temporal context for modern life. Such places and knowledge about them play an essential role in "sustaining the American heritage and the American community" (Kennedy 1997: 33).

Lowenthal (1985: xxiii) comments on this appreciation of archaeological and historic places:

> Memory and history both derive and gain emphasis from physical remains. Tangible survivals provide a vivid immediacy that helps to assure us there really was a past. Physical remains have their limitations as informants, to be sure; they are themselves mute, requiring interpretation; their continual but differential erosion and demolition skews the record; and their substantial survival conjures up a past more static than could have been the case. But however depleted by time and use, relics remain essential bridges between then and now. They confirm or deny what we think of it, symbolize or memorialize communal links over time, and provide archaeological metaphors that illumine the processes of history and memory.

These associations are derived by individuals who use the archaeological and historical context provided by places to evaluate their own personal conditions. In some situations, these associations benefit modern communities, both in terms of community cohesion from a shared historical context and via tourism. The latter benefit, which typically is mixed with costs, is derived when people visit a place to enjoy the archaeological or historical sites in or near the community, enhancing the local economy in the process.

That Americans recognize and appreciate the association of archaeological sites and the commemorative benefit is proven by the large number of archaeological places identified as national, state, regional, and local parks and sites throughout the nation. Some archaeological places are designated for specific events or individuals, such as Franklin Court, part of Independence National Historical Park (NHP) in Philadelphia; Jamestown National Historic Site (NHS), Little Big Horn NHS, Monticello, and

Mount Vernon. Others commemorate broader historical patterns or periods in American history and prehistory, such as Saugus Iron Works NHS in Massachusetts, Hopewell Culture NHP and Serpent Mound State Memorial in Ohio, Etowah Indian Mounds State Historic Site in Georgia, Moundville State Monument in Alabama, Cahokia Mounds State Historic Site in Illinois, Pecos NHP and the Pueblo of Acoma in New Mexico, and Casa Grande Ruins National Monument and Pueblo Grande City Park in Arizona. Such a brief listing mentions only a very few of the rich national assortment of archaeological and historic places that draw tourists intent upon visiting them and other nearby sites and parks (see Slick, this volume).

The heritage benefit of archaeological and historical places for individuals and communities has an important economic aspect. Visitors spend dollars during their visits. Millions of Americans and foreign visitors tour these sites and museums annually. The state of New Mexico, for example, reports that $293 million flow directly into the state from interest in the cultural resources of New Mexico and that $1.6 billion in spending occurs based upon this activity (New Mexico 1995–96). These calculations include money related to performing arts, festivals, fairs, and libraries. However, the number of visitors who come to the state for the archaeological and historic sites, museums, and Indian reservations is 8.2 million of the estimated 19 million visitors coming to the state for appreciation of cultural resources of one sort or another.

In addition to the potential economic benefits, archaeology enriches communities by focusing energy and enthusiasm. Spin-offs from individual projects have rippled through communities touching public schools, museums, neighborhood actions, street names, and the design of public places. To look at a few examples of local programs with community involvement at their core, consider Baltimore, Maryland (Peters et al. 1987); Alexandria, Virginia (Cressey 1987); Pensacola, Florida (Bense 1991, 1995); St. Augustine, Florida (Smith and Piatek 1993); and Tucson (Ellick 1991), Flagstaff (Phagan and Pilles 1989), and other parts of Arizona (Hoffman 1991). Pam Cressey (1987: 6) was not exaggerating when she wrote that "every community in America has an archaeological heritage which, if managed properly as a public resource, can help us recognize and celebrate the accomplishments of our predecessors. Archaeology brings the American legacy to life." The integration of public education and outreach in archaeological programs is increasingly common, as shown by examples from Arkansas (Green and Davis 2000), Rhode Island (Robinson and Taylor 2000), the American Southwest (Lerner and Hoffman 2000), and Utah (Moe 2000).

All archaeology, like politics, is local. In rare instances, archaeological discoveries may have regional, national, or international import, but they always have local interest. "Few archaeologists will ever find a pharaoh's tomb or buried gold. . . . Most finds are of purely local, or perhaps regional, importance, even sometimes, frankly dull. But the information that comes from them is of more than passing local significance and educational value. This is where archaeologists can work miracles with public relations, provided they develop close links with the local media" (Fagan 1991: 18).

In addition to personal considerations and reflections, the commemorative benefit of archaeological places may act on a wider social scale. Writing of the ancient monumental architecture found in the midwestern and southeastern United States, from the Mississippi and Ohio valleys to the Gulf Coast, Roger Kennedy (1994: 1–6) notes that these prehistoric examples of engineering and human social organization ought to give modern Americans an appreciation of the achievements and potential of non-Western cultures and their modern descendants. Following this appreciation, we hope, will come tolerance and the possibility of cooperation.

For Native Americans, the associations with ancient archaeological sites are more directly cultural. The links hold special commemorative value associated with ancient histories of creation, special events, and epic journeys. These associations with archaeological sites provide opportunities for archaeologists to work directly with Native Americans to examine the ways in which their respective approaches to understanding the past are complementary (e.g., Deloria 1992; Reid 1992a, b; Echo-Hawk 1993, 1997, 2000). Pyburn and Wilk (1995: 72) urge archaeologists to act on this challenge and opportunity: "Archaeology can be used in the service of native people by reconstructing some of the heritage that has been lost through conquest and deprivation. Archaeologists can also offer real support for developing tourism, jobs, crafts industries, self-respect, education, and public awareness. It is absolutely crucial that archaeological reconstructions not be framed as 'gifts from the archaeologists' but as the results of scientific research, which is a technique of understanding that is useful and available to anyone." In order for this cooperation to work effectively, however, the representatives of each party must not only respect the position of the other but also be able and willing to serve as effective advocates of their own perspective. Archaeologists must express and support the benefits of an archaeological approach to investigations and understanding the past (McManamon 1994a: 19).

Cultural associations are also important for other groups of Americans in relation to historic period sites. Places such as Jamestown in Virginia and early European settlement sites in Canada, New England, the Southeast, and the Southwest hold cultural associations for Americans of other backgrounds. African Americans recently experienced a cultural connection with the discovery, investigation, and—after some controversy—commemoration of the African Burial Ground in lower Manhattan, New York City (see Crist, this volume).

The History Benefit of Archaeology

The second general benefit of archaeological resources is the information that can be learned about the past through proper investigations. This information helps us to understand larger patterns of the past, such as the development of human settlement or land use over a large area or the development of agriculture or a certain kind of technology. Lipe (1996: 23) has called the ability to provide information about the past the principal benefit of archaeology: "The primary social contribution of archaeology . . . [is] the production and dissemination of new information about the past based on the systematic study of the archaeological record. . . . Most sites in fact gain their primary social value because they have the potential to contribute new information about the past when subjected to archaeological study." This benefit based upon the information about the past that can be learned from the study of archaeological resources overlaps, of course, with the associational and commemorative benefits already described. Sense of place and historical context are enhanced by interpretations derived from archaeological investigations. The importance of scientific investigation of archaeological sites, rather than haphazard individual collecting of artifacts, and the public benefits of the information and artifacts recovered were the primary reasons that the Antiquities Act of 1906 established fundamental aspects of United States law and policy regarding archaeological and historical resources (Lee 2001; McManamon 1996).

The information benefit has particular attractions for educators and schoolchildren as well as for the general American public. Educators, and by extension their students, have discovered that archaeology can provide stimulating subject matter for teaching a wide range of subjects (Rogge and Bell 1989; Selig and London 1998; articles in Smith and McManamon 1991; Stone and MacKenzie 1989; Stone and Molyneaux 1994; Smardz and Smith 2000). Fay Metcalf, a distinguished American educator experienced and familiar with issues at the local, state, and national levels, recognizes the excitement and intrigue that archaeological approaches and information can bring to formal education. She points out that using material culture, its spatial context, and archaeological methodology promotes complex thinking skills involving evaluation of data, construction of inferences, and flexibility of interpretations (Metcalf 1992 and this volume).

Archaeology has obvious connections with history, geography, and social studies generally (e.g., Lavin 1996; MacDonald 1995; Metcalf 1992; KC Smith 1995). All American schoolchildren learn United States history, state history, and ancient history at least twice during a normal twelve-year elementary and secondary education. Information from archaeological investigations can address prehistory, early contact between Native Americans and European colonists, and later periods of U.S. history (e.g., MacDonald 1995; Metcalf 1992). Along with classic texts and ancient writings, archaeology is one basic source of information about ancient civilizations. Many teachers have found that incorporation of archaeological information and discussions of how the investigation of material remains can illuminate aspects of history stimulates student interest. Archaeological examples also can provide intriguing introductions to topics in biology, chemistry, and physics. For example, radiocarbon dating is a natural entrée to a discussion of general atomic structure; two- and three-dimension coordinate geometry can be explored using standard archaeological horizontal and vertical recording of artifacts and features. A majority (90%) of the American public supports the inclusion of archaeology in the school curriculum (Ramos and Duganne 2000).

The General Public and Archaeological Messages

Interpretations of history and prehistory from archaeological resources and archaeological investigations are of interest to millions of Americans. Understanding the levels of knowledge and the views of the general public about archaeology is an important component of effective public outreach. Until recently the few public surveys carried out have been of limited geographical scope. Feder (1984, 1987, 1995), for example, reports on different samples of students at Central Connecticut State University. Households in British Columbia have been sampled as well (Pokotylo and Mason 1991; Pokotylo and Guppy 1999).

The Society for American Archaeology commissioned a national survey on public attitudes about and understanding of archaeology. This survey, performed by Harris Interactive, suggests that the American public sees both heritage and history benefits to archaeology (McManamon 1999; McManamon and Little n.d.; Ramos and Duganne 2000). Respondents to the nationwide survey agreed that the value of archaeological objects and sites is educational (99%), scientific (99%), aesthetic or artistic (94%), related to personal heritage (93%), spiritual (88%), monetary (73%), and political (59%).

In light of the broad spectrum of values placed on archaeology and the widespread public interest, there is no single archaeological message for archaeologists to aim at the public. Potter (1990: 610) offers insightful comment on archaeology and public outreach: "The most significant and meaningful messages are not 'one size fits all.' Instead, they are local. Different communities have different pasts and need to know specific things about those pasts." This echoes Fagan, as earlier quoted, and the useful, practical advice provided by DeCicco (1988) in his public outreach primer. Potter urges archaeologists to explore and discover what the public knows, thinks about, or uses from the past as part of the effort to construct interesting, useful messages. From the perspective of critical analysis, being urged by some archaeologists as an important aspect of the interpretation of archaeological data, such outreach and reflection upon the modern context in which archaeology is being done is essential (e.g., Leone et al. 1987). Certainly from a practical perspective in public education this also is good advice, and again it is emphasized by others in their own work and experience from working with local media (DeCicco 1988; Fagan 1991: 19; Peters et al. 1987).

One of the archaeological messages in any public outreach activity, therefore, must be of at least local interest and sufficiently enticing to attract individuals with no special archaeological training: how people lived in an area at some point in the past, an unexpected event, or an unusual kind of feature or artifact found locally.

Local, community-specific topics are essential to successful public education. Yet, communication with the public also should directly or indirectly make general points related to the value of archaeological resources:

- Interesting and useful knowledge can be learned from archaeological remains if they are properly studied.
- The proper study of archaeological remains is careful, painstaking work that includes fieldwork, laboratory work, and report prepara-

tion and distribution, and ultimately it involves the curation of collections and records.

• Archaeological remains are often fragile, always nonrenewable, and ought not to be destroyed wantonly (e.g., Lerner 1991; Stuart and McManamon 1996).

General points such as these have been identified as important messages to be used in educational, volunteer, and other public outreach programs designed to work over the long term on the prevention of archaeological looting and vandalism (Lerner 1991: 103).

We might consider successful transmission of these general messages as the ultimate goal of public education and outreach. A public with an appreciation for and understanding of archaeology and archaeological resources would be a public who abhorred site destruction and supported archaeological activities and preservation. Only a small percentage of the public explicitly holds these beliefs at present; hence working to increase that percentage is both an important and a worthwhile goal (McManamon 1994b: 65).

These specific and general messages need effective messengers. Archaeologists ought not to be alone in communicating the messages. Educators, reporters, film makers, and a host of others already are enlisted in these efforts. However, archaeologists of all sorts should have some role in public education and outreach, even if only as cheerleaders and supporters for those who actively take on this challenge (Herscher and McManamon 1995; B. Smith 1993; Sabloff 1998; McManamon 2000b). So says Principle No. 4: Public Education and Outreach, in the "Principles of Archaeological Ethics" developed by the Society for American Archaeology (1996: 452):

Archaeologists should reach out to, and participate in cooperative efforts with, others interested in the archaeological record with the aim of improving the preservation, protection, and interpretation of the record. In particular, archaeologists should undertake to (1) enlist public support for the stewardship of the archaeological record; (2) explain and promote the use of archaeological methods and techniques in understanding human behavior and culture; and (3) communicate archaeological interpretations of the past. Many publics exist for archaeology including students and teachers; Native Americans and other ethnic, religious, and cultural groups who find in the archaeological record important aspects of their cultural heritage; lawmakers and government officials; reporters, journalists, and others involved in the media; and the general public. Archaeologists who are unable to undertake public education and outreach directly should encourage and support the efforts of others in these activities.

Archaeologists find employment in different parts of the profession's work force. Among the most common settings are academic research and teaching; conducting investigations as consultants in the planning and conduct of public projects; working for public agencies that manage lands, programs, or resources; and in museum curation, interpretation, and research. In each of these areas of employment, many opportunities exist to include public education and outreach as a part of professional activities. Increasing numbers of references describing public outreach projects and programs are available to provide examples and to guide those unfamiliar with this terrain (e.g., Bense 1991, 1995; DeCicco 1988; Fagan 1991; Jameson 1997; Peters et al. 1987; Potter 1994; Potter and Leone 1987).

Archaeologists should act locally, using local newspapers, magazines, radio, and television to feature archaeological activities, events, and news. Individual archaeologists, no matter which part of the field they work in, should be willing to speak to local elementary and secondary schools, civic organizations, and local archaeological, historical, preservation, and conservation organizations. Of course, professional archaeologists should work with avocational archaeological societies. They need not lead these societies, although some do, but being willing to take part constitutes recognition of the important work that such volunteer organizations can accomplish.

At the local level, there are activities that archaeologists, acting as individuals and citizens, can undertake or support to enhance a local archaeology program, a local environmental ordinance, or historic zoning restrictions that interpret or preserve local archaeology. Individual archaeologists can and should work with local community governments, local service organizations, local libraries, and other educational services.

Within their professional jobs, archaeologists working for public agencies at all levels—national, regional, state, and local—have opportunities to enhance public education and outreach. During the last decade, public agencies at all levels have taken the lead in presenting archaeology to the public (e.g., Brook 1992; Cressey 1987; Hawkins 1988; articles in Jameson 1997; Jameson 2000; Osborn and Peters 1991). This has been so in formal educational settings, especially primary and secondary public schools, as well as in outreach for the general public. These kinds of programs often provide substantial rewards for the public agencies that undertake them.

Many have become regular features of agency programs and should remain as such.

Archaeologists working for consulting firms also have accomplished much with public education and outreach. Many medium-sized and large archaeological projects—for example, for highways, power lines, or water control projects—produce brochures, public lectures, and displays and hold "open house" days at sites. Project sponsors often see these products as tangible public benefits for which they rightly can take credit. The positive public relations obtained render the sponsors willing to support these kinds of programs as outcomes of the archaeological investigations they fund. These kinds of activities should be supported by the archaeological community and encouraged by those who design scopes-of-work for public projects.

Archaeologists teaching at the postsecondary school level are often the only archaeologists that most people encounter personally during their lives. For most of the students in such classes, especially in large introductory and survey courses, the class will be the most extended presentation about archaeology that the students ever receive. It is imperative, therefore, that the professionals teaching these courses use them as effectively as possible to inculcate in their audiences an appreciation for and understanding of archaeology and archaeological resources that will create a supportive, well-informed, educated public. Those teaching adult education courses on archaeological topics have the same opportunities and obligations for creating public advocates and supporters. Professors educating graduate students—those individuals who eventually will replace contemporary practitioners and become the professional corps of archaeologists—ought to provide their students with experience working with the general public through schools, mass media print and electronic publications, and local communities (B. Smith 1993; Sabloff 1998; McManamon 1998).

Individuals among the general public can serve as the eyes and ears of local, state, or even national officials who are responsible for archaeological preservation. Certainly, there are not enough officials or even trained archaeologists in the United States to serve such a widespread monitoring function, nor will there ever be.

An active, informed public that is supportive of archaeology and archaeological preservation can serve as an invaluable source of political, volunteer, and economic backing. If archaeological sites are to be preserved for the very long term, and if archaeological administration, planning, investigations, reporting, and curation are to be supported for the long term, more and better public education must become an actively pursued and highly regarded part of the discipline of archaeology.

References

Bense, Judith A. 1991. The Pensacola Model of Public Archeology. In *Archeology and Education: The Classroom and Beyond,* ed. KC Smith and F. P. McManamon, 9–12. Archeological Assistance Study no. 2. Washington, D.C.: National Park Service.

———. 1995. Putting Pensacola on the Map! Archaeotourism in West Florida. *AnthroNotes* 17(1–2): 17–21.

Brook, Richard A. 1992. Adventures in the Past. *Federal Archaeology Report* 5(1): 1–4.

Cressey, Pamela J. 1987. Community Archaeology in Alexandria, Virginia. *Conserve Neighborhoods* (National Trust for Historic Preservation, Washington, D.C.) no. 69: 1–7.

DeCicco, G. 1988. A Public Relations Primer. *American Antiquity* 53: 840–56.

Deloria, Vine, Jr. 1992. Indians, Archaeologists, and the Future. *American Antiquity* 57(4): 595–98.

Echo-Hawk, Roger C. 1993. Working Together: Exploring Ancient Worlds. *SAA Bulletin* 11(4): 5–6.

———. 1997. Forging a New Ancient History for Native America. In *Native Americans and Archaeologists: Stepping Stones to Common Ground,* ed. N. Swidler, K. E. Dongoske, R. Anyon, and A. S. Downer, 88–102. Walnut Creek, Calif.: AltaMira Press.

———. 2000. Archaeology and Native American Oral Tradition. *American Antiquity* 65(2): 267–90.

Ellick, Carol. 1991. Archeology Is More than a Dig: Educating Children about the Past Saves Sites for the Future. In *Archeology and Education: The Classroom and Beyond,* ed. KC Smith and F. P. McManamon, 27–32. Archeological Assistance Study no. 2. Washington, D.C.: National Park Service.

Fagan, Brian M. 1991. The Past as News. *CRM* 14(1): 17–19.

Feder, Kenneth L. 1984. Irrationality and Popular Archaeology. *American Antiquity* 49: 525–41.

———. 1987. Cult Archaeology and Creationism: A Coordinated Research Project. In *Cult Archaeology and Creationism: Understanding Pseudoscientific Beliefs about the Past,* ed. F. B. Harrold and R. A. Eve, 34–48. Iowa City: University of Iowa Press.

———. 1995. Ten Years After: Surveying Misconceptions about the Human Past. *CRM* 18(3): 10–14.

Green, Thomas J., and Hester A. Davis. 2000. The Arkansas Archeological Survey: A Statewide Cooperative Programme to Preserve the Past. In *Cultural Resource*

Management in Contemporary Society: Perspectives on Managing and Presenting the Past, ed. F. P. McManamon and A. Hatton, 120–41. One World Archaeology no. 33. London: Routledge.

Hawkins, Nancy W. 1988. *Classroom Archaeology: A Curriculum Guide for Teachers*. Baton Rouge, La.: Division of Archaeology, Department of Culture, Recreation, and Tourism.

Herscher, E., and F. P. McManamon. 1995. Public Education and Outreach: The Obligation to Educate. In *Ethics in American Archaeology: Challenges for the 1990s*, ed. M. J. Lynott and A. Wylie, 42–44. Washington, D.C.: Society for American Archaeology.

Hoffman, T. L. 1991. Stewards of the Past: Preserving Arizona's Archaeological Resources through Positive Public Involvement. In *Protecting the Past*, ed. G. S. Smith and J. E. Ehrenhard, 253–59. Boca Raton, Fla.: CRC Press.

Jameson, J. H., Jr. 2000. Public Interpretation, Education, and Outreach: The Growing Predominance in American Archaeology. In *Cultural Resource Management in Contemporary Society: Perspectives on Managing and Presenting the Past*, ed. F. P. McManamon and A. Hatton, 288–99. One World Archaeology no. 33. London: Routledge.

———— (ed.). 1997. *Presenting Archaeology to the Public: Digging for Truths*. Walnut Creek, Calif.: AltaMira Press.

Kennedy, Roger G. 1994. *Hidden Cities: The Discovery and Loss of Ancient North American Civilization*. New York: Free Press.

————. 1997. Conversation, Preservation, and the Cause Conservative. *Preservation Forum* 11(2): 33–41.

Lavin, Meggett B. 1996. So, You're Still Not Sure about Archaeology and Eighth Graders? *Archaeology and Public Education* 6(2): 4–5, 14.

Lee, Ronald F. 2001. *The Antiquities Act of 1906*. Originally published 1970. Online publication, Archeology and Ethnography Program, National Park Service, Washington, D.C. <http://www.cr.nps.gov/aad/pubs/INDEX.HTML>

Leone, Mark P., Parker B. Potter, Jr., and Paul A. Shackel. 1987. Toward a Critical Archaeology. *Current Anthropology* 28(3): 283–302.

Lerner, Shereen. 1991. Saving Sites: Preservation and Education. In *Protecting the Past*, ed. G. S. Smith and J. E. Ehrenhard, 103–8. Boca Raton, Fla.: CRC Press.

Lerner, Shereen, and Teresa Hoffman. 2000. Bringing Archaeology to the Public: Programmes in the Southwestern United States. In *Cultural Resource Management in Contemporary Society: Perspectives on Managing and Presenting the Past*, ed. F. P. McManamon and A. Hatton, 231–47. One World Archaeology no. 33. London: Routledge.

Lipe, William D. 1996. In Defense of Digging: Archeological Preservation as a Means, Not an End. *CRM* 19(7): 23–27.

Lowenthal, David. 1985. *The Past Is a Foreign Country*. Cambridge: Cambridge University Press.

————. 1996. *Possessed by the Past: The Heritage Crusade and the Spoils of History.* New York: Free Press.

MacDonald, Cathy. 1995. Historical Archaeology Meshes Learning Experiences for Kids. *Archaeology and Public Education* 6(1): 5.

McManamon, Francis P. 1991. The Many Publics for Archaeology. *American Antiquity* 56(1): 121–30.

————. 1994a. Changing Relationships between Native Americans and Archaeologists. *Historic Preservation Forum* 8(2): 15–20.

————. 1994b. Presenting Archaeology to the Public in the USA. In *The Presented Past: Heritage, Museums, and Education,* ed. P. G. Stone and B. L. Molyneaux, 61–81. London: Routledge.

————. 1996. The Antiquities Act: Setting Basic Preservation Policies. *CRM* 19(7): 18–23.

————. 1998. Public Archaeology: A Professional Obligation. Archaeology and Public Education 8(3): 3, 13.

————. 1999. Understanding the Public's Understanding of Archeology. *Common Ground* 4(2): 3. Washington, D.C.: NPS, Archeology and Ethnography Program.

————. 2000a. Archaeological Messages and Messengers. *Public Archaeology* 1(1): 5–20.

————. 2000b. Public Education: A Part of Archeological Professionalism. In *The Archaeological Education Handbook: Sharing the Past with Kids,* ed. K. Smardz and S. J. Smith. Walnut Creek, Calif.: AltaMira Press.

McManamon, F. P., and A. Hatton (eds.). 2000. *Cultural Resource Management in Contemporary Society: Perspectives on Managing and Presenting the Past.* One World Archaeology no. 33. London: Routledge.

McManamon, Francis P., and Barbara J. Little. N.d. What the American Public Knows and Thinks about Archaeology. Manuscript in possession of the authors.

Metcalf, Fay. 1992. Knife River: Early Village Life on the Plains. A "Teaching with Historic Places" Supplement. *Social Education* 56(5): 312 ff.

Moe, Jeanne M. 2000. America's Archeological Heritage: Protection through Education. In *Cultural Resource Management in Contemporary Society: Perspectives on Managing and Presenting the Past,* ed. F. P. McManamon and A. Hatton, 276–87. One World Archaeology no. 33. London: Routledge.

New Mexico, Office of Cultural Affairs. 1995–96. *On Fertile Ground: Assessing and Cultivating New Mexico's Cultural Resources.* Santa Fe: New Mexico Office of Cultural Affairs.

Osborn, J. A., and G. Peters. 1991. Passport in Time. *Federal Archaeology Report* 4(3): 1–6.

Peters, K. S., E. A. Comer, and R. Kelly. 1987. *Captivating the Public through the Media While Digging the Past.* Technical Series no. 1. Baltimore, Md.: Baltimore Center for Urban Archaeology.

Phagan, C. J., and P. J. Pilles, Jr. 1989. Public Participation Archaeology at Elden Pueblo. In *Fighting Indiana Jones in Arizona: American Society for Conservation Archaeology, 1988 Proceedings*, ed. A. E. Rogge and J. Montgomery, 13–16. Portales, N.M.: American Society for Conservation Archaeology.

Pokotylo, David L., and Neil Guppy. 1999. Public Opinion and Archaeological Heritage: Views from Outside the Profession. *American Antiquity* 64(3): 400–416.

Pokotylo, David L., and Andrew R. Mason. 1991. Public Attitudes towards Archaeological Resources and Their Management. In *Protecting the Past*, ed. G. S. Smith and J. E. Ehrenhard, 9–18. Boca Raton, Fla.: CRC Press.

Potter, Parker B., Jr. 1990. The "What" and "Why" of Public Relations for Archaeology: A Postscript to DeCicco's Public Relations Primer. *American Antiquity* 55: 608–13.

———. 1994. *Public Archaeology in Annapolis: A Critical Approach to History in Maryland's Ancient City*. Washington, D.C.: Smithsonian Institution Press.

Potter, P. B., Jr., and M. P. Leone. 1987. Archaeology in Public in Annapolis: Four Seasons, Six Sites, Seven Tours, and 32,000 Visitors. *American Archaeology* 6(1): 51–61.

Pyburn, K. Ann, and Richard R. Wilk. 1995. Responsible Archaeology Is Applied Anthropology. In *Ethics in American Archaeology: Challenges for the 1990s*, ed. M. J. Lynott and A. Wylie, 71–76. Washington, D.C.: Society for American Archaeology.

Ramos, Maria, and David Duganne. 2000. *Exploring Public Perceptions and Attitudes about Archaeology*. Prepared by Harris Interactive for the Society for American Archaeology. <http://www.saa.org>

Reid, J. Jefferson. 1992a. Editor's Corner: Recent Findings on North American Prehistory. *American Antiquity* 57(2): 195–96.

———. 1992b. Editor's Corner: Quincentennial Truths and Consequences. *American Antiquity* 57(4): 583.

Robinson, Paul A., and Charlotte C. Taylor. 2000. Heritage Management in Rhode Island: Working with Diverse Partners and Audiences. In *Cultural Resource Management in Contemporary Society: Perspectives on Managing and Presenting the Past*, ed. F. P. McManamon and A. Hatton, 107–19. One World Archaeology no. 33. London: Routledge.

Rogge, A. E., and P. Bell. 1989. *Archaeology in the Classroom: A Case Study from Arizona*. Archaeological Assistance Program Technical Brief no. 4. Washington, D.C.: National Park Service. <http://www.cr.nps.gov/aad>

Roper and Starch. 1995. *Americans' Attitudes toward History*. Conducted for the History Channel, New York.

Sabloff, J. A. 1998. Distinguished Lecture in Archaeology: Communication and the Future of American Archaeology. *American Anthropologist* 100(4): 869–75.

Selig, R. O., and M. R. London (eds.). 1998. *Anthropology Explored: The Best of Anthro Notes*. Washington, D.C.: Smithsonian Institution Press.

Smardz, K., and S. Smith (eds.). 2000. *The Archaeological Education Handbook: Sharing the Past with Kids.* Walnut Creek, Calif.: AltaMira Press.

Smith, B. 1993. A New Goal for Academia. *Archeology and Public Education* 3(3): 1.

Smith, KC. 1995. Picture This: Using Photographs to Study the Past. *Archaeology and Public Education* 6(1): 6–8.

Smith, KC, and F. P. McManamon (eds.). 1991. *Archeology and Education: The Classroom and Beyond.* Archeological Assistance Study no. 2. Washington, D.C.: National Park Service.

Smith, KC, and Bruce John Piatek. 1993. New Discoveries in the Oldest City. *Archaeology and Public Education* 4(2): 7–8.

Society for American Archaeology (SAA). 1996. Society for American Archaeology Principles of Archaeological Ethics. *American Antiquity* 61(3): 451–52.

Stone, Peter G., and R. MacKenzie (eds.). 1989. *The Excluded Past: Archaeology in Education.* London: Unwin Hyman.

Stone, Peter G., and Brian L. Molyneaux (eds.). 1994. *The Presented Past: Heritage, Museums and Education.* London: Routledge.

Stuart, George E., and Francis P. McManamon. 1996. *Archaeology and You.* Washington, D.C.: Society for American Archaeology.

4

Hopi Understanding of the Past

A Collaborative Approach

Leigh (Jenkins) Kuwanwisiwma

Out of respect for our ancestors, and a desire to know about our past, the Hopis want to collaborate with archaeologists in contemporary research conducted at our ancestral sites. It is the position of the Hopi tribe that in order to perform a thorough archaeological investigation and interpretation, it is essential that research be conducted in conjunction with the living descendants of the people who created the archaeological sites.

The Hopis want to be treated as peers in archaeological research projects, so that our knowledge, values, and beliefs are regarded with the same respect that archaeologists afford one another when there are differences in research methods and interpretation of the archaeological record. The Hopis do not, however, want to superimpose sacred knowledge indiscriminately on the archaeological record. Nor do we want to constrain archaeological interpretation unfairly. We have no desire to censor the ideas of archaeologists, nor do we wish to impose research designs on archaeologists.

Archaeological research concerns the Hopis particularly when our ancestors are the subject of that research. The findings of archaeologists are important and have real impact on how Hopis perceive themselves. The destruction of archaeological sites by construction projects and land development, or by scientific excavation, is of great concern to the Hopis, in part because the record established by our ancestors is obliterated. Hopi participation in archaeological research will help ensure that Hopi perspectives and concepts are incorporated in the written record that will remain after archaeological sites are destroyed. Inclusion of the Hopi information and interpretation in the written history of an archaeological site will help off-set the losses that occur with the destruction of a site created by Hopi ancestors.

Bringing in a Hopi perspective necessitates a brief historical look at how the Hopi tribal program on cultural resources developed. I came into cultural resource management with little sense of what it entails. That was in 1989. Since then, I have learned to be much more sensitive to the archaeological record. As I walk into Oraibi, for example, it bothers me to see architectural changes occurring. I wish we could do more to educate the Hopi public to save a lot of our archaeology out on the reservation. I have likewise gained sensitivity as I work with archaeologists. Today we have a staff of professional archaeologists and a progressive archaeology program that has allowed us, for example, to collaborate with law enforcement agencies. We have conducted several investigations under the Archaeological Resources Protection Act in which our team of archaeologists has gone in and done the damage assessment. We are now active in doing our own surveys in compliance with section 106 of the National Historic Preservation Act. We are also active within the Hopi tribe in bringing in an array of perspectives as we conduct consultation with the professional communities in traditional cultural property investigations.

As I look around the tribal programs now, I see a lot of interaction between the tribal programs and the traditional tribal communities. We draw upon people from the various societies, clans, and villages of the Hopi people. We meet monthly; we deliberate; we make decisions and recommendations on various projects in which the Hopi tribe is involved. Many tribal programs have developed today and people want them to be a viable part of the whole dimension of cultural resource management. No longer do the Hopi desire to be treated merely as informants. In some cases the Hopi tribe has itself developed proposals and research designs. A good example involves the Glen Canyon environmental studies, in which six or seven tribes—the Hopi tribe among them—are now active in the process. We conducted our own archaeological review and investigations; we have supplied comments. Now we are producing our own report on Hopi tribal history and ethnohistory in the Grand Canyon.

This field is a changing environment with significant new issues arising. One of them is the issue of confidentiality. How do you protect tribal information that is considered to be confidential but that is so necessary, particularly now with traditional cultural properties, to evaluate these sites adequately so that they are given full weight of the merits presented by both sides: the scientific as well as the tribal perspective? We are now discussing at the tribal level the impact of the utilization of public funds through federal grants and programs to do research and the legal issues that arise as a result of having publicly funded projects generating information, because we then have to deal with the proprietorship issue of who owns that information. It is a very significant issue and problem that has to be addressed by all. Certainly the tribes want to contribute; certainly the tribes want to be a partner in various projects; but in order to bring in tribal perspective and participation, we must deal with the protection of the information. There is now the issue of intellectual property rights when archaeologists and ethnologists come into Hopi, interact with the Hopi tribe through a formal contract, and must then deal with the issue of proprietorship. Who owns that information?

Because of these issues, interpretation and the requirement of consultation have challenged the Hopi people to be very careful as they contribute information. One good example is in the excavation of kivas. In Hopi information there is a specific reason why kivas, especially ceremonial kivas, are predominantly round, versus the rectangular configuration of Hopi and Zuni kivas. We are the only two pueblos with rectangular kivas and there is a very specific reason why. There is a reason why we strongly object to the excavation of kivas, especially kivas demonstrated to be ceremonial in nature.

There is always the problem of correct interpretation. The word *kiva* is a Hopi word that comes from two words: house and underground. Thus it literally means "house underground." In concept it does not necessarily mean a religious ceremonial chamber underground. It literally means a structure, house, or place underground. This causes a significant problem when I read archaeological and technical reports. As I now know, every round depression is classified as a kiva, but reports often do not qualify them any further. Look at Chaco and Pueblo Bonito. There are some such structures that are truly ceremonial in nature, but there are also others that I think the Pueblo people, in my case the Hopis, would interpret as something else.

I took some of my staff and several people from the Smithsonian Institution up to Old Oraibi, and among the significant features of Oraibi are about a dozen ceremonial cisterns. These are similar to kivas in structure but are not kivas in the classic sense. We took a hike up to several of our local clan sites up there and looked at some of the ceremonial cisterns perched right on the tip of the mesa. I would like to comment here on the fact that it does not make me feel like a real contributor when I share some of this information and people respond by saying to me, "Well, that's oral tradition." *Oral tradition* is a relegated term. I don't like it and I don't use it. Rather I would substitute *traditional knowledge* or *cultural knowledge*, because in Hopi what I am referring to is still supported in a social context in perspectives about how our society interacts, how our clan system works, and what some of the original and ceremonial functions of each of these Hopi clans and societies were and how they work. This kind of traditional knowledge is also supported extensively by ceremony and ritual, which are very tangible if you have the opportunity to be initiated into several of our societies. Therefore, *oral tradition* is a term I do not endorse. I would prefer traditional and cultural knowledge of the Hopi people.

These ceremonial cisterns, according to our traditions, were manifested through prayer and ritual. Hopi clans had to practice that sense of spirituality and humility and, through the use of ceremony and prayer, brought about a blessing we see as ceremonial cisterns. As I was sitting on top of one of these little buttes and looked at one of these ceremonial cisterns, because that's what it is in clan history, I have to ask myself how can water flow up? Generally you see cisterns or springs at the bottom where you have seepage, but when you have ceremonial cisterns there's that very specific Hopi element attached to it. That's another interpretive perspective into archaeology of our program.

I'm very interested today in the ceramic distribution sites reveal because of how this relates to clans. As they were arriving in Oraibi, clans were assigned specific areas. For example, there are two bands of Coyote clans at Oraibi, and they were among the last clans to arrive. They were assigned lands for a number of reasons. They did not have any major ceremonies to add to the Hopi ceremonial cycle, but rather they pledged to defend the Hopi villages, and through this pledge the Hopi chiefs allowed them into Oraibi. In examining the documentation of genealogy and the clan structure around Oraibi, it would not be surprising to find Coyote clans surrounding Oraibi. Ceramic distribution, I feel, will corroborate Hopi information about the assignment of clans to specific areas. I would be interested to see if we can look at traditional knowledge and some of the clan stories and see how these dovetail with the archaeological tracing of ceramics.

I am interested in that sort of research. I think it would verify traditions that Hopi still hold. For instance, I am personally interested in Aztec National Monument, which we call the Place of the Arrow. Some of our clans migrated from Mesa Verde and met up with the Rabbit, Tobacco, Crow, and Kachina clans over at Aztec National Monument.

In summary, we have an archaeological program, and when necessary we have conducted excavations on Hopi. When a shopping center development was proposed on First Mesa, and because clan ownership is very specific in terms of the land base, the village of Walpi had no choice but to ask the Hopi tribe's Cultural Preservation Office to come in and conduct not only a survey but also some testing. Once we had done the testing and found that there was nothing subsurface, the project went ahead. We processed mitigation requirements. Walpi also called us on a road project. In stabilizing the sides of the road they had encountered one burial, and a few more were endangered by the clay for the stabilization. Our team of archaeologists went up and removed three sets of human remains and the Hopis reinterred them in a safer place. Human remains were encountered on a pipeline project. Our office was called and, with clan consultation, was allowed to remove those remains and reinter them in a safe area close by.

I hope that the Hopi program has developed far enough to be a technical resource to the profession of anthropology and particularly to archaeology. We will continue to depend on the discipline of archaeology to have our program expand in a sensitive way so as to function as a resource not only for anthropology and archaeology but for the education of the whole American public to understand its past.

Author's Note

For more extended discussion about Hopi and other Native American perspectives on issues raised in this chapter, see *Working Together: Native Americans and Archaeologists,* ed. Kurt E. Dongoske, Mark Aldenderfer, and Karen Doehner (Washington, D.C.: Society for American Archaeology, 2000). For current and updated information on the Hopi Cultural Preservation Office, consult our web page: <www.nau.edu/~hcpo-p/index.html>.

5

Neat Stuff and Good Stories

Interpreting Historical Archaeology
in Two Local Communities

Adrian Praetzellis

As a historical archaeologist working in California, I deal with sites from the nineteenth and twentieth centuries. When I go back to England, every year or so, I usually end up in a conversation that begins, "And what do you do?" At this point, I often find myself having to answer the one of the key questions in publicly financed archaeology today: Why would Americans spend their money on *that*? This is a reasonable question, even if it does wear one down after a while. The answer, at least for me, is to be found in a profound difference between the way many British people and North Americans view their respective pasts and the effect that this has on how they view their present.

To many Europeans, old is good and older is better. As one who began his career on medieval and Roman sites I can testify that no British person I have ever met has even once suggested that he or she personally identifies with the Roman conquerors of Britain or with the Saxon or medieval folk who followed them. Stonehenge, for example, is experienced by most British people almost as a theatrical set, the site of ancient goings-on that have no relevance to modern life and no connection to living people— except, of course, to latter-day druids who feel themselves to be the spiritual descendants of the builders of this great monument. Stonehenge is undeniably dramatic, but for most people its meaning is in the past. Strangely, while the British are willing to stand in line for an hour or more to look at the reconstructed remains in the Yorvik Viking Centre in York, they would turn their noses up at the archaeology of the nineteenth century.

Over the last twenty-six years of participant observation, I have come to believe that Americans are far more aware than their European cousins that, as a nation, we are the product of our immediate past. Many people to whom I have spoken understand that historical archaeology truly is "the archaeology of us" and how we got to be as we are. It is not a second-best kind of archaeology, plied only by those who could not make it as Meso-American specialists. In fact, it seems to me that the only people who actually care about the trade relations of the Classic Period are academics, who engage in esoteric discussions for vaguely aesthetic reasons, in the words of the theologian Thomas Merton. Yet when I talk to a television reporter about a nineteenth-century working-class neighborhood where people of half a dozen races and ethnicities managed to "get along" (to borrow a phrase from Rodney King of the notorious Los Angeles Police Department beating case), the lessons for modern life are so obvious that the story makes the six o'clock news. It is clear that archaeology has a lot to contribute. However, for ordinary people to get any benefit from it, we professionals have to engage them in our work; and this brings me to the first case study.

As I wrote the first draft of this chapter in 1995, the U.S. General Services Administration (GSA) was constructing a huge new federal building and courthouse in the middle of what had been the historic Chinese district of Sacramento, California. This neighborhood had been largely Chinese from the time of the Gold Rush until the greatest threat of all—urban renewal—had transformed some of this "blighted" area into a parking lot. Even today the district is very Asian in appearance and has an active Chinese community, a mix of families who have lived in Sacramento for several generations and others who arrived after the Communist takeover in 1949.

My first abortive contact with the community was in 1981 when an office building was to be built on what had been an "urban-renewed" parking lot. Naively, I imagined that mailing out a friendly letter inviting all the members of the local Chinese-American historical society to visit the archaeological excavations would do the job. I recall that we got one local visitor. Next time, I vowed, we would do better.

In 1994 my organization was contracted to deal with the archaeology of the proposed courthouse site, across the street from our first excavation. We began to lay the groundwork for public involvement early: first by supplying artifacts to community members who were putting together an exhibit at a local museum and later by speaking on Sacramento's Chinese archaeology at the Sun Yat Sen Hall, in the heart of Chinatown. Both events involved the Chinese American Council of Sacramento, whose leadership of local business and community activists saw the archaeological work as a way of focusing attention on the modern Chinese community as well as the achievements of their forebears. Albert Yee, a doctoral candidate in history at Ohio State University who did historical research on the site, pointed out that although several blocks of the city's historic district had been restored as Old Sacramento State Historic Park, there is nothing to show the contributions of Sacramento's Chinese pioneers in the part of the town that was and is the center of the Chinese-American population. Perhaps, we thought, there was a way to remedy this oversight.

The archaeological site at the courthouse was remarkable. It was certainly one of the best I had seen since I first began work in Sacramento in the mid-1970s. In the early 1850s it was the location of boardinghouses run by the principal Chinese family associations. The entire block had been razed by fire in 1855 and, in true Gold Rush spirit, people had simply built over the debris. It was a kind of California Chinese Pompeii, with all the remains of everyday life left where they had fallen.

Our archaeological treatment plan for the federal building project specified that depending on what we discovered on the site, GSA might authorize a "product" for public interpretation. The plan used the word *might* because, after all, one never knows what one may find on a site, including nothing at all. GSA's district historic preservation officer, Joan Byrens, and her successor, Esther Timberlake, were enthusiastic about the site. They encouraged us to pursue the idea of a permanent exhibit in the federal building—if there was grassroots support for the project. Since we now had a relationship with specific individuals in the Chinese American Council, I went to them with the idea of an exhibit that would focus on local Chinese-American history and archaeology. From the outset, I tried to emphasize to my friends at the council that the plan was to put the community in the driver's seat as far as the theme of the display was concerned. The archaeologists would act merely as consultants on technical matters. The council immediately got to work and began to gather support for the project. Meanwhile, GSA hired a local architect and historian of Chinese America, Philip Choy, to work with GSA's architects on a specific design for the exhibit. Mr. Choy visited our archaeological laboratory to see the artifacts from the site and developed a plan for a display dealing with the history of Chinese immigration and the local community as well as the archaeological evidence of the lifeways of the nineteenth-century

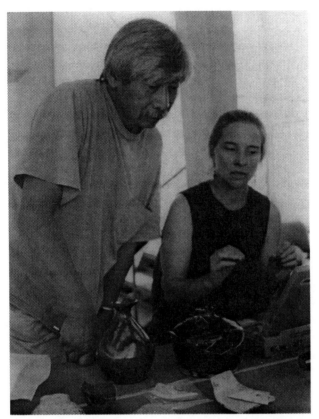

Fig. 5.1. Celebrating Sacramento's Chinese pioneers. Poring over tens of thousands of computer records of the ceramics, glass containers, and food bone from the site of the General Services Administration's new courthouse in Sacramento, California, archaeologist Sunshine Psota and exhibit designer Philip Choy select artifacts for a permanent exhibit in the building's foyer. The site, located in Sacramento's historic Chinese district, contained the remains of Chinese-run boardinghouses and businesses that were destroyed by fire in 1855. Photograph by Adrian Praetzellis.

pioneers who lived and worked on the site. Later, we all met with Chief Judge Robert Boyle of the U.S. District Court, who expressed his support for the project.

As a result of all this and thanks to a supportive federal agency and some highly effective lobbying, there is now a 900-square-foot permanent exhibit on archaeology, entitled "Uncovering Sacramento's Chinese Pioneers," in the lobby of one of the busiest public buildings in California's state capital.

My second case study takes us down to the San Francisco Bay Area. Those who remember the 1989 World Series may recall that as the fourth game was due to begin, the announcers commented that a major earthquake had just jolted Candlestick Park. Tragically, this shaker demolished a portion of Interstate 880, the Cypress Freeway, in Oakland, and more than eighty people died when the upper deck of the freeway crashed down, crushing the vehicles below. Responding to local pressure, the California Department of Transportation (CALTRANS) decided not to rebuild the freeway in the same location but rather to reroute it through part of what had been Oakland's historic residential and industrial neighborhoods. More than thirty archaeologically sensitive city blocks would be affected by the construction. With the support of CALTRANS archaeologist Janet Pape, we successfully made a case in the project's Archaeological Treatment Plan that if important archaeological remains were found, the agency should make an effort to let the public in on the excitement.

Initially, some CALTRANS engineers were skeptical that anything of interest would have survived in this heavily built up area. They were profoundly wrong. At the final count, the field archaeologists had exposed more than 2,500 archaeological features—such as building remains, refuse-filled pits, and post holes—of which more than 130 were determined to be eligible for the National Register of Historic Places.

In the nineteenth century, the area was made up of both solid working-class neighborhoods and mixed neighborhoods of middle- and working-class families. It was noticeably multiethnic, with boardinghouses of eastern European immigrants or Irish next door to transplanted Italians and New Englanders. In the 1870s, many African Americans moved in to work at the huge railroad yards, making West Oakland one of the earliest black communities in the West and an established destination for people looking for a new life after the Civil War. Many locals can trace their family connections in Oakland over several generations, back to the 1880s. For example, Gertrude Blake, a local real estate agent, has been researching the U.S. population census schedules and found members of her family on several city blocks where archaeologists have been working.

With this context in mind, we would have found it difficult to ignore immigrant and African-American archaeology when our project's research design was written. Up to the mid-1990s, almost no archaeology had been done in the West that emphasized black Americans. This is not to

Fig. 5.2. A capitalist's dining room. Erica Gibson, archaeological lab director, shows off the contents of a single refuse-filled privy excavated in West Oakland in advance of the Cypress Freeway (Interstate 880) project. It is clear that the resident, who gave his occupation to the U.S. census taker in 1880 as "Capitalist," could have set a sumptuously equipped table. Yet food bones from the privy show that the household was eating cheaply, mainly stews and tough steaks. Photograph by Adrian Praetzellis.

suggest that some kind of conspiracy was at work but merely that these sites are relatively few and far between. However, within the first few weeks of excavation on the Cypress project, the archaeologists had uncovered several collections of artifacts that we can say with certainty were the property of specific African-American families whom we have identified in historical records.

Unlike the situation in Sacramento, where the identities of the individuals who used the things we found will never be known, in Oakland we have named individuals and families, including some of Mrs. Blake's distant relatives, who have unique histories as well as shared life experiences. There are railroad laborers, retired military officers, barbers and teachers, and factory workers and business owners; people from every section of society are represented in the archaeological remains.

Even before the excavation began, it was clear that we would uncover collections from African-American households. Furthermore, it was equally clear that this material would be of use and interest to local people who were looking for ways to revitalize their neighborhood by presenting its present population with a view of their historical continuity. A natural contact point in the community was the African American Museum and Library at Oakland (AAMLO) and its director, Robert Haynes, who by good fortune has a degree in anthropology and has worked on archaeological sites. After discussions with AAMLO, CALTRANS decided to sponsor a movable display that could travel around local libraries, public buildings, and transportation hubs—places where it would receive good exposure. As a museum curator, Robert Haynes knows all about the "hook"—that element of an exhibit that piques people's interest. He suggested that we tie the archaeology to a readily understandable and important local theme—the history of unionism.

Oakland was the western hub of the Brotherhood of Sleeping Car Porters, an all-black union of men who worked the Pullman sleeping cars. We archaeologists had excavated collections of artifacts from porters' homes. This was a natural connection that brought together something readily understandable and something a little esoteric—the idea that we can learn about past ways of life from things that people have left behind. Haynes even persuaded a retired porter to get his old gear out of storage and talk about the porters' lives at each new venue when the traveling display opened there. The mobile exhibit toured libraries, museums, and other public buildings in California for a remarkable three years before its run was concluded and the panels were given to AAMLO. I was delighted to hear that a high-level CALTRANS manager recently commented that the archaeology has generated most of the construction project's positive press coverage and is one of the few elements of the project of which the community actually approves!

Archaeologists are convinced that work showing the historical bases of modern society is both important and interesting. But how can we share our enthusiasm with the public? With this in mind, I would like to make a couple of suggestions about how the public can learn about what we are doing. And this involves an effort by all of us: the regulators, agency archaeologists, and consulting archaeologists. First, since publicly financed archaeology is regulated by the various state historic preservation officers (SHPOs), the effort must start there. SHPOs have to push the idea that public interpretation is an essential component of all major archaeological studies. There is ample support for this position in federal regulations and many examples of successful programs exist. We can make sure that public interpretation gets its foot in the door by regularly building it into the memoranda of agreement and treatment plans that archaeologists must prepare before the work gets official approval. Next, agency archaeologists must think about public interpretation when soliciting archaeological professionals to perform work in advance of road projects, building of public facilities, and any other government-sponsored construction.

Finally, what is the responsibility of consulting archaeologists? Most of the for-the-public products that my organization, the Anthropological Studies Center at Sonoma State University, has produced were initiated when we made the case to the sponsoring agency that any large public archaeology project should take the information gathered back to the people who paid for it. I have been seeing a bumper sticker around recently that says "Real Musicians Have Day Jobs." Archaeology is like music—it is not just a job; it's a vocation. It is what we would be doing even if we made our livings as dentists, foresters, or junior high school teachers. Once in a while we *do* have to risk losing a project for the sake of principle. I urge archaeological consultants to include in the next budget a line item for public interpretation and hope for the best.

British television has three regularly scheduled series about archaeology. They air not at 3:00 A.M. but during prime viewing hours. Imagine the potential interest in a nation like the United States, where identity is tied so much more intensely to the recent past. There really is no need for archaeologists to suffer angst over whether members of the public think archaeology is worth doing. Of course they do. But it is up to us to give them something in which they can be interested.

6

Underwater Heritage and the Diving Community

Lynn Harris

South Carolina was one of the first states to recognize the potential benefits of public and professional cooperation in the management of submerged cultural resources. The idea that recreational divers have the potential to be the archaeologist's worst enemies or best allies has often been part of the professional outlook, although the state's approach to working with the diving public has evolved considerably since the 1970s. Since the formative years of underwater work as a specialization within the context of the broader discipline of archaeology, the South Carolina Institute of Archaeology and Anthropology (SCIAA), the administrative repository for the state's archaeological site inventory, has actively worked toward developing a rapport with the local diving community and including the public in state-sponsored maritime archaeology projects. In 1989 the Underwater Archaeology Division's Sport Diver Archaeology Management Program (SDAMP) was established specifically to address the role of sport divers and to meet management needs in regard to the state legislation, submerged resource inventory, and research objectives. The program has a full-time position devoted to public education. A beneficial two-way exchange of information and ideas and a historical appreciation shared between avocationalists and professionals in South Carolina have resulted from this program, in addition to an extension of the training program to international venues.

Underwater archaeology is labor intensive and costly. There are only a few professional underwater archaeologists in South Carolina—a situation shared by most other states in the nation. Trained scuba divers provide a large and effective workforce in a time of dwindling state budgets. It has already been convincingly demonstrated that in South Carolina amateur divers find the majority of sites by virtue of their numbers and the frequency with which they dive. Combining professional and avocational skills is considered necessary by many archaeologists to maximize the potential information from our underwater resources. To utilize sport divers efficiently as an avocational workforce resource, it is essential to provide the basic archaeological training and information.

In return, divers use archaeology as a new recreational direction to apply practical diving skills, and they gain new insights and appreciation of submerged historical sites. Education programs targeting diving communities promote a better understanding of the necessity for site preservation and the enforcement of antiquities legislation restricting certain destructive activities on underwater sites. The perception that underwater sites are managed only for historical research objectives is often considered too abstract and esoteric by the general public. Additionally, preserving and enhancing sites for public recreation and as a boost for heritage tourism and local watersport businesses must become a vital part of the message.

Legislation and Site Management

The South Carolina Underwater Antiquities Act of 1991 (article 5, chapter 7, of title 54) permits small-scale, recreational, nonmechanical, surface collecting in state waters by divers licensed through the South Carolina Institute of Archaeology and Anthropology. The conditions of the "hobby" license require responsible collecting and reporting of sites to the state. Quarterly reports on finds are assessed by staff of the Sport Diver Archaeology Management Program and followed up by site visitation, collections documentation, and finally the submission of site data to the SCIAA Information Management Division for inclusion in the South Carolina State Site Files. Through the legislation divers are entitled to keep their finds while archaeologists, in return, gain information on the locations and types of cultural resources located within state waters.

This legislation, which amends a 1976 act, is distinctive to South Carolina's underwater site management and presents a controversial ethical issue to many professionals, who often are not comfortable with the concept of private ownership of artifacts and random public collecting without a coherent research design. As state archaeologists, we do not condone collecting; yet realistically we cannot effectively harness it, given the budget and staff constraints of our profession. The legislation contrasts with that enacted for terrestrial archaeological sites in the state. The reason for the discrepancy is that most terrestrial sites are either situated on private property (where there is no regulation, except for grave sites) or on regulated state or federally owned land such as parks, forests, and reserves. Underwater sites are all located on state-owned bottomlands. The assistance of state wildlife officers to enforce the law is a help but is not entirely satisfactory. The answer lies in greater efforts toward public education rather than in enforcement alone. The state hobby licensing system also allows the state to manage the collecting activities of sport divers to some degree. Assessments of how much collecting is taking place and to what extent the resources are being impacted can be monitored. This is conducted through quarterly reports, liaisons with dive shops, and encouraging and directing sport diver projects. Balancing the loss of state artifact ownership with gains in management information and a long-term investment in public education about preservation principles is a price the state has decided to pay.

The Education Program

The central characteristic of the licensing system is that it does not work unless it is accompanied by a strong education program that equips divers to make preliminary site assessments and to acquire meaningful management information. The Sport Diver Archaeology Management Program provides a number of services to the diving community, including educational literature, a field training certification course, and workshops and conferences. A field manual familiarizes sport divers with archaeological concepts and the objectives of the program (Harris 1990a). It also describes and explains affordable ways to record the locations of sites and artifacts; lists basic conservation techniques; and provides detailed information on artifact identification. Lists of references for further reading and names of people with speciality interests to contact are included. The quarterly SDAMP newsletter *Flotsam and Jetsam*, produced by state-employed archaeologists, keeps divers informed of conferences, workshops, and fieldwork opportunities and includes articles by both professionals and avocationalists. An annotated bibliography (Naylor 1990) provides a useful reference guide to local repositories and maritime collections in South Carolina for nondivers and divers who are interested in becoming involved in historical research. Site and survey reports by divers who have graduated from the state's archaeology training courses are continually being added to our compilation of public educational materials.

The literature produced by the program is complemented by annual field training courses and a continuing education program. This South Carolina certification system consists of four courses. Course 1 is the only formally taught course, combining theoretical and practical components. A series of lectures is given by SCIAA staff and advanced former students. This preliminary weekend session is aimed at familiarizing the participants with archaeological concepts and underwater archaeology techniques. It provides a broad-based view of the subject, yet draws on experiences of the training staff at local sites and through participation in projects.

The objectives of Course 1 are that participants should

- be introduced to the basic principles, concepts, techniques, and aims of archaeology;
- appreciate the need for recording, protecting, and preserving the underwater heritage;
- be familiar with state legislation and the types of sites and artifacts likely to be encountered in South Carolina waters; and
- have the necessary knowledge to undertake a basic pre-disturbance survey of a site.

Lectures are complemented with a practical session in artifact identification and a series of pool training exercises on a replica shipwreck and scattered artifact assemblage simulating an underwater site. This exercise familiarizes students with methods of recording ship construction components and with conventional mapping and surveying techniques.

Courses 2 and 3 require continued involvement in projects, workshops, archaeological meetings, and conferences. To obtain higher certification credits, students receive a logbook to list further fieldwork experience, site report submissions, and workshop or conference attendance. Workshops are offered by SCIAA on a monthly basis and include topics such as (1) artifact identification (prehistoric and historic, water control structures, docks, and watercraft), drawing, and photography; (2) ship construction; (3) site photography; (4) drafting; (5) artifact labeling and cataloguing; (6) conservation; and (7) historical research.

Specific fieldwork skills obtained during project participation include (1) the use of surveying and remote sensing equipment; (2) site stabilization; (3) excavation and dredge operation; (4) taking lines from watercraft; and (5) using a grid.

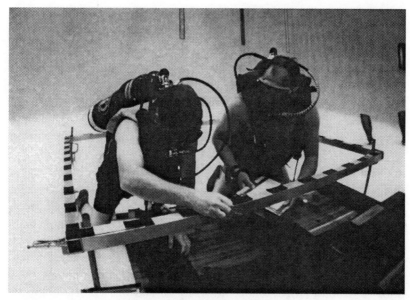

Fig. 6.1. Divers on an underwater archaeology field training course for the public in South Carolina learn in a swimming pool how to map a shipwreck.

By attending six workshops and five field training sessions, students advance to the highest level (Course 4), which involves directing a project lasting a total of fourteen days or participating in a project conducted by SCIAA for a similar time. The final products required in Course 4 are a written project report, a lecture delivered at a meeting or conference, and setting up an artifact or photographic exhibit.

To date, more than 200 members of the public have been certified through South Carolina's training program. The majority of participants are locals from around the state. However, an increasing number of out-of-state divers from Georgia, North Carolina, Alabama, and Tennessee have enrolled because similar programs are not currently offered in these states. Student groups have included scuba instructors, museum curators, university students, terrestrial archaeologists, anthropologists, high school students, law enforcement officers, judges, historic preservation officials, environmentalists, Sea Scouts, boaters, historians, business executives, and other diverse professionals with a common interest in maritime preservation. Nondivers are encouraged to attend these courses as many shipwrecks and other submerged cultural resources are located in marshes or intertidal areas like beaches. Underwater projects also require dry work, such as establishing land-based datum points, and post-fieldwork tasks such as artifact sorting, cataloguing, and photography.

Upon completing Underwater Archaeology Course 1, divers receive a South Carolina certificate that enables them to participate in local projects.

Research Projects

In comparison to most underwater archaeological projects, working in the riverine environment of South Carolina is challenging. Tidal windows limit working hours, and strong currents can tear and scrape inexperienced river divers off the river bottom. Underwater visibility, in water the color of iced tea, ranges from zero to six feet. Dealing with clinging aquatic weed, aggressive water snakes, and inquisitive alligators are other exciting parts of the job.

Various projects have been conducted by advanced certified divers to date. For example, in 1990 a project directed by Hampton Shuping was initiated with the idea of conducting historical and archaeological research in the waterfront zone of three Georgetown area plantation sites—Richmond Hill, Laurel Hill, and Wachesaw (Harris 1992). The primary goal was to document architectural features of four barges, the plantation workhorses, which reflect the carpentry techniques used by the builders and the possible function of the vessels. Each watercraft displayed significant architectural distinctiveness, which could be attributable to the work of a master carpenter or apprentice on the plantation. Alternatively, the boats may have been utilized for different work tasks. Limited surface artifact sampling was conducted to provide some insights into activities and date ranges associated with the local riverine area.

This project was also intended as an opportunity for the Sport Diver Archaeology Management Program to teach volunteer sport divers the concepts of underwater archaeology, barge construction, and documentation methodology. Divers from around the state assisted in all aspects of the project, ranging from conducting simple surveying tasks and keeping field logbooks to search techniques, excavation, hull documentation, artistic renderings of the site and hull components, artifact cataloguing, and producing a final report. An equally important goal was the creation of a glossary or nomenclature for the various architectural components. In the past, ship terminology had been adapted to small watercraft. Unusual features like stretchers and end logs associated with the rectangular hull design of these craft required more specific definition.

In 1993, local divers under the direction of Jimmy Moss conducted a preliminary archaeological and historical survey of the west branch of the Cooper River, one of the most popular recreational diving areas in the state. South Carolina's inland riverine waterways were the historical highways and byways for watercraft, many of which were wrecked or abandoned or became casualties of military conflict. Rivers were also economic arteries for Native Americans, plantation owners, and African slave communities. The objectives of the project were twofold: first, involving divers in an avocational riverine archaeology project to promote diver education, and second, systematically locating and comprehensively assessing the underwater cultural resources in this historically significant two-mile stretch of the river. Sites included prehistoric and historic artifact scatters, dock structures, and shipwrecks. Participating divers were involved in a range of tasks, including historical research, plotting sites on topographic maps, cataloguing and labeling artifacts, and compiling the project report.

Unpublished literature about past archaeological surveys (previously undertaken by SCIAA) was examined. This background study also instigated a closer look at SCIAA's early site inventory system. The reviews identified various site management problems that would be pertinent for future work on underwater sites in the state. Based on the results, ideas were gleaned about underwater site distribution and interpreting fluvial processes, thus providing insight into riverine geomorphology and how terrestrial topographic features relate to underwater features. An analysis of artifact samples reflected distinctive assemblages relating to plantation sites on the nearby riverbanks. This project, conducted and directed by sport divers, provided an ideal opportunity to combine public outreach and education with research, an important goal of SDAMP.

Nondiving members of the public who participate in the state's program also have opportunities to become involved in maritime projects, such as documenting boats in museum collections or vessels embedded in riverbanks or beaches. In 1992, SCIAA conducted a terrestrial excavation of a small historic sailing craft, the Malcolm Boat (38CH803), in a mudbank of the Ashley River (Amer et al. 1993). The investigations revealed that the vessel was a small oceangoing hull dating to the last quarter of the eighteenth or first quarter of the nineteenth century. The project provided information about the vessel's age, method of construction, and function as a coastal or possibly interisland trader. The project placed the site within a regional maritime historical context in shipbuilding practices and typology of small craft. Methods of site stabilization for intertidal zones were also explored using the site as a testing ground. Members of the public were included in all aspects of the project, including excavation, documentation, and site stabilization.

A project of an entirely different scope was undertaken by avocational archaeologist Drew Ruddy with the guidance of our staff in 1999 and 2001. In 1969 Ruddy, then a college student, had secured one of the first hobby collecting licenses in the state to recover artifacts from the underwater environment around Willtown, one of the oldest English settlements in colonial Carolina. Today, thirty-one years later, Drew Ruddy has undertaken to tell the story of his earliest experiences as a diver and a collector. As a current SCIAA research associate, he has produced a unique and highly readable report on his Willtown findings. He writes in his introduction: "It is with amazement that I reflect today on how two teenagers with some diving experience and no archaeological training or background were able to secure a salvage diving license. . . . Today I find myself in a different place in my life, a different level of maturity, and although not a professional archaeologist, I have acquired a sense of appreciation for the precision required to document an underwater historic site." Going back to his early maps and diving logs, Drew and his diving partner of long ago attempted to map and reconstruct where they had found artifacts in former years. In his overview of collected materials, Ruddy explores possible reasons for distribution patterns related to both land and water usage during historic times. His report, which recently earned the 2001 Avocational Archaeologist of the Year Award, provides a historic background of Willtown slanted toward maritime activities, including early English explorations in the area, tensions with the Spanish, Indian trade, the Yammassee War, Stono Rebellion, and the 1863 Gunboat Expedition. Filled with colorful graphics like historic maps, aerial views of the Willtown waterfront, and photographs of artifacts, Drew's work is an extremely valuable addition to the growing body of literature by avocationalists on South Carolina's underwater heritage (Ruddy 2000).

Heritage Tourism: River Trails Form Flowing Time Lines

A wealth of submerged cultural material lies on our river bottoms and is embedded in the muddy banks of marshes. Hulks of oceangoing ships and riverine craft and the remains of ferry landings and dock structures belonging to a bygone era litter these aquatic thoroughfares. Each archaeological site on the trail represents an important piece of South Carolina's mosaic of transportation, technology, plantation, and labor history. A gigantic outdoor museum lies on our doorstep. Bringing up a shipwreck from an underwater environment is financially exorbitant and a logistical nightmare in terms of display and continued maintenance. Another alternative is in situ display as part of a trail or preserve.

In an effort to make the submerged sites of South Carolina available to the public, in the past five years the SCIAA has developed a scuba diving and canoeing trail in partnership with the local community and trained archaeological avocationalists. Trained volunteers assisted in all aspects of trail creation, including research, mapping the sites, and the logistics of making the sites more accessible. The project was funded in part by South Carolina Parks, Recreation, and Tourism. County and state agencies and local business also provided in-kind support in terms of services, equipment, and use of facilities.

The canoeing trail on the Ashley River is a tidal float of approximately six miles that affords captivating views of historic shipwrecks, wharves, and old river houses. The river is narrow and twisting with many overhangs. Charleston's historic Middleton Rice Plantation is located at one end of the trail, and a historic bridge is at the other. Dorchester, formerly a frontier village and now a state park, is an ideal midway point for the two trail legs. Most of the shipwrecks are visible only at low tide. The tidal range is as much as four feet, and trips have to be scheduled around the tides. Eight sites, including examples of colonial period sailing vessels, a nineteenth-century steam tug, and an early twentieth-century motorboat, all form part of the trail. There are several possible reasons for the demise of these vessels scattered along the riverbanks. Archaeologists speculate that these unserviceable hulks of the past were discarded or scuttled in navigation headwaters, reflecting a riverine disposal pattern and technological time line.

The Ashley River plantations are an integral part of tourism in the Charleston area, transporting the public back in time to experience the grandeur, elegance, and labor history of the old South. The river and the watercraft that provided the vital connection with Charleston form an important part of the story that maritime archaeologists thought needed to be told. Interpretive staff of Dorchester State Park and Middleton Plantation now offer regular canoe trips on the shipwreck trail in conjunction with their walking tours on land, thus linking the history of the land with the water.

The scuba diving trail on the Cooper River was officially opened in October 1998. In order to enhance the sites and make them more accessible to the diving public, waterproof slates with maps of shipwrecks and historical information about the river and each site were designed by our staff and distributed to scuba diving stores for sale to the diving community. When arriving at a site, dive boats secure to mooring buoys anchored to underwater concrete monuments identifying each site and the sponsors who contributed to the trail. A guideline leads across the river bottom to the shipwreck. The intention was to make it easier to dive in murky water and provide an orientation for less experienced divers.

The trail allows a diver to visit several sites in one day. These include examples of a Revolutionary War vessel, a nineteenth-century river barge, a locally built plantation boat, an oceangoing schooner, and historic waterfront access structures like wharves and ferry landings. There is also plenty to see above the water, like the former rice paddies and remnants of rice cultivation irrigation structures. Trail boats carry diving tourists through a golden spiderweb of marshland creeks and tracts of properties that were the family plantations of some of the wealthiest members of the colonial elite. An abundance of wildlife inhabits the riverbanks, including water birds, turtles, and alligators. The trail is essentially an effort to blend aquatic recreation with education, historic preservation, and—to coin a new word—eco/archaeo-tourism.

International Outreach Program

South Africa

From 1993 to 1994, as part of an international consultancy, SCIAA was invited to assist in laying the groundwork for a public underwater archaeology training program for the National Monuments Council (NMC) in South Africa. This program was established in conjunction with the development of a national shipwreck database. At present there are an approximately 2,000 historically known shipwrecks within South African territorial waters, representing an international heritage. These include seventeenth- and eighteenth-century British, Dutch, Portuguese, and French East Indiamen; nineteenth-century British troopships; passenger and mail steamships of the latter part of the century; and a variety of twentieth-century shipwrecks such as Taiwanese and Japanese fishing vessels and bulk cargo carriers. Diving on shipwrecks is a popular recreational pastime, and diver visitation to these sites has escalated rapidly with increased tourism during the last few years. Unless the public is educated about preserving submerged natural and cultural resources, these sites will not be a viable source of tourist income or future attraction. Rather than dismantling shipwrecks for the recovery of portholes and other mementos, these sites could potentially be managed as underwater museums, training grounds for educational programs, and sources of potentially useful information for the national shipwreck database.

During the one-year consultancy period with the National Monuments Council, public training courses were offered around the country in coastal centers such as Cape Town, Knysna, Port Elizabeth, East London, and Durban. Over a hundred participants were certified, including historical archaeologists, museum curators, historians, wildlife officers, hydrographic surveyors, and other professionals who would be working closely with the diving community. An essential ingredient for offering courses in regional centers was the inclusion in the program of an invited local historian or scuba diver who was familiar with the history and submerged resources of the area. Discussions with participants were geared toward how the archaeological techniques and management concepts taught in the courses would be applicable to that particular cultural and natural environment. In the larger setting, the South African shipwreck legislation (Act 28 of 1969), the necessity for national resource management, the availability of funding for underwater archaeology, and the level of expertise for regional consultation and guidance were discussed within the context of what could realistically be achieved on a local level within the existing infrastructure.

In contrast to the legislation in South Carolina, South Africa's law does not permit recreational collecting. Activities on shipwreck sites are restricted to surveying exercises such as photography and mapping. Commercial salvage permits are issued through the NMC provided that the applicants have the cooperation of a local museum and a professional archaeologist to oversee the project. Currently there is only one maritime archaeologist, Bruno Werz, working in South Africa, through the University of Cape Town (Werz 1993). Most activities on underwater sites are monitored by regional museum historians and curators. State funding for maritime archaeology is nonexistent and any financial support is likely to be derived from the private sector. The political agendas and basic economic priorities of the new South African government are improvements to housing and education, not archaeology.

Any preservation efforts on underwater archaeological sites in South Africa will of necessity have to be generated by local communities with historically oriented rather than commercial goals. Guidance by local interdisciplinary specialists with common or overlapping management objectives would be the desirable course of action.

For example, sport divers surveying shipwrecks in the Simons Bay area of Cape Town are affiliated with, and supervised by, the South African Institute of Maritime Technology. Underwater mapping and surveying exercises provide application-testing opportunities for equipment and methodologies developed by the institute for hydrographic surveying in general. The team involved in our project there included archaeologists from the South African Maritime Museum and the National Monuments Council. Both agencies were interested in obtaining historical information, and trained scuba divers who had attended the public archaeology training course were keen to utilize their newly acquired skills to move to a more advanced certification level.

Divers who attended courses were also encouraged to utilize their skills independently to conduct preliminary, nondestructive surveys of sites and to submit for the NMC database data reports listing specific categories of information. These data could be utilized further for a shipwreck route being developed around the Cape Peninsula. The planned route is to consist of underwater trails for dive charters visiting shipwreck concentrations. Laminated underwater sheets with site plans are envisaged to orient divers on site layout and to familiarize them with the history and legislation. The route will be used as an educational training ground for future underwater archaeology workshops and as a boost to maritime tourism. The project is being funded by the local tourism board and business community. Trained volunteers play an important role in collecting information from these sites to produce underwater trail maps and displays, land-based story boards, and interpretation centers. The route displays will provide information on the marine flora and fauna as well as shipwreck features, thereby highlighting both cultural and environmental preservation issues.

Namibia

The Underwater Federation in Namibia, a neighboring African country well known for its diamond-mining history, also requested underwater archaeology educational courses for divers. This agency is responsible for training recreational divers as well as commercial diamond-mining divers who work in the alluvial deposits of the west coast surf zones. The training course was followed by an expedition composed of the trained participants to inventory shipwrecks along the Skeleton Coast. This area is named for the numerous shipwreck skeletons that litter the treacherous coastline adjoining the Namib Desert. The dynamic geomorphological processes along these beaches and littoral dune fields have resulted in many shipwrecks lying as much as a kilometer inland. These sites have not been inventoried, and the expedition would serve as the first part of a local management plan.

Surveys in this remote area were undertaken on foot, by vehicle, and in light aircraft. Wreckage was plotted using GPS units and was drawn and photographed. These data were linked to historical research conducted by the group historian, and a report was submitted to the Namibian National Monuments Council. Shipwrecks and disarticulated wreckage located during the survey included artifacts from an eighteenth-century Dutch vessel, hull components of American whaling vessels, supply watercraft associated with the diamond-mining settlements of the nineteenth century, and the remains of early twentieth-century fishing vessels. Additionally, the locations of diamond-mining settlements and whaling stations were recorded, including features such as houses, paraphernalia associated with diamond mining, human graves, supply wagons, and vehicles. The littoral dunes yielded evidence of trade or shipwreck scavenging activities among the indigenous peoples. Shell middens contained coins from the Dutch shipwrecks that had been made into a form of jewelry and hull sheathing shaped into projectile tools.

A World of Opportunity

Experiences in three distinctive geographic, cultural, and administrative environments support the notion that the discipline of archaeology is most likely to succeed by effective integration of public education, trained volunteers, private sector involvement, and tourism with the research objectives management strategies of the region's state and national organizations. Although it is possible to transplant basic concepts of cultural resource management to another state or country, the program has to be adapted to the local variations within the particular infrastructure.

Like South Africa, many countries lack funding and professional expertise yet have a wealth of archaeological resources still to be inventoried at a baseline level. This is the ideal phase to enlist the help of trained volunteers and to combine research with public education. The creation of a full-time position to coordinate such a program is highly recommended. A suitable arrangement is combining site assessments and database processing in the position description.

By working within established public programs like that of South Carolina, we might be able to achieve a viable worldwide network of research cooperation and communication. In terms of shared cultural resources, shipwrecks prominently represent an international heritage. Many historic vessels were not wrecked at their port of origin but on distant shores of other countries. These sites have important implications for trade, economics, and other cultural interactions between nations.

References

Amer, C. F. 1993. The Malcolm Boat (38CH803): The Discovery, Stabilization, Excavation, and Preservation of an Historic Sea Going Smallcraft in the Ashley River, Charleston County, South Carolina. Research Manuscript Series 217. Columbia: South Carolina Institute of Archaeology and Anthropology, University of South Carolina.

Boshoff, J. 1994. *A Proposal for the Establishment of a Tourist Shipwreck Route.* Cape Town, South Africa: National Monuments Council.

Deacon, J. 1993. *The Protection of Historical Shipwrecks through the National Monuments Council Act.* Proceedings of the Third National Maritime Conference. Durban, South Africa.

Harris, L. 1990a. *An Underwater Archaeology Manual for South Carolina Sport Divers.* Columbia: South Carolina Institute of Archaeology and Anthropology, University of South Carolina.

———. 1990b. Future Plans for the South Carolina Sport Diver Archaeology Management Program. Proceedings of the 1990 Tucson Conference of Underwater Archaeology. Society for Historical Archaeology.

———. 1992. *The Waccamaw-Richmond Hill Waterfront Project 1991: Laurel Hill Barge No. 2.* Research Manuscript Series no. 214. Columbia: South Carolina Institute of Archaeology and Anthropology, University of South Carolina.

———. 1995. Integrating Shipwreck Management, Research and Public Education in Southern Africa. Paper delivered at the 28th Annual Conference on Historical and Underwater Archaeology, Washington, D.C.

Harris, L., J. Moss, and C. Naylor. 1993. *A Preliminary Underwater Archaeological and Historical Reconnaissance of the West Branch of the Cooper River.* Research Manuscript Series no. 218. Columbia: South Carolina Institute of Archaeology and Anthropology, University of South Carolina.

Naylor, C. 1990. *South Carolina's Maritime History: An Annotated Bibliography of the Colonial Period*. Columbia: South Carolina Institute of Archaeology and Anthropology, University of South Carolina.

Ruddy, D. 2000. Willtown Bluff "A convenient fertill piece of land fitt to build a towne on. . .": An Avocational Underwater Archaeological Report. Columbia: South Carolina Institute of Archaeology and Anthropology, University of South Carolina.

Werz, B. 1993. South African Shipwrecks and Salvage: The Need for Improved Management. *International Journal of Nautical Archaeology* 22: 237–44.

7

On the Power of Historical Archaeology to Change Historians' Minds about the Past

James P. Whittenburg

My purpose is to represent the point of view of historians in a discussion of the public benefits of archaeology—to explain how archaeology benefits the public through its impact upon historical research. That assumes, of course, that there are public benefits to my own field. Archaeology may be easier to defend. Indeed, the public benefits of historical archaeology seem self-evident to this resident of Williamsburg, Virginia. Colonial Williamsburg rests—literally—on archaeological evidence. If we could take archaeology out of the picture by means of some time machine, I think we could be certain that there would have been no restoration—at least as we now know Duke of Gloucester Street. In a nonacademic vein, I would suggest that there would now be no economic base to modern Williamsburg. The College of William and Mary might well have ceased to exist at all. Certainly, there was little beyond stubbornness to keep either the town or the school going between the time when the state capital moved to Richmond during the Revolution and the first stirring of John Rockefeller's interest in restoration at the beginning of the Great Depression.

Still, Williamsburg is a peculiar place where archaeology has become woven into the fabric of the community—and is therefore seen as unexceptional. Over the course of my career, I have dealt with, used, and felt the influence of archaeology on almost a daily basis in my role as scholar and teacher. It is hardly surprising, then, that I have strong and positive opinions about the benefits of archaeology, public or otherwise. I do not, however, have wide experience in explaining those benefits to other people. My intention here is to illustrate the manner in which archaeology has the power to inform historians such as myself about the past, even to cause us to change our minds, which is no small feat. To do that I will stick closely to the single example of the history of the early Chesapeake.

A Model of Early Chesapeake Society

At some point in the late 1970s, historians reached a near consensus on the general outlines of British colonization in Virginia and Maryland over the course of the seventeenth century. That assertion might strike some of my colleagues—who are given to intellectual fisticuffs over any point of dis-agreement—as very odd. But in overview, our model of the early Chesapeake was one of anarchy, early death, and brutal exploitation leading to social degradation and political instability. Dependent for decades upon immigration for its very survival, the English presence in the Chesapeake slowly righted itself demographically toward the end of the first century of settlement. After two massive Indian revolts and a fierce rebellion among the English settlers themselves, the chaos finally gave way to sta-bility, deference, and the ordered Georgian mindset of Washington's Vir-ginia, sometime after 1720 or so (Greene 1988: 81–100).

The first and in many ways the most effective tool in this 1970s "new social history" reconstruction of the seventeenth-century Chesapeake world was demography. Very careful and often highly quantitative research gave us an image of the Chesapeake between the founding of Jamestown in 1607 and the decision to transfer the capital to Williamsburg in 1699 as the ragged end of the British world. There life expectancy was so low and the gender ratio so skewed that families could hardly exist at all, much less pass wealth or power from one generation to the next. The im-migration upon which the region depended for its very life produced con-tinual turnover at all levels of leadership and worked against the establish-ment of communities. At length, the unanticipated discovery of a veritable money tree—the tobacco plant—opened the door first to temporary sla-very in a particularly vicious form of indentured servitude and then to outright enslavement of Africans for life (Morgan 1975; Tate and Ammer-man 1979; Rutman and Rutman 1984). The 1970s boom in Chesapeake archaeology played a role in reaffirming this Virginia-as-hell-hole model. In the next ten years, certainly by the time we celebrate the 400th anniver-sary of the founding of Jamestown, the model will undergo significant change, and this time archaeology will be at the forefront, not merely play-ing a supporting role.

Native Americans, Englishmen, and Jamestown Island

In comparison to later colonial history, we know rather little about the Jamestown era. Until recently, most historians assumed that this first enduring British mainland outpost had long ago fallen victim to erosion and lay somewhere offshore in the James River. William M. Kelso and Nicholas M. Luccketti have proven that assumption false—if only by a few feet—by uncovering John Smith's fort during work for the Association for the Preservation of Virginia Antiquities.

Every inch a for-profit corporation, the Virginia Company of London began Jamestown in 1607 as a capitalist enterprise. Even so, practitioners of the new social history such as Edmund S. Morgan, Carville V. Earle, and Karen Ordahl Kupperman told us years ago that, between marching to the fields by drumbeat under martial law, the Jamestown folk died of salt poisoning—or simply apathy (Earle 1979; Kupperman 1979; Morgan 1971). Hanging on in the New World by their fingernails, these solders of fortune did not seem a very enterprising lot. What Kelso, Luccketti, and material culture specialists such as Beverly A. Straube have pieced together from the Jamestown site, however, presents a different image—one of vigorous activity aimed at making a profit from trade with local Indians as soon as the boats docked in 1607. In turn, the nature of that trade with the Powhatans has added a key piece of evidence required to answer the question historian J. Frederick Fausz asked in 1987: "Why did Powhatan and his people allow Jamestown to survive?" (Fausz 1987).

The standard answer to Fausz's query, thanks mainly to Nancy Oestreich Lurie, had long been that Powhatan saw the colonists as potential allies against his Native-American, not European, enemies (Lurie 1959). In 1990, anthropologist Jeffrey L. Hantman suggested that another factor may have been even more important: copper, a metal essential to Powhatan as a symbol of authority among his own people. Prior to the arrival of the English, Hantman explained, Powhatan seems to have acquired copper from the Monacan people of the Virginia interior. Yet the Monacans were at best an uncertain trading partner and at worst a hostile military force. Hantman hypothesized that the availability of English copper after 1607 may explain why the Powhatans tolerated the fragile Jamestown settlement at all (Hantman 1990).

The ongoing archaeology at Jamestown Island has established that almost from the time they set foot on land, the colonists produced copper items with which to barter supplies from the Powhatans. In particular, the Jamestown Rediscovery Project has turned up large quantities of tubelike copper beads that the colonists manufactured at Jamestown and the Powhatans strung together into necklaces or fashioned into bracelets (fig. 7.1). There is also clear archaeological evidence of the manufacture of clay pipes for the Indian trade as well as a number of other items—including medi-

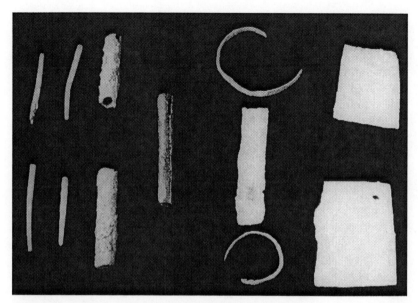

Fig. 7.1. Jamestown copper. Courtesy of William M. Kelso.

cine—for export. Indeed, early Jamestown begins to resemble a manufacturing center (Kupperman 1996).

Impermanent Architecture in the Chesapeake

It is hardly surprising that the people involved in the current Jamestown work recognized the profusion of copper at Jamestown as an industrial site, for they had seen something similar in their excavations at Fort Raleigh on Roanoke Island. In fact, they have long been interested in early sites in the Chesapeake, and from their work—building, of course, upon the findings of the Martin's Hundred excavations by Ivor Noel Hume—we now have a reasonably clear image of typical "company era" settlements such as this one, drawn by extrapolating from the stains that marked the placement of posts forming the early seventeenth-century stockade (fig. 7.2). For drawings and descriptions of structures and forts from the Roanoke Island and Virginia Company era, see Noel Hume (1982, 1994).

The journey from excavation of a fence line to the artist's conception of the fort may have been simple enough, but the buildings are not so straightforward—and are far more important to historical interpretation. In fact, posts set upright in holes dug to receive them formed a framework that could hold clapboards or, as at Jamestown, wattle and daub. It was

Fig. 7.2. Excavation of the bastion section of Fort Raleigh. Courtesy of Nicholas M. Luccketti.

certainly surprising that British colonists resurrected a building technique that had all but disappeared from England two centuries and more before Jamestown, but the archaeology was clear—once we played connect-the-dots.

Excavations of seventeenth-century post-hole houses in the 1970s became the key to our interpretation of early Chesapeake architecture as "impermanent." Archaeologists had seen these holes before, but we did not know what to make of them until the 1970s. Then, in a 1981 *Winterthur Portfolio* article that was as remarkable for its accessibility to historians as for the brilliance of its conclusions, Cary Carson, Norman F. Barka, William M. Kelso, Gary Wheeler Stone, and Dell Upton synthesized a decade's worth of site reports on this "impermanent" style of building in both Maryland and Virginia. Here was affirmation for the dismal Chesapeake world that the new social historians had outlined in a truckload of publications; here was exactly the sort of building style one would expect of a frontier society that reeked of crudity, death, and avarice.

Outliers

Ah, but then there was the great "outlier," a term from the classes I teach on quantitative methods, describing a case so wildly atypical that to include it in the analysis would mislead the researcher about the general pattern. Bacon's Castle, far off the river (also not typical) in Surry County (again, hardly the expected), could not be trusted. What could we learn from this single surviving aboveground example of seventeenth-century Virginian domestic architecture? Not much, according to the accepted wisdom of the time. It loomed over the seventeenth-century landscape, true, but like its builder, Arthur Allen, Bacon's Castle (fig. 7.3) was an enigma—rather like the Sphinx (Andrews 1984).

Fig. 7.3. End view of Bacon's Castle. Courtesy of Carl R. Lounsbury.

No, Virginians lived not in castles but in earth-fast hovels. These structures were routinely no more than twenty feet wide by thirty feet long, and at the very top of the heap (a nice way to illustrate the early Virginia social scale), the richest planter might crown his showplace with a coating of pitch and a thatched roof. Unfortunately, this made it difficult to explain places like Causey's Care, a site near Shirley Plantation just below Richmond on the James River. This plantation was home to Walter Aston, a man of some means, at least in an early Virginia context. Walter obligingly followed one of the key Chesapeake patterns by dying young—while his ill-fated son was a minor—so that the Aston name almost disappeared from the colonial record. But the entirely fortuitous excavation of the plantation, only a few steps ahead of the largest earth-moving equipment I have ever seen revealed a large, tile-paved cellar with a dairy room. It can only be described as an industrial complex—so complex that the functions of some of the structures, most of them stone, are not absolutely certain—and a motherlode of impressive artifacts that connote wealth and status. Was Aston, like Arthur Allen, merely an outlier? (Styrna 1985).

The problem with progressively classifying observations as outliers is that they soon form the bulk of the cases. In the last few seasons, more places—especially from the era of Bacon's Rebellion in the third and fourth quarters of the seventeenth century—have begun to push that envelope. For example, Richneck, about a mile beyond the College of William and Mary in the direction of Jamestown, is a complex of overlapping sites that archaeologists under the direction of Marley R. Brown III of the Colonial Williamsburg Foundation have unearthed in the midst of a new subdivision. According to the lights of the Virginia-as-end-of-the-civilized-world thesis, it should not exist at all until the dawn of the Georgian era a half-century later, when—like magic—the great halls such as Westover and Corotoman appeared along the grand river system of Virginia to symbolize the wealth and power of men such as William Byrd and Robert "King" Carter.

But Richneck did exist—right along with Bacon's Castle. They were not isolated exceptions to the elite norm. Construction adjacent to the Colonial Williamsburg restoration recently forced the excavation of the John Page House, a structure much on the order of Bacon's Castle: cruciform in cross section, brick, two or three stories high, and decorated with castings that bear the initials of the family who built it and the date 1662. The date marks it as earlier than Bacon's Castle and possibly a model that Arthur

Fig. 7.4. Cruciform cellar of the Page House. Courtesy of Marley R. Brown III.

Allen copied when he designed his Surry County estate. Even given the necessity of crossing the James River, it was certainly possible for the late seventeenth-century traveler to view Bacon's Castle, Richneck, and the Page House in a single day. Perhaps the seventeenth-century landscape looked quite a bit different from the one proposed in the impermanent architecture thesis (fig. 4).

Large castings of hearts, perhaps originally covered with white plaster, link the Page House, at least stylistically, to Arlington, a lavish plantation on the Eastern Shore, where recess heart-shaped castings decorated the main structure. It should not pass unnoticed that the Eastern Shore was as isolated a region as any in Virginia—not the sort of place we might expect to find the cutting edge of anything in the seventeenth century. Yet Arlington, built sometime in the third quarter of the century, was remarkable not only for appointments like the hearts. It was also exceedingly large. The mansion rested on a double pile of brick, possessed four chimneys for heat, and rose three stories above the ground. Equally important, its footprint closely resembles the footprint of the Governor's Palace in Williamsburg, which the colony completed in 1720.

Archaeology and the Interpretation of the Early Chesapeake

The landscape of early Virginia is about to change in front of your eyes. My friends who are archaeologists and architectural historians warn me to be cautious. Most of humanity, they say, lived in tiny, ill-equipped, impermanent hovels. True, I'm sure; but our image of a seventeenth century all but sinking into chaos under the weight of its own crudity—a society characterized by the celebrated vignette in which Governor Harvey assaulted a member of his own council with a cudgel, knocking the teeth from the man's mouth—is founded upon assumptions about the dismal lifestyle of the *elite*, not the *masses* (see Bailyn 1959: 95).

Arlington, the Page House, and Richneck will change our perception of that lifestyle by making it necessary to incorporate into our mental template of the era many more houses such as Greenspring, Governor Berkeley's seventeenth-century seat about ten miles outside Williamsburg and nothing now but a mound of dirt. More important to me as a social historian, the revised image of the people who built those homes will force a reevaluation of their society. It may well be that even in the context of a miserable demographic situation, the Chesapeake elite achieved political and economic hegemony much earlier than most historians have thought possible. Perhaps historian Jon Kukla was correct in his 1985 assertion that the seventeenth century may have been an age of heretofore unsupposed stability (Kukla 1985). Kukla was all but alone in that opinion a decade ago, and as yet the supposed stability of seventeenth-century Chesapeake society is conjecture, but if historians do alter their vision of what early Virginia was like, archaeology will have been a primary force in propelling us down that path.

The Window Is Open

If it is important that we understand the nature of early American society, then archaeology is going to be key to this public benefit. The early Chesapeake is merely one example. There will be others—if the funding for archaeology continues to flow. It would indeed be ironic if the money stopped now. The flowering of Chesapeake archaeology in the 1970s and 1980s depended upon funds that in one way or another resulted from governmental action, whether by grant or regulation, at the federal, state, or local level. During that span of about ten years we moved rapidly from a time when all the historical archaeologists in the country might gather in one medium-sized lecture hall to a critical mass of youngish scholars—most with exciting subspecialties—whose technical skills and academic training dwarf those of the earlier generation of men and women who more or less made historical archaeology up as they went along. Over the same decade and a half, resistance to material culture among academic historians has waned, as the presentation of material culture studies has grown ever more sophisticated and as the older, more tradition-bound historians have retired.

The newest recruits to history faculties come to us raised on the Annales school of French history, often taken along with healthy infusions of ethnography. Ever eager to plunder yet another discipline for its shiny new methodology, these *enfants terribles* have already spied out, among other targets, literary criticism, and they speak the names Foucault and Derrida in the same revered tones my generation reserved for names like Geertz and Deetz. My point is that the long-awaited full integration of material culture, specifically archaeology, and history has already begun; the union is entirely possible, right now. The window of opportunity, then, is open—if the funding continues. Otherwise, the next sound you may hear is that window slamming shut again.

References

Andrews, S. B. (ed.). 1984. *Bacon's Castle*. Richmond: Association for the Preservation of Virginia Antiquities.

Bailyn, B. 1959. Politics and Social Structure in Virginia. In *Seventeenth-Century America: Essays in Colonial History*, ed. J. M. Smith, 90–115. Chapel Hill: University of North Carolina Press.

Carson, C., N. F. Barka, W. M. Kelso, G. W. Stone, and D. Upton. 1981. Impermanent Architecture in the Southern American Colonies. *Winterthur Portfolio* 16: 135–96.

Earle, C. V. 1979. Environment, Disease, and Mortality in Early Virginia. In *The Chesapeake in the Seventeenth Century: Essays on Anglo-American Society*, ed. T. W. Tate and D. L. Ammerman, 96–125. Chapel Hill: University of North Carolina Press.

Fausz, J. F. 1987. The Invasion of Virginia: Indians, Colonialism, and the Conquest of Cant: A Review Essay on Anglo-Indian Relations in the Chesapeake. *Virginia Magazine of History and Biography* 95: 133–56.

Greene, J. P. 1988. *Pursuits of Happiness: The Social Development of Early Modern British Colonies and the Formation of American Culture*. Chapel Hill: University of North Carolina Press.

Hantman, J. L. 1990. Between Powhatan and Quirank: Reconstructing Monacan Culture and History in the Context of Jamestown. *American Anthropologist* 92: 676–90.

Kukla, J. 1985. Order and Chaos in Early America: Political and Social Stability in Pre-Restoration Virginia. *American Historical Review* 90: 275–98.

Kupperman, K. O. 1979. Apathy and Death in Early Jamestown. *Journal of American History* 66: 24–40.

———. 1996. The Founding Years of Virginia—and the United States. *Virginia Magazine of History and Biography* 104: 106–8.

Lurie, N. O. 1959. Indian Adjustment to European Civilization. In *Seventeenth-Century America: Essays in Colonial History,* ed. J. M. Smith, 33–60. Chapel Hill: University of North Carolina Press.

Morgan, E. S. 1971. The Labor Problem at Jamestown, 1607–1618. *American Historical Review* 76: 595–611.

———. 1975. *American Slavery, American Freedom: The Ordeal of Colonial Virginia.* New York: W. W. Norton.

Noel Hume, I. 1982. *Martin's Hundred: The Discovery of a Lost Colonial Virginia Settlement.* New York: Knopf.

———. 1994. *The Virginia Adventure: Roanoke to James Towne, an Archaeological and Historical Odyssey.* New York: Knopf.

Rutman, D., and A. Rutman. 1984. *A Place in Time: Middlesex County, Virginia, 1650–1750.* New York: W. W. Norton.

Styrna, C. A. 1985. The House of Walter Aston: The Historical and Architectural Reconstruction of a Seventeenth-Century House in Tidewater Virginia. Unpublished research paper, College of William and Mary.

Tate, T. W., and D. L. Ammerman (eds.). 1979. *The Chesapeake in the Seventeenth Century: Essays on Anglo-American Society.* Chapel Hill: University of North Carolina Press.

8

Garbology

The Archaeology of Fresh Garbage

W. L. Rathje

Gold cups, jade beads, mummies, temples lost in rainforests. To me, these were the essence of archaeology. How I longed to become an archaeologist and to journey back to the days of our ancient ancestors by following breadcrumb trails of artifacts they had left behind. When I was nine, that was the archaeology I dreamed about as I drifted to sleep beside my dog-eared copy of *The Wonderful World of Archaeology* (Jessup 1956).

Fourteen years later I found myself in graduate school and immersed in the stifling smell of dusty potsherds, the quiet punctuated every so often by the thunderous explosions of 200 or 300 broken pieces of pottery being poured out of linen bags onto masonite laboratory tables. These potsherds had become my path to ancient lives. By this time I had learned enough of archaeology's arcane secrets to appreciate fully the stories that could be told by potsherds and other commonplace discards about a society's rise and fall and its day-to-day existence. I was, in fact, excited to be systematically and scientifically analyzing the vast expanse of discards to discover replicated patterns of human behavior that we can still recognize today. At the time, I believed I was about to add my own small piece to understanding the puzzle of the Classic Maya collapse (see Rathje 1971, 1973). By 1968 that was the archaeology I dreamed about when I dozed off late at night on top of my well-worn copy of *Uaxactun, Guatemala: Excavations of 1931–1937* (Smith 1950).

Today, twenty-seven years later still, I look back on my past dreams of archaeology with a bemused smile, my hands full of fresh garbage and my mind dancing with thoughts of the calories from fat in our diet or of the recyclables mixed into garbage instead of separated for curbside collection.

As for today's dreams—who could fall asleep while perusing the Environmental Protection Agency's Report 530–R–96–001, *Characterization of Municipal Solid Waste in the United States: 1995 Update* (Franklin Associates 1996)?

What happened to my visions of archaeology? Nothing, really. Diverse as they appear, the three perspectives pivot upon the same point: coming to understand some basic threads in the fabric of humanity—which our ancestors wove into us and which we are likewise weaving into our descendants—by touching as a person and by measuring as a scientist the artifacts people make and leave behind. With this personal preamble as background, I will now describe the history, nature, and public benefits of a type of archaeology called garbology, which I believe is currently adding one small piece of understanding to help solve the puzzle of the human enigma.

"Buried Alive: The Garbage Glut" was the cover headline of *Newsweek*, November 27, 1989. "Are We Throwing Away Our Future with Our Trash?" had been the title of the "American Agenda" segment of *ABC Evening News with Peter Jennings* on December 2, 1988. In the late 1980s, the amount of garbage America generated had reached crisis proportions for the media and its public. The vast majority of refuse was sent to landfills, and those landfills were filling up and closing down. Where was the garbage to go?

Concerned citizens, convinced that action had to be taken without delay, quickly identified garbage culprits among the discards that visibly shocked them everyday—litter. Editorials in prestigious newspapers, such as the *New York Times*, echoed popular perceptions that fast food packaging, disposable diapers, and plastic grocery bags were singularly responsible for "straining" our landfills. Public officials in communities nationwide proposed banning the accused perpetrators. In the meantime, into what kinds of holders were responsible folks to put their burgers, hot coffee, groceries, and infants? Oddly enough, the answer was not clear, because in all the commotion there had been few facts presented about what actually was in garbage and landfills. It was at this point that a new kind of archaeologist, the garbologist studying fresh garbage, was able to unearth a few relevant facts that began to fill the information vacuum surrounding our discards.

At the time, workers around the country were regularly digging into landfills to install methane vents, but no one paid much attention to the refuse that was exhumed in the process. After all, it was just smelly, disgusting garbage. The smell and look of discards were not deterrents to archaeologists, who always expect to get their hands dirty. To archaeologists, in fact, contemporary garbage is a gold mine of information. No society on earth has ever discarded such rich refuse—much of it packaging, which identifies its former contents by brand, type, cost, quantity, ingredients, nutrient content, and more. Yielding to this temptation, between 1987 and 1995 archaeologists from the Garbage Project at the University of Arizona systematically excavated, hand-sorted, weighed, measured for volume, and recorded thirty tons of contents from fifteen landfills around North America—located from California to Toronto and from the deserts of Arizona to the Everglades of Florida. The information that emerged from these "digs" was unexpected (see Rathje 1989, 1991; Rathje and Murphy 1992a).

In contrast to all of the concern directed at fast food packaging and disposable diapers, the archaeological data demonstrated that both items *together* accounted for less than 2 percent of landfill volume within refuse deposited over the last ten years. Even more surprising, because of industry-wide "light-weighting"—that is, making the same form of item but with less resin—plastic grocery bags had become thinner and more crushable, to the point that a hundred plastic bags consumed less space inside a landfill than did twenty paper bags. If all three items of central public concern had been banned and had not been replaced by anything, the garbage archaeologists were certain that landfill managers would not have noticed the difference.

At the opposite end of the spectrum of contents were materials that occupied large portions of landfill space but received little public attention. Construction/demolition debris (C/D) was one. Because of definitional issues, C/D was not even included in the EPA's national estimates of the refuse going to municipal solid waste (MSW) or standard community refuse landfills. Nevertheless, C/D accounted for 20 percent or more of excavated refuse by volume in Garbage Project digs and was the second largest category of discarded materials recovered from MSW landfills.

The largest category occupying MSW landfill space was paper. This was true for refuse buried in the 1980s as well as for refuse dating as far back as the 1950s, because in most landfills, paper seemed to biodegrade very slowly. As a result, by volume nearly half of all of the refuse excavated by the Garbage Project has been newspapers, magazines, packaging paper, and nonpackaging paper, such as computer printouts and phonebooks.

Not long after the Garbage Project's first reports of its landfill digs, the energy directed at passing bans was largely redirected toward curbside recycling. A number of communities began placing emphasis on reuse and recycling programs for C/D. Paper recycling promotions started stressing the need to keep paper out of landfills because it did not biodegrade as quickly as most of us had once hoped. An association of state attorneys general determined from dig data that several products claiming to be bio-degradable, including some brands of disposable diapers and plastic garbage bags, did not biodegrade in landfills, and the false advertising of these products was eradicated. All of this was evidence that some crucial views about garbage on the part of policy planners, the media, and the public had changed—and that garbology had been validated as a new kind of archaeology, one that could make an immediate public contribution.

The Rationale for Garbage Archaeology

For as long as there have been archaeologists, there have been jokes, cartoons, and stories guessing at what it would be like for an archaeologist to dig through our own refuse (see Macaulay 1979). While often humorous, such speculations are based on a serious rationale: if archaeologists can learn important information about extinct societies from patterns in ancient garbage, then archaeologists should also be able to learn important information about contemporary societies from patterns in fresh garbage. The pieces of pottery, broken stone tools, and cut animal bones that traditional archaeologists dig out of old refuse middens provide a surprisingly detailed view of past lifeways, just as all the precisely labeled packages and the food debris and the discarded clothing and batteries in modern middens reveal intimate details of our lives today.

During the summer of 1921, A. V. Kidder seemed to understand this when he took the trouble to observe the artifacts that were coming out of a trench being cut for a sewer line through a "fresh" garbage dump in Andover, Massachusetts. From at least this point onward, archaeologists have studied contemporary urban refuse informally and sporadically in class exercises and methodological experiments. A variety of subspecialties—ethnoarchaeology, historic sites archaeology, industrial archaeology, and experimental archaeology—have been edging ever closer to analyzing what citizens of the industrialized world discarded last year, last month, and even yesterday. All archaeologists are aware that contemporary rubbish will inevitably be studied in due course by traditional archaeologists in the same manner we now study the middens of Troy and Tikal, perhaps in a hundred or so years from now.

If indeed there are useful things to learn from an archaeological study of *our* garbage—things that can enrich human lives and minimize the undesirable environmental consequences of the industrialized world—why wait until we (and I literally mean you and I) are all dead and buried to find out? This was what a group of students and I thought when we founded the Garbage Project at the University of Arizona in the spring of 1973. Today all of us who are a part of the project, including codirector Wilson Hughes, who was one of the founding students, are still thinking along these same lines. Garbology now!

After nearly three decades of sorting, recording, and interpreting MSW, garbology, or the archaeological study of contemporary urban refuse, has become a recognizable subspecialty within archaeology and other behavioral sciences (Thomas 1979; Fagan 1985, 1991a, 1991b; Podolefsky and Brown 1993; *American Heritage Dictionary* 1992; *Oxford Dictionary* 1995; Encyclopaedia Britannica 1996; Turnbaugh et al. 1996; Rathje in press). Perhaps the defining characteristic of all garbology digs is that they combine traditional concerns of archaeological method and theory to produce results that are immediately relevant to understanding and mitigating current social dilemmas (see Rathje 1996). The highly publicized "garbage crisis" more or less had the Garbage Project's name on it and made it relatively easy to convince the public at large that the study of contemporary refuse provided a significant contribution to society. The crisis did not erupt in the media, however, until the *Mobro* garbage barge sailed in 1987 and gained an enduring place in the nation's environmental consciousness when it wandered for weeks looking for a place to dump its cargo.

Fresh Sort Rationale and Results

The Garbage Project's first data collection format, called the Regular Sort, was designed to sample and record household pickups of fresh refuse (a *pickup* is all of the materials placed out by a single household on one regular refuse collection day). From the beginning, project procedures have rigorously protected the anonymity of the households discarding the refuse sampled.

Solid waste managers have been characterizing wastes by material composition (paper, plastic, glass, etc.) and weight since the 1880s. To these traditional measures, the Garbage Project added a series of innovations, including records from package labels (brand, cost, solid weight or fluid volume of original contents, specific type of contents, packaging materials) and more detailed breakdowns of broad refuse categories, such as "food waste" (which was separated into "once-edible food" versus "food preparation debris," both being identified by specific food item; see Hughes 1984). Because of their exacting level of detail, the Regular Sort data files documenting residential refuse are ideal for analyzing the role of specific household behaviors in generating wastes. Today the Garbage Project's fresh refuse records, compiled from a long-term ongoing study in Tucson, Arizona, and short-term studies in five other cities, form a one-of-a-kind database now spanning close to thirty years.

Garbage Project studies of fresh refuse have consistently documented a few basic patterns in the way we interact with the material world around us. First, *what people say they do and what they actually do are often different.* For example, while respondents rarely report to interviewers that they waste any food at home, nearly three decades of Garbage Project studies have documented that households generally waste about 15 percent of the solid food they buy (Rathje 1976, 1986; Fung and Rathje 1982). Such misreports characterize a broad range of household behaviors. In other words, people who are interviewed or fill out surveys do not accurately report how much food they waste, what they eat and drink, what they recycle, or the household hazardous wastes they throw away (see Rathje and Murphy 1992a, 1992b).

This discovery, of course, is not a great surprise. It is common knowledge among behavioral scientists that any methodology depending upon the accuracy of answers people give to interviewers or on surveys suffers from problems of informant bias (Webb et al. 1966). Respondents may not be able to recall specific behaviors accurately and quantitatively, such as how many ounces of green beans they ate the day before or how often they discard a half-full container of pesticide; and even if respondents can recall behaviors accurately, such as beer drinking or changing the oil in their cars, they may not want to admit to the specifics.

At this point it should be noted that systematic garbage sorts avoid informant biases. Refuse data, like virtually all archaeological data, are quantitative: packaging and commodity wastes can be weighed, measured for volume, and chemically analyzed, and their labels can be read for further information, all without relying upon the memory or honesty of respondents. When refuse is identified by specific household (as opposed to recording only the generating household's census tract), the Garbage Project obtains permission for its sorts from the discarders. Even under these conditions of self-awareness, project analyses show that, except for fewer alcohol containers, discards adhere to the same patterns found in garbage collected anonymously at the census tract level (Ritenbaugh and Harrison 1984).

Although independent of informant-based distortions, refuse analysis is susceptible to other forms of bias. The most obvious one is garbage disposals, and the Garbage Project has included studies not unlike those of ethnoarchaeology, to develop correction factors for ground-up food (Rathje and McCarthy 1977). Other biases include people who drop off recyclables at buy-back centers and the fact that behavior can only be characterized at the household level and not for individuals.

Overall, the advantages of garbage sorting as an alternative to self-reporting and as a quantitative measure of behavior outweigh its limitations, and the first pattern identified—that self-reports differ from refuse records—has opened up a broad new research arena.

The second conclusion drawn from refuse analysis is that *there is clear patterning in the differences between what people report they do and what they actually do.* This conclusion was drawn from a number of Garbage Project studies designed to verify consumer responses to various kinds of diet questionnaires by comparing self-reports about food use against packaging and food debris in fresh refuse. One specific self-report/refuse pattern the Garbage Project has documented is the "good provider syndrome": a female adult reporting for a household as a whole has a tendency to overreport everything the household uses by 10 to 30 percent or more. Another pattern is the "surrogate syndrome": to find out how much alcohol is consumed by household members, do not ask a drinker; drinkers consistently underreport their alcohol consumption by from 40 to 60 percent. Instead, ask a nondrinker; nondrinkers report accurately what drinkers drink (Johnstone and Rathje 1986; Dobyns and Rathje 1987). The second conclusion is again no real surprise.

Unlike the first two, the third conclusion was full of surprises: the differences between respondent reports and the material remains in refuse frequently indicate directly opposed behaviors. To be more specific, *respondents normally report rational behaviors, while their actual behaviors often appear irrational.* One of the best examples of this kind of counterintuitive relationship between self-reports and refuse occurred during the highly publicized "beef shortage" in the spring of 1973. At this time, when consumers were complaining bitterly about high prices and erratic availability, the Garbage Project was recording the highest rate of edible beef waste it has ever documented (Rathje and McCarthy 1977).

Several other instances of this kind of counterintuitive report/refuse pattern have been documented. In 1977, the Garbage Project gave meat fat its own separate category. Using the long-term Tucson database, the Garbage Project determined that in 1983 people began cutting off and discarding much larger than normal quantities of the separable fat on fresh cuts of red meat; at the same time they also bought less fresh red meat. Both actions seemed to be responses to a National Academy of Sciences study which was widely reported in the media and which identified fat from red meat as a cancer risk factor (Committee on Diet, Nutrition, and Cancer 1983). There was just one problem. The consumers under study replaced the fresh red meat in their diet with processed red meat—salami, bologna, sausage, hot dogs, etc.—which contained large quantities of hidden fat, so that the level of fat intake in the diet did not fall; instead, it stayed the same or rose (Rathje and Ho 1987).

A third case involved household hazardous wastes (Rathje et al. 1987). In 1986 Marin County sponsored a "Toxics Away! Day" to collect household hazardous wastes, such as used motor oil and unused pesticides. The Garbage Project recorded residential refuse two months after the collection day and compared it to household discards sorted before the collection day. The results were completely unexpected: there were nearly twice as many potentially hazardous wastes recorded in the refuse *after* the collection day than there had been beforehand. The data clearly demonstrated that all of the increase in hazardous wastes was due to the discarding of large quantities of items from only a few households (such as three or four half-full cans of paint or several full containers of pesticide in just one pickup). The Garbage Project's interpretation was that the media activity surrounding the collection day had made people aware of potentially hazardous commodities in their homes. For those who missed the collection day, however, no other appropriate avenue of discard had been identified. As a result, some residents disposed of their hazardous wastes via the only avenue available to them—their normal refuse pickup. The same pattern was verified in subsequent studies in Phoenix and Tucson (Rathje and Wilson 1987). The lesson learned: communities that initiate hazardous waste collection days should inform residents of future collection times or of other avenues for appropriate discard.

Counterintuitive interview/refuse patterns of this kind indicate that consumers may not be aware of how much their reported behaviors differ from their actual behaviors and that the Garbage Project is beginning to document a previously unmeasurable phenomenon in the gap between what people think is happening and what is really going on. Such studies have already led to some general principles of the differences between people's awareness of their behavior and their actual behavior (see Rathje 1996).

The Garbage Project's contribution to understanding more clearly the relationship between what people report and what they do (Rathje and Murphy 1992a; Rathje 1996) is based entirely on the use of archaeological methods and theory to document actual behaviors quantitatively from refuse. This is the grist of any archaeologist's mill, and the validity of the Garbage Project's data records and interpretations is based upon a hundred years of previous archaeological studies analyzing refuse to reconstruct behavior.

For a hundred years, archaeologists have also been studying refuse in attempts to count the number of people who lived within particular sites or regions at particular times. The Garbage Project has now done the same thing at the request of the federal government. The U.S. Census Bureau has long been aware of the criticism that its interview-survey methods lead to significant undercounts of ethnic minorities, especially young adult males, who may be undercounted by 40 percent or more. In 1986 the Quality Assurance Branch of the Census Bureau funded a study to answer the question: Could the Garbage Project count people based on the types and quantities of residential refuse they generate? The answer was yes (Rathje and Tani 1987). For any unit of time, the overall weight of total refuse discarded (minus yard wastes, which change markedly between suburbs and inner cities) varies directly with the number of resident discarders. The Garbage Project converted quantities of refuse thrown out per week to numbers of people by using per-person generation rates documented in test areas. Overall, a series of garbage-based estimates of population came within 5 percent of the actual number of residents. The Garbage Project now stands ready to verify census counts with a method that does not violate subjects' anonymity.

Ongoing Research

During the last two decades, researchers in the Garbage Project have worked on a large number of specialized topics similar to the census study, all of which are the focus of continuing inquiry. Landfill excavations, for example, are gauging the impact of recycling programs on the volume of wastes that reach landfills. The first reported results indicated that Toronto's "blue box" curbside recycling program has conserved some 20 percent of landfill space in the metropolitan area since 1982 (Tani et al. 1992).

Recovery of 2,425 datable, readable newspapers from Garbage Project excavations dramatically changed the view that biodegradation is commonplace in landfills. To understand better why biodegradation does and does not occur in landfill environments, the Garbage Project has so far conducted four cooperative digs involving microbiologists and environmental engineers from the University of Arizona, University of Oklahoma, University of Wisconsin–Madison, Argonne National Laboratories, and Procter and Gamble's Environmental Laboratory (Suflita et al. 1993).

Recently, the Garbage Project has initiated several studies integrating fresh and landfill data on hazardous wastes in MSW. The heavy metal assays of fines (that is, finely crushed samples) are being compared with detailed item-by-item lists (such as 2 light bulbs, 1 drain opener can, two newspapers, etc.) of the refuse identified within each 150-pound landfill sample. The goal is to determine the rate of movement of heavy metals in commodities and inks and other hazardous wastes from refuse into the landfill matrix (Rathje et al. 1992).

Garbage Project Students and Staff

The Garbage Project does not consist merely of systematic records compiled by hands-on sorting of household garbage; it is also made up of the sorters and project staff attached to the hands. While many people find the results of our studies interesting, most of them also find the sorting process itself revolting. A few market researchers realized in the 1950s that household refuse contained useful information, but after repeated experiments they found that they could not pay people to sort refuse. Those hired either quit quickly or kept sloppy records. Who would possibly be willing to rummage through someone else's smelly trash and keep accurate records of its contents? That is a good question.

The answer is a matter of public record. *Rubbish!* (Rathje and Murphy 1993—the paperback edition of Rathje and Murphy 1992a) contains a list of more than 900 university students and others who sorted refuse with the Garbage Project between 1973 and 1991. The intimate archaeological view these and subsequent sorters have had of the materials discarded from households much like their own has provided them with a unique perspective; and while they do not preach to others, they are enthusiastically dedicated to providing everyone possible with the same insights they have drawn from their own hands-on sorting of residential refuse.

In attempting to share results, we at the Garbage Project have focused most directly on schools, museums, and other avenues of access to students. The rationale is that the archaeology of our own society will mean the most to the young people who can do the most with archaeological insights. Currently, project members are especially proud of two endeavors. The first is the compilation of *The WRAP (Waste Reduction Alternatives Program) Resource Manual* (Dobyns and Hughes 1994), which has been distributed to schools throughout Arizona and the United States. The manual is designed to help students and teachers learn how their individual behaviors produce significant quantities of garbage and how they can make changes that will greatly decrease that garbage. The second endeavor resulted in "The Garbage Dilemma," an interactive video on permanent display in the Hall of Science in American Life at the Smithsonian's National Museum of American History. The video was the product of cooperation among Garbage Project staff, the Smithsonian's design staff, and the Chedd-Angier Production Company. Schools and museums—not landfills—are the kinds of environments where we hope Garbage Project results will eventually come to reside.

Garbology in the Twenty-First Century

What has set the archaeologists of the Garbage Project apart from other behavioral science researchers is that all of our studies have been grounded in the hands-on sorting of quantifiable bits and pieces of garbage, in place of collecting data through interview-surveys, government documents, or industry records. In other words, the Garbage Project is studying consumer behaviors directly from the material realities they leave behind rather than from self-conscious self-reports. The exhaustive level of detail Garbage Project student sorters use to record data has also set the studies apart from other data sources. Many local plans by engineering consultant firms and even by solid waste managers are based on national characterizations of solid waste generation, which involve estimating residential and other discards by using government and industry records of solid waste production—items of questionable validity—together with an untold number of untested assumptions. Even if national estimates are accurate, they are available only at the level of categories of material composition—so much plastic, glass, aluminum, paper, steel, and so on. But how can anyone plan with these data? Most of these materials come from the packaging with which people emerge from stores; but no one goes shopping for five ounces of glass, three ounces of cardboard boxes, or eight ounces of aluminum cans. Instead, they shop for a jar of Best Foods mayonnaise, a box of Cap'n Crunch cereal, and a twelve-pack of Bud Light beer. This brings us back full circle to our item-by-item Regular Sorts of fresh refuse. In other words, in contrast to virtually all other sources of information, the Garbage Project looks at refuse the way all archaeologists do—as the material result of human behavior.

Ultimately, the contribution of the Garbage Project comes down to one simple component: in order to understand and mitigate important problems, we must first become aware of the problems and measure their material impact. Measuring material impacts can lead to some surprising results. Consider the greatest irony of the so-called garbage crisis.

Since 1987 communities everywhere have been promoting recycling, reuse, source reduction, and everything else they can to decrease the amount of refuse being discarded. At the same time, to cut collection costs and reduce worker injuries, many communities have converted to automated systems that depend on standard-sized garbage containers. The containers that most families used to buy for themselves were usually sixty gallons in size, about what one person could carry a short distance. The new standardized containers have wheels and are one-third bigger, ninety gallons, to accommodate the needs of the largest families. By all accounts, the result of these changes has been that recycling is increasing and on-the-job injuries are down. So far, so good.

The Garbage Project hands-on sorts, however, add another dimension—a darker side that no other source has mentioned (Rathje 1993). When the Garbage Project first studied Phoenix residential refuse, the city of Phoenix, unlike Tucson, already had an automated system. Garbage Project personnel were surprised to discover that Phoenix households discarded nearly double the refuse thrown out by households a hundred miles away in Tucson. The mystery was greatly clarified when the city of Tucson switched to the automated system and its household refuse generation rate increased by more than one-third. At this point, the Garbage Project identified a "Parkinson's Law of Garbage" with implications for every city's solid waste management strategy (Rathje 1993).

The original Parkinson's Law was formulated in 1957 by C. Northcote Parkinson, a British bureaucrat, who concluded, "Work expands so as to fill the time available for its completion." Parkinson's Law of Garbage similarly states, "Garbage expands so as to fill the receptacles available for its containment."

Parkinson's Law of Garbage is really quite simple. When people have small garbage cans, larger items—old cans of paint, broken furniture perpetually awaiting repair, bags of old clothing—are not typically thrown away. Rather, these materials sit in basements and garages, often until a residence changes hands. But when homeowners are provided with plastic mini-Dumpsters, they are presented with a new option. Before long, what was once an instinctive "I'll shove this in the cellar" becomes an equally instinctive "I'll bet this will fit in the dumper."

The Garbage Project has compared the components of Tucson residential refuse collected before and after mechanization. Solid waste discards went from an average of less than fourteen pounds per biweekly pickup to an average of more than twenty-three pounds. The largest increase was in the yard waste category, followed by "other" (broken odds and ends), food waste, newspapers, and textiles. The first pickup of the week was substantially heavier than the second, reflecting the accomplishment of weekend chores, and the discards in that pickup were loaded with consistently larger quantities of hazardous waste than the Garbage Project has come to expect in a typical load. These findings suggest that the introduction of 90-gallon containers should be of concern for three reasons.

First, the increase in discarded newspaper suggests that one counterproductive result of larger containers may be a lower participation rate in any form of recycling. For those who find separating out recyclables a bother, the 90-gallon bin is a no-penalty means to circumvent the issue. Likewise, the increase in "other" and textiles could mean that people are using the bin as an alternative to the donation avenue, whereby unwanted resources wind up with the Salvation Army and other charities, or even as an alternative to yard sales.

Second, the substantial increase of hazardous waste indicates that the large bins are a convenient alternative to storing toxic items at home until they are used up or until the next household hazardous waste collection day.

Third, at the same time as all-out recycling programs are being implemented to try to decrease the flow of garbage, collection techniques are being installed that may unwittingly be *increasing* the overall flow of garbage to an even higher rate.

The evidence for Parkinson's Law of Garbage is not yet conclusive. The only way to know whether it is a behavioral pattern is through hands-on garbology. This archaeological research question is important to answer for the method and theory of archaeology, for culture history, and for our cities' immediate economic and environmental future. Garbologists, grab your gloves and face masks! One day the results of your efforts may be enough to convince Indiana Jones to turn his trowel on his own discards— and then recycle them.

References

The American Heritage Dictionary of the English Language. 1992. 3rd ed. Boston: Houghton Mifflin.

Committee on Diet, Nutrition, and Cancer, Assembly of Life Sciences, National Research Council. 1983. *Diet, Nutrition, and Cancer.* Washington, D.C.: National Academy Press.

Dobyns, S., and W. W. Hughes. 1994. *The WRAP (Waste Reduction Alternatives Program) Resource Manual.* Phoenix: Final Report to the Reduce, Reuse, and Recycle Grant Program, Arizona Department of Environmental Quality.

Dobyns, S., and W. L. Rathje (eds.). 1987. *The NFCS Report/Refuse Study: A Handbook of Potential Distortions in Respondent Diet Reports.* 4 vols. Final Report to the Consumer Nutrition Division. Washington, D.C.: U.S. Department of Agriculture.

Encyclopaedia Britannica. 1996. *Yearbook of Science and the Future.* Chicago: Encyclopaedia Britannica.

Fagan, B. M. 1985. *The Adventures of Archaeology.* Washington, D.C.: National Geographic Society.

———. 1991a. *Archaeology: A Brief Introduction.* 4th ed. New York: Harper Collins.

———. 1991b. *In the Beginning.* 7th ed. New York: Harper Collins.

Franklin Associates. 1996. *Characterization of Municipal Solid Waste in the United States: 1995 Update.* Publication no. 530–R–96–001. Washington, D.C.: Environmental Protection Agency, Office of Solid Waste.

Fung, E. E., and W. L. Rathje. 1982. How We Waste $31 Billion in Food a Year. In *The 1982 Yearbook of Agriculture,* ed. J. Hayes, 352–57. Washington, D.C.: U.S. Department of Agriculture.

Hughes, W. W. 1984. The Method to Our Madness. *American Behavioral Scientist* 28(1): 41–50.

Jessup, R. 1956. *The Wonderful World of Archaeology.* Garden City, N.Y.: Garden City Books.

Johnstone, B. M., and W. L. Rathje. 1986. Building a Theory of the Difference between Respondent Reports and Material Realities. Symposium on "Different Approaches to Using Food Consumption Data Bases for Evaluating Dietary Intake." Institute of Food Technologists Annual Meeting, Dallas.

Macaulay, D. 1979. *Motel of the Mysteries*. Boston: Houghton Mifflin.

New York Times Editors. 1988. Serious about Plastic Pollution. In "Topics of *The Times.*" *New York Times*, January 8.

Oxford Dictionary and Usage Guide to the English Language. 1995. Oxford: Oxford University Press.

Podolefsky, A., and P. J. Brown (eds.). 1993. *Applying Anthropology: An Introductory Reader*. 3rd ed. Mountain View, Calif.: Mayfield Publishing Company.

Rathje, W. L. 1971. The Origin and Development of Lowland Classic Maya Civilization. *American Antiquity* 36(3): 275–85.

———. 1973. Classic Maya Development and Denouement. In *Classic Maya Collapse*, ed. T. P. Culbert, 405–54. Albuquerque: University of New Mexico Press.

———. 1976. *Socioeconomic Correlates of Household Residuals: Phase 1*. Final Report to the Program for Research Applied to National Needs. Washington, D.C.: National Science Foundation.

———. 1986. Why We Throw Food Away. *Atlantic Monthly* 257(4): 14–16.

———. 1989. Rubbish! *Atlantic Monthly* 246(6): 99–109.

———. 1991. Once and Future Landfills. *National Geographic* 179(5): 116–34.

———. 1993. A Perverse Law of Garbage. *Garbage* 4(6): 22–23.

———. 1996. The Archaeology of Us. In *Encyclopaeia Britannica's Yearbook of Science and the Future—1997*, ed. C. Ciegelski, 158–77. Chicago: Encyclopædia Britannica.

———. In press. Archaeology and Solid Waste Management. In *The Oxford Companion to Archaeology*, ed. B. Fagan. New York: Oxford University Press.

Rathje, W. L., and E. E. Ho. 1987. Meat Fat Madness: Conflicting Patterns of Meat Fat Consumption and Their Public Health Implications. *Journal of the American Dietetic Association* 87(10): 1357–62.

Rathje, W. L., and M. McCarthy. 1977. Regularity and Variability in Contemporary Garbage. In *Research Strategies in Historical Archaeology*, ed. S. South, 261–86. New York: Academic Press.

Rathje, W. L., and C. Murphy. 1992a. *Rubbish! The Archaeology of Garbage*. New York: Harper Collins.

———. 1992b. Beyond the Pail: Why We Are What We Don't Eat. *Washington Post*, June 28.

———. 1993. *Rubbish! The Archaeology of Garbage*. New York: Harper Perennial.

Rathje, W. L., and M. K. Tani. 1987. *MNI Triangulation Final Report: Estimating Population Characteristics at the Neighborhood Level from Household Refuse*. 3 vols. Final Report to the Center for Survey Methods Research. Washington, D.C.: Bureau of the Census.

Rathje, W. L., and D. C. Wilson. 1987. Archaeological Techniques Applied to Characterization of Household Discards and Their Potential Contamination of Groundwater. Paper read at the Conference on Solid Waste Management and Materials Policy, New York City.

Rathje, W. L., D. C. Wilson, W. W. Hughes, and R. Herndon. 1987. *Characterization of Household Hazardous Wastes from Marin County, California and New Orleans, Louisiana.* U.S. EPA Environmental Monitoring Systems Laboratory, Report no. EPA/600/x-87/129, Las Vegas.

Rathje, W. L., W. W. Hughes, D. C. Wilson, M. K. Tank, G. H. Archer, R. G. Hunt, and T. W. Jones. 1992. The Archaeology of Contemporary Landfills. *American Antiquity* 57(3): 437–47.

Ritenbaugh, C. K., and G. G. Harrison. 1984. Reactivity and Garbage Analysis. *American Behavioral Scientist* 28(1): 51–70.

Smith, A. L. 1950. *Uaxactun, Guatemala: Excavations of 1931–1937.* Publication no. 588. Washington, D.C.: Carnegie Institution of Washington.

Suflita, J. M., G. P. Gerba, R. K. Ham, A. C. Palmisano, W. L. Rathje, and J. A. Robinson. 1993. The World's Largest Landfill: Multidisciplinary Investigation. *Environmental Science and Technology* 26(8): 1486–94.

Tani, M. K., W. L. Rathje, W. W. Hughes, D. C. Wilson, and G. Coupland. 1992. *The Toronto Dig: Excavations at Four Municipal Solid Waste Disposal Sites in the Greater Toronto Area.* Toronto: Trash Research Corporation.

Thomas, D. H. 1979. *Archaeology.* New York: Holt, Rinehart and Winston.

Turnbaugh, W. A., R. Jurmain, H. Nelson, and L. Kilgore. 1996. *Understanding Physical Anthropology and Archeology.* 6th ed. Minneapolis/St. Paul: West Publishing Company.

Webb, E. J., D. T. Campbell, R. D. Schwarts, and L. Sechrest. 1966. *Unobtrusive Measures: Nonreactive Research in the Social Sciences.* Chicago: Rand McNally.

9

Empowerment, Ecology, and Evidence

The Relevance of Mortuary Archaeology to the Public

Thomas A. J. Crist

In October 1992, the skeletonized face of the "Iceman," a Neolithic hunter found in the ice in the Alps, beckoned readers from magazine racks across the country. Gazing at us across 5,000 years, from the cover of *Time*, the Iceman was about to reveal to an eager public his secrets and those of his ancient counterparts. So intriguing was this mountain wanderer's story to millions of Americans that the October 26 edition of *Time* became one of the best-selling issues in the magazine's history.

At about the same time in New York City, an eighteenth-century cemetery in lower Manhattan was also becoming the focus of international attention. Excavated under historic preservation law prior to the construction of a federal office building, the African Burial Ground sparked a highly charged public debate that focused in part on the choice of scientists who would analyze the remains of close to 400 formerly enslaved individuals. In numerous public hearings and other meetings, members of New York City's descendant African-American community forcefully demanded that an African-American anthropologist direct the laboratory investigation of the excavated bones and artifacts. They further insisted that they be given a significant voice not only in the disposition of the human remains but in the treatment and preservation of the burial ground site itself. A congressional subcommittee hearing was convened to review the matter and a federal steering committee was appointed to act as a liaison between the community and the General Services Administration, the federal agency responsible for the project. The site evolved into a national symbol of African-American pride and empowerment (LaRoche and Blakey 1997); indeed, plans for the portion of the site that would not be part of the new building's footprint now include a memorial, not yet built, to commemorate the lives of the early African Americans buried there.

As the Iceman and the African Burial Ground both made headlines, thousands of Muslims and Serbs were dying in the war in Bosnia. Four years later a team of forensic investigators from the United Nations War Crimes Commission sifted through hundreds of human remains buried in mass graves to document the vicious atrocities committed during the Balkan war. These scientists, including two forensic physical anthropologists from the United States, carefully excavated and analyzed the bones to gather unimpeachable skeletal evidence against the military commanders who allegedly ordered the genocidal executions of thousands of civilians.

Each of these seemingly disconnected events involved the analysis of human skeletal remains, whether to learn about health and disease in the past or to incarcerate military leaders guilty of crimes against humanity. For centuries the effects of discovering and studying skeletal remains have reverberated throughout society, establishing international borders, supporting racial inequality and justifying slavery, validating religious doctrines and biblical passages, and identifying missing persons. Yet in these days of budgetary shortfalls and government cutbacks, archaeologists often find it difficult to justify spending public funds on the archaeological excavation and analysis, even the forensic analysis, of human remains. Because of this, many archaeologists consider proactive engagement with the public an essential component of good practice (Osborn 1994: 15). Archaeologists now more than ever seek to make their research relevant to current events.

In this chapter I explore both the substantive and the intangible benefits the public receives when federal and state funds are spent to excavate historical burial grounds. Examples of these wide-ranging benefits are outlined and discussed, specifically focusing on how the results of these projects are relevant to our own society.

Social Uses and Abuses of Human Remains

History and archaeology can both be used to serve different interests. The same event or site can be interpreted by different groups to support their respective political agendas, financial goals, or religious traditions. In much the same way, human remains and burial grounds can be manipulated to serve opposing views, to legitimize claims to power, or to accommodate the dominant group's moral and economic positions. Some scholars argue that mortuary remains, particularly gravestones, can be studied as part of social ideology, an active component in the struggle between the powerful and the powerless (McGuire 1988; Pearson 1982). In this view, funerary memorials emphasize an idealized expression of the social relations of power in an attempt by the dominant group to maintain the social order. Human remains can likewise be interpreted by scientists representing the dominant group to promulgate racist beliefs and other agendas by offering allegedly objective evidence to support their predetermined conclusions—whether the scientists are professionally trained or self-appointed.

Examples of the social uses and abuses of human remains abound. Between about 1820 and his death in 1851, prominent Philadelphia physician and scientist Samuel George Morton, building on the typological foundations Linnaeus had created in the previous century, collected more than a thousand skulls from around the world to test his hypothesis that the various human races could be ranked objectively using calculable criteria such as brain size (Gould 1981: 51). To collect data on brain size, Morton measured the cranial capacities of the skulls in his collection. By statistically manipulating his data he concluded that Europeans were the most superior of the human races, with Native Americans in the middle, and people of African descent at the bottom (Morton 1849). He and his colleagues also believed that innate criminality was reflected by the morphology of the body and that "born criminals" could be identified even as children (e.g., Lombroso 1911). As Gould (1981: 54–69) demonstrates after reviewing the original data, Morton committed several scientific blunders that reduce his famous findings to meaningless statistics. Yet American proponents of slavery hailed his work, claiming that Morton's results "scientifically" supported their assertion that African Americans represented an inferior human species. Morton's work laid the foundation for the rise of eugenics (the field of human genetic engineering) in both Europe and the United States, the most devastating effect of which was the horrendous Nazi campaign during World War II to cleanse Europe of those peoples the German "scientists" deemed inferior. Most Americans of the postwar period know little about the eugenics movement and its association with the infant discipline of physical anthropology during the late nineteenth century (Stocking 1987). Even fewer realize that American immigration law in the 1920s was largely based on the concepts of eugenics and the pseudoscientific ranking of various ethnic groups' mental abilities (Haller 1984; Larson 1995; Selden 1999). Building on the work of Morton and his nineteenth-century colleagues in the field of craniometry, a group of mathematicians and psychologists devised a series of intelligence tests designed to identify individuals and ethnic groups who exhibited reduced mental capacity (e.g., Yerkes 1917). Once identified, these "feeble-minded" individuals were barred from entering the United States. Those who were already American citizens were severely limited in their constitutional freedoms and were subject to federal sterilization programs (Gould 1981: 335).

Among the most onerous results of the mental testing (and racial ranking) movement in the United States was the federal Immigration Restriction Act of 1924. The hallmark of this law was the imposition of severely restrictive quotas against people of "inferior" mental ability, identified by American eugenicists as immigrants from eastern and southern Europe and the Mediterranean nations. It is particularly stunning to realize that a national policy on immigration that was passed into law by the world's most democratic country arose from the comparative study of skulls by a small cadre of Victorian scientists interested in ranking the mental abilities of the human species.

Social policies like immigration law are often based directly on "scientific" research, but other components of everyday modern life have been more indirectly influenced by this research, even decades after the results were published. Apart from its early practitioners' attempts to quantify racial differences (e.g., Hrdlicka 1899, 1919), the fledgling field of physical anthropology supplied a scientific foundation for the eugenics movement in the early part of the twentieth century. When it was founded in 1918 the *American Journal of Physical Anthropology* included a section on War Anthropology (Blakey 1987: 23), a practical application of the discipline to the perceived needs of the United States Army during World War I. This section described the physical and psychological criteria that American army recruits were required to meet in order to be accepted into the service, and it was supplemented by an extensive series of mental tests administered to over 1.75 million men during World War I (Yerkes 1921, 1941; Gould 1981: 194). The results of these tests were used in part to formulate American immigration law in the 1920s, as already discussed, and have been further used not so much to prop up the discredited field of eugenics as to support racial segregation after World War II (Molnar 1992: 269–70). Modern cousins related to these early mental tests include the intelligence quotient (IQ) test developed in 1912, the Scholastic Aptitude Test (SAT), the American College Test (ACT), and the Graduate Record Examination (GRE), now used as part of the admissions criteria upon which thousands of American universities depend. As recently as 1994 the

controversial book *The Bell Curve* (Herrnstein and Murray 1994) reig-
nited the nineteenth-century contention that race or ethnicity somehow
determines the intelligence and potential of an individual (e.g., Fraser
1995). Currently, researchers are seeking genes that determine behavioral
traits like aggressive personality and the propensity for criminal behavior,
rekindling memories of the Victorian scientists who sought morphological
features to indicate mental aptitude and criminal thought.

Undoubtedly, the major sustained source of conflict between archaeologists and non-archaeologists is the treatment of Native American human
remains. Beginning in the late nineteenth century and continuing as recently as the 1960s, archaeologists and physical anthropologists conducted
widespread, systematic excavations of pre-Columbian burial grounds
seeking skeletal remains to send back to their institutions for examination
and analyses. Often sponsored by government-funded museums, including the Smithsonian Institution, these expeditions unearthed the remains
of thousands of Native Americans and their associated burial goods. In
retrospect, many view this anthropological research as supporting, if not
perpetuating, the repression of Native Americans (see Thomas 2000 for an
archaeologist's sympathetic view of this position).

Although rekindled in 1990 when President George Bush signed the
Native American Graves Protection and Repatriation Act (NAGPRA) into
law, tensions between physical anthropologists and Native Americans
reached a crescendo of national proportions in 1996 when a well-preserved
male skeleton more than 9,000 years old was discovered eroding from the
banks of the Columbia River in Washington State. The skeleton was found
on federal land administered by the U.S. Army Corps of Engineers and
came to be called "Kennewick Man" by the media. Five Northwest Native
American tribes claimed the individual under the provisions of NAGPRA,
with the sole intention of reburying his remains without any scientific
study. Eight prominent physical anthropologists representing several universities and the Smithsonian Institution sued the federal government to
release the remains for examination, setting the stage for a series of acri-
monious public debates regarding the appropriate treatment of these and
other Native American remains. After five years the case is still in adjudi-
cation. Regardless of its outcome, the case of Kennewick Man dramatically
illustrates the chronically antagonistic relationship that has existed between Native Americans and archaeologists and physical anthropologists
for more than a century and a half. The heated debates that have followed
the skeleton's discovery, often engaging commentators who are neither

Native Americans nor anthropologists, underscore both the public's serious interest in the origins of New World peoples and the long-unresolved issues that continue to divide science from Native American religions. Other uses of human remains include the legitimization of biblical references and religious traditions. One of the most notable instances in which skeletal remains were used as evidence to support a religious doctrine centers on a discovery made by construction workers under St. Peter's Basilica in Rome. Among the central tenets of the Roman Catholic Church is that the apostle Peter, who was crucified between about 64 and 68 A.D., was the first pope. In 1968, Pope Paul VI announced that the skeletal remains of St. Peter had been found and satisfactorily identified after almost three decades of scientific analysis (Walsh 1982). During renovations under the basilica in 1939, workers discovered human remains in a vault that bore the partial inscription of "Petros Eni," Greek for "Peter is within." Studied in the early 1960s by Venerando Correnti, an anthropologist at Palermo University, the fragmented skeletal remains were identified as those of a powerfully built male about 65–70 years old who stood about 5 feet, 7 inches tall (Guarducci 1965). Based on this osteological information and in conjunction with historical evidence, the Catholic Church declared conclusively that the bones were those of St. Peter, noting that the evidence supported traditional versions of the Church's founding and early activities. In this case human remains were employed to validate and support the ideology of the Roman Catholic Church, furnishing powerful testimony regarding its history and giving credence to its ecclesiastical positions.

Forensic Anthropology, Human Rights, and War Criminals

Of more immediate value to the American public, the information provided by the skeleton allows forensic anthropologists to determine the personal identification of decomposed remains and to document perimortem trauma that may be related to the cause of death. In a larger context, this type of analysis can be directed toward gathering evidence of war crimes and human rights abuses.

Forensic physical anthropologists have long relied on studies of historical and prehistoric skeletal remains to help them analyze the remains of missing persons and to reconstruct the events that occurred around the time of death. Analysis of remains from archaeological sites has allowed researchers to document age-related changes that affect the human skeleton, to develop methods for determining the sex and ancestry of unknown individuals, and to establish criteria for distinguishing perimortem and postmortem trauma to the bones. All of the roughly 150 practicing forensic anthropologists in the United States have learned their skills by working with human remains from archaeological sites and have successfully applied their knowledge to solving hundreds of modern crimes throughout the country.

Coincidentally enough, at the end of the first day of the "Public Benefits of Archaeology" conference in Santa Fe in 1995, municipal workers performing sewer repairs discovered fragmented human remains under a street adjacent to San Miguel Mission, a church built in 1819 over the remains of a 1598 mission. Located just blocks from the conference setting, this discovery prompted a request to me from the New Mexico state historic preservation officer to examine the remains. I conducted an examination in the mission's back office that evening and determined that the remains represented historical period burials and did not require a police investigation. Similar accounts of such anthropological true-crime mysteries are described in four popular books recently published by forensic anthropologists (Joyce and Stover 1991; Ubelaker and Scammell 1992; Maples 1994; Manhein 1999) and one written especially for children (Jackson 1996). Aimed at a public audience, these books describe in clear, nontechnical language how physical anthropologists apply the methods and theories of their field to solving questions of medicolegal significance.

Studies of human remains are also essential to investigations of war crimes and human rights abuses (Burns 1991, 1995). After World War II, British anthropologists studied the human remains at former Nazi concentration camps to collect evidence for the War Crimes Tribunal. In 1994, several archaeologists from the National Park Service visited the former Yugoslavia under the auspices of the United Nations War Crimes Commission to confirm reports of mass graves and to document atrocities recounted by Croats in Serb-dominated territory (Calabrese 1994: 9). The United Nations estimates that more than 28,000 people are missing in Croatia, their remains buried in more than a hundred mass graves. Forensic archaeologists and anthropologists apply skills "learned over a lifetime of studying past cultures to a very real and dramatic modern context . . . [giving us] the chance to resolve the disappearance of many families' loved ones" (Calabrese 1994: 9).

One war criminal in particular was the focus of an unusually intense anthropological investigation. In 1985, skeletal remains purported to be those of Josef Mengele, the notorious Auschwitz concentration camp doctor, were unearthed in Brazil. Mengele had reportedly drowned in 1979 and was buried in a small village cemetery outside São Paulo. Three teams of physical anthropologists from West Germany and the United States were sent to Brazil to confirm the identity of the remains. The bones recovered by the Brazilian police were ultimately identified based on the osteological examination, comparisons of writing samples, and an anthropological technique called video superimposition whereby an antemortem photograph of Mengele from his Nazi party file was superimposed over the image of the recovered skull for comparison of facial features (Posner and Ware 1986; Joyce and Stover 1991). Dental records later provided positive identification of the remains, confirming that Mengele had indeed escaped prosecution after almost thirty-five years of hiding in South America.

Ecosystems and the History of Disease

Analysis of past human remains provides unique information about how modern people respond to pollution and disease. Analyzing archaeological bone samples allows modern researchers to document past environments and their effects on human health. Archaeological sites can be considered "scientific monitoring stations" for the study of past ecosystems (McManamon 1995: 2). Historic and prehistoric human remains likewise act as recorders of past environments, and through bone chemistry analysis the toxic materials to which past peoples were exposed can be ascertained. This information provides baseline levels against which current chemical concentrations in human tissue can be assessed and allows environmental scientists to document the effects of industrialization on people around the world (Ericson and Coughlin 1981). Such studies have documented the effects of lead poisoning among colonial American populations (Aufderheide et al. 1985) and enslaved individuals in Barbados (Corruccini et al. 1987). Archaeological toxicology promises to yield information about the pollutants common in the past and the physiological and genetic effects of such materials on modern populations.

During the course of history, nearly every population was affected at some time by plague and pestilence. Some epidemics have altered the course of history itself, decimating peoples, halting settlements in new lands, and forcing changes in economic and social conditions. Epidemics of formerly common diseases, like bubonic plague, syphilis, cholera, tuberculosis, and smallpox, have exerted their influence over vast numbers of people; more recently, diseases like polio, influenza, and AIDS have continued to remodel our social and cultural views. Learning how past peoples responded socially and politically to disease epidemics is important if we are to address the needs of infected individuals in our society effectively and humanely. In this regard paleopathology, the study of abnormal lesions in dry bone, provides medical personnel with long-term case studies in the progression and outcome of certain diseases. Disorders like tuberculosis and scurvy, once thought of as almost eradicated, are being found in increasing numbers of patients, particularly those from urban areas and in institutions like nursing homes and prisons. For instance, scurvy, although commonly considered an antique disease, has been documented among numerous types of patients, including otherwise healthy individuals with poorly balanced diets, athletes, food faddists, and those on fixed incomes (Crist 1997). Documenting the lesions associated with scurvy and other nutritional disorders in past human remains allows modern physicians to distinguish these conditions from other types of diseases and often to make simple changes in the patient's diet that lead to quick and total recovery.

Racism, Empowerment, and Historical Cemeteries

Of more intangible but no less important value than the practical applications already noted, the archaeological excavation of a historical burial ground often provides compelling links to the past for the site's descended community, especially when the remains represent a minority group. A group's social past, ancestral history, and national appreciation constitute much of how that group's members view themselves and how they are perceived by others in modern society (Blakey 1990: 38; Fraser and Butler 1986). From our heritage we draw a sense of social worth and meaning, and biases in the historical record often obscure or dismiss the pasts of disenfranchised minorities whose real contributions are unrecognized and underappreciated. Archaeology may serve to fill many of these gaps in American history. But both archaeology and physical anthropology also shape this group ideology and historical knowledge, generating far-reaching social implications that have included such nefarious political theories as eugenics and social Darwinism. In recent years, the descendants of socially oppressed and economically disadvantaged groups have begun pressing to have traditional historical events reinterpreted from other perspectives. For example, New York City's African Burial Ground has been described "not only as an icon for the struggle of African Americans but as a symbol of their direct involvement in the recovery and preservation of their past" (Barbour 1994: 13). The archaeological excavation of historical burial grounds thus can enable disenfranchised groups to reclaim their past. These projects also encourage the public to reassess traditional notions regarding the obscured history of such groups.

Most of the archaeological excavations of historical cemeteries in the United States over the last two decades have been performed to comply with federal preservation legislation, including section 106 of the National Historic Preservation Act of 1966 (NHPA), as amended. These laws and their implementing regulations make cultural resource management a regular component of the land-planning process. In general, projects supported by state or federal funds and those licensed or approved by federal agencies require environmental assessments that document the impacts of such projects on a variety of natural and historical resources. In cases where archaeological resources that are eligible for listing in the National Register of Historic Places (including historical burial grounds; see Potter and Boland 1992) will be adversely affected, data recovery excavations of the site become the principal means of mitigating the impacts. The costs of excavating, analyzing, and reporting on the resource are typically the responsibility of the sponsoring agency or developer. Since many of these projects are associated with government-sponsored construction, public funds are expended whenever these particular sites undergo the section 106 review process.

Because of these legislative requirements, the number of historical cemeteries relocated by archaeologists has increased significantly since the 1970s. In many cases the effects of undertaking these projects extend far beyond simple compliance with federal and state preservation laws.

A recent focus on "descendant community partnering," as well as new revisions to NHPA regulations (36 CFR 800) requiring public involvement, have begun to engage the public in the decision-making processes surrounding discoveries of historical cemeteries. Among the results of these initiatives is enhanced communication between anthropologists and the public. Rather than involvement after the project is under way, community partnering refers to the proactive participation of the affected community from the earliest phases of the project, so that the resultant course of action addresses both the scientific and the sociocultural concerns of all interested parties (Roberts and McCarthy 1995). Marked community dissatisfaction with the original course of the African Burial

Ground project in New York City (Cook 1993; Harrington 1993; Parrington 1993; LaRoche and Blakey 1997) has emphatically reinforced the role of descendant communities in projects that arouse sufficient spiritual and social interest; true community involvement is another method through which archaeologists and physical anthropologists make their research relevant to the public. When properly planned, compliance-based excavation of a historical burial ground has the potential to contribute much toward the amelioration of racist ideas and other public misperceptions and historical fallacies. Anthropologists occupy a unique position as an educational force within the public sphere due to their specialized understanding of the biological basis for human variation and behavior. The archaeological excavation of a historical burial ground provides a natural educational forum through which the public can be introduced to the anthropological concepts of human variability and adaptation. Physical anthropologists must, and do, reinforce the notions of racial equality by seizing each opportunity offered through the public exposure associated with the excavation of a historical cemetery.

Community Involvement and Philadelphia's First African Baptist Church Cemeteries

The number of African-American cemeteries excavated in the United States has increased over the last decade, particularly in urban areas undergoing redevelopment. This is because African-American cemeteries were often relegated, commonly unmarked, to the margins of early American cities. In Philadelphia, the First African Baptist Church Cemetery projects allowed archaeologists and physical anthropologists to engage the public early on in the planning phases for both cemetery relocations. The resulting projects effectively focused public attention on the urban experience of free African Americans during the early years of the Industrial Revolution.

The First African Baptist Church was founded in 1809 and split into two congregations in 1816. The splinter group relocated to Eighth and Vine streets by 1824 and remained on the property owned by Pastor Henry Simmons until about 1842. The original group worshipped at Tenth and Vine streets, using their property as a burial ground between about 1810 and 1822. The Tenth Street church relocated to a building in south Philadelphia in 1906, where the congregation currently meets.

The Eighth Street cemetery, in use between about 1823 and 1841, was discovered during archaeological monitoring activities associated with the construction of a commuter rail tunnel in 1980 (Parrington et al. 1989; Parrington and Roberts 1990). Excavated by archaeologists from John Milner Associates (JMA) in 1983 and 1984, the remains of 140 individuals and associated funerary artifacts were discovered at the site. The human remains were analyzed at the Smithsonian Institution and reinterred in 1987 at the cemetery used by the modern First African Baptist Church congregation. Community involvement from the beginning of the project was essential to its successful completion (Roberts 1984). In recognition of the keen public interest in the cemetery, a wooden platform was erected at the site so that visitors could safely view the archaeological proceedings in a panorama-like setting. Staff members from the Afro-American Historical and Cultural Museum, located three blocks from the former cemetery, were available to provide organized tours from the platform's vantage point as the site was excavated. More than 2,600 people took advantage of these tours over the two field seasons, connecting Philadelphia's current citizens with those from the city's antebellum past.

An effective plan to bring the public into the archaeology laboratory was mounted by JMA during the analysis of the Tenth Street First African Baptist Church cemetery, excavated three years after the remains from the Eighth Street cemetery were reinterred. The Tenth Street site was discovered during construction of the Vine Expressway through center-city Philadelphia and was funded through the Pennsylvania Department of Transportation and the Federal Highway Administration (Crist et al. 1996). The skeletal remains of eighty-nine individuals were excavated and transferred to the JMA Osteology Laboratory, located four blocks from the site; numerous funerary artifacts, including well-preserved coffin hardware and clothing, were likewise moved to the lab. During the course of the subsequent five-year study, the firm hosted over fifty school groups and tours in the lab. These groups ranged from first graders to graduate students, with a particular emphasis on children from the inner-city schools, who rarely are exposed to archaeology. Groups from the Phil-A-Kids program sponsored by the local Atwater Kent Museum also toured the laboratory each summer during this phase of the project. Here they were given the opportunity to handle bones and artifacts selected for their educational value and durability. Unlike most museum displays, which are accompanied by "do not touch" signs, these tours provided hundreds of children with tangible links to the heritage of a social group not commonly discussed in traditional history textbooks.

The group tours culminated in an ancestral homecoming ceremony conducted by the project's cultural anthropologist, bringing together the scientific project team and the current members of the First African Baptist Church congregation in June 1993. In the months following the ceremony, church leaders actively planned the reinterment of the human remains from the Tenth Street site at Eden Cemetery, adjacent to the burial plot in which the Eighth Street remains had been reburied in 1987. The reburial ceremony took place in May 1995 and was attended by more than forty members of the current church. At the congregation's request, the mortuary artifacts from the Tenth Street site have been curated at the Afro-American Historical and Cultural Museum in Philadelphia, completing the circle of involvement that had begun with the excavation of the Eighth Street cemetery twelve years earlier.

Neither First African Baptist Church Cemetery project elicited the forceful involvement of the descendant community, as happened with excavation of the African Burial Ground in lower Manhattan. The reason, in part, involved the relationship that began during the first cemetery project and extended through the second. This interactive partnership demonstrated the great potential that exists for mutually beneficial cooperation between the scientists who excavate and analyze historical cemeteries and the descendant communities affected by such projects. The publicly funded First African Baptist Church Cemetery projects served to heighten awareness among church members and the larger Philadelphia community about the scientific value of studying ancestral remains while enhancing knowledge about the African-American role in shaping early American society. Both projects fostered a sense of cultural pride among Philadelphia's African-American community and introduced thousands of people to an important part of American history that the buildings at Independence National Historic Park and other major tourist attractions do not reflect. The scope of the public forum created by the seminars and presentations made by the project team members encompassed archaeology, physical anthropology, history, and religion, attracting the public to the wide range of information learned from the archaeological excavation of these and other forgotten burial grounds.

The Public Has a Vested Interest

The November 1994 cover of *Discover* magazine posed the rhetorical question "Race: What Is It Good For?" Archaeologists and physical anthropologists are uniquely qualified to address this and other public issues that affect our national community. From the celebration of a past group's achievements to the resolution of a missing persons case, mortuary archaeology and forensic anthropology provide benefits to the public that are often unrecognized but never unutilized.

Informing the public about the significance of historical cemeteries and the value of skeletal studies is often not difficult. Many people, it seems, already intuitively accept this position and are willing to support the expenditure of public funds on the appropriate treatment of such remains. However, too often people equate archaeology with fieldwork because they never see the results of research conducted in the laboratory. This is probably due to the technical nature of osteological research, which involves specialized knowledge that the public may feel is too overwhelming to understand. Yet, as the Iceman stories and the media attention given the African Burial Ground indicate, not only are people interested in these types of projects but they want to play an active role in how the work is conducted and reported.

Given examples of the past uses and abuses of human skeletal remains, the question of whether the public should support mortuary archaeology is easily answered. The public maintains a vested interest in the future of our biological and cultural past, a heritage entrusted to archaeologists and physical anthropologists. By engaging people in the excitement of archaeology, historical cemetery projects will continue to benefit our society by portraying the past through its relevance to the present.

Acknowledgments

I would like to thank the organizers of the "Public Benefits of Archaeology" conference for asking me to participate in this timely assessment of our discipline. I am particularly indebted to Donna J. Seifert, John H. Sprinkle, and C. Esther White. I greatly appreciate Barbara J. Little's encouragement and suggestions regarding my conference presentation and the preparation of this chapter. I am also grateful for editorial comments provided by Daniel G. Roberts and the suggestions offered by Rebecca Yamin, Molly Hickey Crist, and Arthur Washburn. Ted A. Rathbun and Douglas W. Owsley have both strongly influenced my research in mortuary archaeology and my commitment to public education. Finally, I would not be in the position to offer these comments had I not participated in the Tenth Street First African Baptist Church Cemetery project. I am particularly grateful to the leaders and members of the First African Baptist Church for their active involvement, especially Mrs. Amy Alexander and Mr. Robert Ivory, and to the many other individuals who made the project a success, including John P. McCarthy, Reginald H. Pitts, and my other colleagues at John Milner Associates. I sincerely appreciate their support and that of my more recent colleagues at Kise Straw and Kolodner.

References

Aufderheide, A. C., J. L. Angel, J. O. Kelley, A. C. Outlaw, M. A. Outlaw, G. Rapp, Jr., and L. E. Wittmers. 1985. Lead in Bone III: Prediction of Social Correlates from Skeletal Lead Content in Four Colonial American Populations (Catoctin Furnace, College Landing, Governor's Land, and Irene Mound). *American Journal of Physical Anthropology* 66: 353–61.

Barbour, W.T.D. 1994. Musings on a Dream Deferred. *Federal Archeology Report* 7(1): 12–13.

Blakey, M. L. 1987. Skull Doctors: Intrinsic Social and Political Bias in the History of American Physical Anthropology. *Critique of Anthropology* 7(2): 7–35.

———. 1990. American Nationality and Ethnicity in the Depicted Past. In *The Politics of the Past*, ed. P. Gathercole and D. Lowenthal, 38–48. London: Unwin Hyman.

Burns, K. R. 1991. Protocol for Disinterment and Analysis of Skeletal Remains. *Manual on the Effective Prevention and Investigation of Extra-Legal, Arbitrary, and Summary Executions.* Publication E.91.IV.1. New York: United Nations.

———. 1995. Forensic Anthropology: The Application of Skeletal Biology to Human Identification. *ASTM Standardization News* 23(4): 28–33.

Calabrese, C. 1994. Investigating Mass Graves for the United Nations. *Federal Archeology* 7(2): 9.

Cook, K. 1993. Bones of Contention. *Village Voice,* May 4, 23–27.

Corruccini, R. S., A. C. Aufderheide, J. S. Handler, and L. E. Wittmers. 1987. Patterning of Skeletal Lead Content in Barbados Slaves. *Archaeometry* 29: 233–39.

Crist, T. A. J. 1997. Scurvy, the Skeleton, and Samuel de Champlain: A Bioarchaeological Investigation of Vitamin C Deficiency. Ph.D. diss., Temple University. University Microfilms, Ann Arbor.

Crist, T. A. J., R. H. Pitts, A. Washburn, J. P. McCarthy, and D. G. Roberts. 1996. "A Distinct Church of the Lord Jesus": The History, Archeology, and Physical Anthropology of the Tenth Street First African Baptist Church Cemetery, Philadelphia, Pennsylvania. Prepared for Gaudet and O'Brien Associates/Urban Engineers and the Pennsylvania Department of Transportation. Philadelphia: John Milner Associates.

Ericson, J. E., and E. A. Coughlin. 1981. Archaeological Toxicology. *Annals of the New York Academy of Sciences* 376: 393–403.

Fraser, G., and R. Butler. 1986. Anatomy of a Disinterment: The Unmaking of Afro-American History. In *Presenting the Past: Essays on History and the Public*, ed. S. P. Benson, S. Brier, and R. Rosenzweig, 121–32. Philadelphia: Temple University Press.

Fraser, S. (ed.). 1995. *The Bell Curve Wars: Race, Intelligence, and the Future of America*. New York: Basic Books.

Gould, S. J. 1981. *The Mismeasure of Man*. New York: W. W. Norton.

Guarducci, M. 1965. *Le Reliquie di Pietro*. Vatican City: Libreria Editrice Vaticana.

Haller, M. H. 1984. *Eugenics: Hereditarian Attitudes in American Thought*. New Brunswick, N.J.: Rutgers University Press.

Harrington, S. P. M. 1993. Bones and Bureaucrats: New York's Great Cemetery Imbroglio. *Archaeology* 46(2): 28–38.

Herrnstein, R. J., and C. Murray. 1994. *The Bell Curve: Intelligence and Class Structure in American Life*. New York: Free Press.

Hrdlicka, A. 1899. *Anthropological Investigations on One Thousand White and Colored Children of Both Sexes, the Inmates of the New York Juvenile Asylum; with Additional Notes on One Hundred Colored Children of the New York Colored Orphan Asylum*. New York: N.p.

———. 1919. *Physical Anthropology: Its Scope and Aims; Its History and Present Status in the United States*. Philadelphia: Wistar Institute of Anatomy and Biology.

Jackson, D. M. 1996. *The Bone Detectives: How Forensic Anthropologists Solve Crimes and Uncover Mysteries of the Dead*. Boston: Little, Brown.

Joyce, C., and E. Stover. 1991. *Witnesses from the Grave: The Stories Bones Tell*. Boston: Little, Brown.

LaRoche, C. J., and M. L. Blakey. 1997. Seizing Intellectual Power: The Dialogue at the New York African Burial Ground. *Historical Archaeology* 31(3): 84–106.

Larson, E. J. 1995. *Sex, Race, and Science: Eugenics in the Deep South*. Baltimore: Johns Hopkins University Press.

Lombroso, C. 1911. *Crime: Its Causes and Remedies*. Boston: Little, Brown.

Manhein, M. H. 1999. *The Bone Lady: Life as a Forensic Anthropologist*. Baton Rouge: Louisiana State University Press.

Maples, W. R. 1994. *Dead Men Do Tell Tales: The Strange and Fascinating Cases of a Forensic Anthropologist*. New York: Doubleday.

McGuire, R. H. 1988. Dialogues with the Dead: Ideology and the Cemetery. In *The Recovery of Meaning*, ed. Mark P. Leone and Parker B. Potter, Jr., 435–80. Washington, D.C.: Smithsonian Institution Press.

McManamon, F. P. 1995. Hidden Data: Learning about Ecosystems from Archeological Sites. *Federal Archeology* 8(1): 2.

Molnar, S. 1992. *Human Variation: Races, Types, and Ethnic Groups*. 3rd ed. Englewood Cliffs, N.J.: Prentice Hall.

Morton, S. G. 1849. Observations on the Size of the Brain in Various Races and Families of Man. *Proceedings of the Academy of Natural Sciences Philadelphia* 4: 221–24.

Osborn, J. A. 1994. Engaging the Public. *CRM* 17(6): 15. Washington, D.C.: National Park Service.

Parrington, M. 1993. The African Burial Ground: An Adventure in Urban Archaeology. Ms. on file, Office of Public Education and Interpretation of the African Burial Ground and Five Points Archaeological Projects, New York.

Parrington, M., and D. G. Roberts. 1990. Demographic, Cultural, and Bioanthropological Aspects of a Nineteenth-Century Free Black Population in Philadelphia, Pennsylvania. In *A Life in Science: Papers in Honor of J. Lawrence Angel,* ed. J. E. Buikstra, 138–70. Scientific Paper no. 6. Kampsville, Ill.: Center for American Archaeology.

Parrington, M., D. G. Roberts, S. A. Pinter, and J. C. Wideman. 1989. *The First African Baptist Church Cemetery: Bioarcheology, Demography, and Acculturation of Early Nineteenth Century Philadelphia Blacks.* 3 vols. Prepared for the Redevelopment Authority of the City of Philadelphia. Philadelphia: John Milner Associates.

Pearson, M. P. 1982. Mortuary Practices, Society and Ideology: An Ethnoarchaeological Study. In *Symbolic and Structural Archaeology,* ed. Ian Hodder, 99–114. Cambridge: Cambridge University Press.

Posner, G. L., and J. Ware. 1986. *Mengele: The Complete Story.* London: Macdonald.

Potter, E. W., and B. M. Boland. 1992. *Guidelines for Evaluating and Registering Cemeteries and Burial Places.* National Register Bulletin 41. Washington, D.C.: National Park Service, U.S. Department of the Interior.

Roberts, D. G. 1984. Management and Community Aspects of the Excavation of a Sensitive Urban Archeological Resource: An Example from Philadelphia. *American Archeology* 4(3): 235–40.

Roberts, D. G., and J. P. McCarthy. 1995. Descendant Community Partnering in the Archaeological and Bioanthropological Investigation of African American Skeletal Populations: Two Interrelated Case Studies from Philadelphia. In *Bodies of Evidence: Reconstructing History through Skeletal Analysis,* ed. Anne L. Grauer, 19–36. New York: Wiley-Liss.

Selden, S. 1999. *Inheriting Shame: The Story of Eugenics and Racism in America.* New York: Teachers College Press.

Stocking, G. W. 1987. *Victorian Anthropology.* New York: Free Press.

Thomas, D. H. 2000. *Skull Wars: Kennewick Man, Archeology, and the Battle for Native American Identity.* New York: Basic Books.

Ubelaker, D. H., and H. Scammell. 1992. *Bones: A Forensic Detective's Casebook.* New York: Edward Burlingame.

Walsh, J. E. 1982. *The Bones of St. Peter.* Bungay, Suffolk, Eng.: Chaucer Press.

Yerkes, R. M. 1917. How May We Discover the Children Who Need Special Care. *Mental Hygiene* 1: 252–59.

———. 1941. Man Power and Military Effectiveness: The Case for Human Engineering. *Journal of Consulting Psychology* 5: 205–9.

——— (ed.). 1921. Psychological Examining in the United States Army. *Memoirs of the National Academy of Sciences,* vol. 15.

III

Learning from an Authentic Past

10

Protecting the Past to Benefit the Public

George S. Smith and John E. Ehrenhard

Sometime during the third century B.C., the great library of Alexandria—the most famous library of antiquity and the center of Greek literary history—was leveled by fire. The collected wisdom of the civilized world of that time was forever lost. Twenty-three hundred years later, scholars continue to lament the loss of this irreplaceable knowledge, knowledge of the human past.

Loss of the accumulated knowledge of the human past, such as that contained in the library of Alexandria, can be compared with the demise of uncountable species of plants and animals. In both cases, that which is lost is gone forever. Archives of cultural history, languages, technologies, religions, built and natural environments, and even memories, are "spilling into oblivion, leaving humanity in danger of losing its past and perhaps jeopardizing its future" (Linden 1991: 46). It is within this context that public benefits of protecting the past are framed.

Answers to the fundamental questions of what the past is and why it is important must be sought within a larger anthropological framework. It should come as no surprise that archaeologists are not the only ones concerned with connections to the past. All cultures have some means of relating to the past. Even though cultural diversity in defining the past includes linear and cyclic approaches, it is clear that an accurate representation of the past is a critical element of all social life (Layton 1994). No matter how the past is structured, understanding the past and protecting symbols of it are an integral part of the collective human experience.

The Past in Perspective

Fundamental differences in understanding time dimensions exist between social groups, and these differences highlight the intellectual ethnocentricities that dominate societies' attitudes about the past (Ehrenhard 1993). The anthropological and ethnographic literature is filled with examples of cultural differences in perceptions of the past. Many of these perceptions depart from Western notions of the passage of time as natural, real, moving, and based on the ordered movement of the heavenly bodies (Williams and Manunggurr 1994). For example, the Inuit of the Northwest Territories of Canada have been described as always living in the present. This use of a timeless present is marked by the fact that there is no chronological chain through which the Inuit can relate events to one another. In fact, they have no word for history (Carpenter 1956). As such, the past is understood as part of the present (Bielawski 1994). This combining of the past and present is seen as an integral part of Inuit survival in the harsh environment of the Far North. Chase (1994) in his study of aboriginal communities in Australia discusses how events are structured as occurring during an individual lifetime, a long time ago, or during the creation period. These are just two of the numerous examples of structuring time. Although cultural perspectives of the past vary, one fact holds: the past consists of observable but irreversible phenomena.

Regardless of how the past is perceived, it is clear that every society has a connection with the past serving to assure group survival, to identify and verify shared behavior, and to provide a means of passing on patterned behavior to future generations. This process, within which revisionist history and national myths—manifested as glorification or even exclusion of selected portions of the past—operates in the larger sense to define cultures (Mangi 1994; Stone and MacKenzie 1994).

Modern archaeology requires the past to be considered within a cultural context. It also requires that some portion of the past be available for study and interpretation and that important places continue to exist to provide a tangible link to the past. The framers of the 1906 Antiquities Act were aware of this when they acknowledged that almost every civilized government of the world has enacted laws for the preservation of the remains of the historic past (U.S. House of Representatives 1906). Regardless of how the past is defined, it plays a critical role in how national patrimony is interpreted, managed, and protected. Archaeological sites and the information they contain are an important part of this process.

Protecting the Past in the Public Interest

When speaking of the "public benefit," McManamon (1991, 1994) reminds us that, in fact, we have not one public to consider but many. Because the public, in the broadest sense, includes all of humanity, it is important to remember that we are serving individuals with varying interests and degrees of understanding. As McManamon (1991) points out, 25 percent of people are informed about or interested in science and 70 percent are more or less uninterested in scientific topics but maintain a positive view of scientific endeavors. All, however, in some way, benefit from and influence our understanding and protection of the past.

Historical Background

As with politics, all archaeology is local. Sites exist and are protected or destroyed in local settings influenced by local concerns. It is within this climate that historic preservation in the United States began. Early efforts to protect the past were undertaken by private citizens and organizations without the benefit of the laws that today provide critical support for site protection. Many such efforts were successful; some were not. However, even those that failed helped build the historic preservation movement through increased public awareness and a resolve to maintain a link with the past.

Beginning in the early 1800s and continuing through the nineteenth century, there were numerous attempts to save, in the public interest, places associated with important events in American history, such as Independence Hall and George Washington's and John Hancock's homes. Exploration of the western portion of the country identified numerous Native American sites, many of which were being looted. Narratives written about these explorations increased public awareness of the sites and of the need to protect them. As a result, sites such as Casa Grande and Chaco Canyon were placed in public trust and protected. All these efforts would contribute to future historic preservation legislation. The public would not be denied its link with the past.

There has always been public interest in protecting the past. In fact, early development of American archaeology can be traced to work conducted and observations made by none other than Thomas Jefferson. His excavations into mounds on his Virginia estate established a model for American archaeology. For this reason, many consider Jefferson to be the father of American archaeology. It is interesting to note that this title was bestowed on someone who could best be described as an avocational archaeologist. Jefferson would not be the only president interested in the past. William Henry Harrison described sites in the Ohio Valley (Willey and Sabloff 1974), and President Jimmy Carter's interest in collecting arrowheads had a profound impact on the language included in the final version of the Archaeological Resources Protection Act of 1979.

The Legal Framework

One of the first laws resulting from early preservation endeavors was the Antiquities Act, passed in 1906, as indicated earlier. It is interesting to note that testimony was given to members of Congress not only by professional archaeologists representing major universities and museums but also by representatives of various avocational archaeological societies. Archaeologists of note providing testimony in support of the Antiquities Act included A. L Kroeber, G. B. Gordon, M. H. Saville, W. H. Holmes, F. W. Putnum, F. Boas, G. A. Dorsey, G. G. MacCurdy, J. W. Fewkes, and E. L. Hewett, to name a few (U.S. House 1906). It took six years and three sessions of Congress to pass the act. Given the complexity of the legislative process, it is amazing that the Archaeological Resources Protection Act of 1979 was drafted and passed in less than one year.

Since 1906 there has been additional federal legislation passed supporting the continued protection of archaeological and historical resources (see, e.g., Friedman 1991). With the exception of a few states that established protective legislation much earlier (notably Illinois, Alabama, Iowa, and Michigan), most states developed statutes promoting archaeological resource protection at the state level beginning in the late 1960s and early 1970s (McGimsey 1972; Carnett 1995). These laws provide protection for sites representing the whole of human history and the full range of cultural diversity in the United States.

Given all the federal and state legislation and the impact it has had, the greatest opportunity to protect our nation's heritage may in fact be at the local level. Simple methods such as municipal ownership of sites, conservation easements, and—possibly most important—zoning regulations can have a profound and positive impact on protecting the past (Carr 1990; Kearns and Kirkorian 1991). The consideration of local values and concerns is another example of the public benefit of protecting the past.

Public Response

Enacting legislation at federal and state levels and using ordinances, regulations, and permit systems at local levels can be very effective means to codify the public's vested interest in the past and to further the public benefits. Government agencies have contributed in other ways. For example, the federal government organizes archaeological programs within the framework of a National Archaeological Program. Strategies include public education, anti-looting measures, information exchange, programs to inventory lands managed by the federal government, and collections management. Federal programs designed to enhance public understanding, appreciation, and enjoyment of the nation's rich heritage, such as Passports in Time (U.S. Forest Service) and Adventures in the Past (Bureau of Land Management), have been implemented. Various site stewardship programs at all levels of government have encouraged partnerships in protecting the past.

Training to enhance the ability to protect archaeological resources has been incorporated into many federal agency programs, such as those developed and implemented by the National Park Service and the Federal Law Enforcement Training Center. Training programs have also been developed for nonfederal participants, such as attorneys, judges, and law enforcement personnel. These initiatives have improved site protection and increased the rates of prosecution and conviction of those who commit crimes against our national heritage. In addition, federal grants from organizations such as the National Center for Preservation Technology and Training (NCPTT) provide funding for projects that benefit archaeological site protection and public education about the past.

In the past ten years, the federal government has undertaken studies to identify the extent of archaeological looting. Statistics on archaeological resource crime have been compiled by the National Park Service and submitted to Congress. The resulting data have been instrumental in amending federal laws to strengthen archaeological site protection; in providing funding for archaeological resource protection programs and training; in securing funding for programs to inventory and evaluate archaeological resources on lands managed by the federal government; and in promoting public education.

Many state and local governments and organizations have adopted programs—state archaeology weeks, for example—that highlight their heritage. Professional and avocational archaeologists work in cooperation with the public and sponsors to organize state and local programs. Typical archaeology week activities include developing and distributing posters and educational materials, conducting site visits, giving lectures on history and prehistory, holding demonstrations of historic and prehistoric technologies, and preparing exhibits on archaeological topics. Many states also have grant programs to further archaeological endeavors.

Private Response

The Society for American Archaeology, the Society for Historical Archaeology, the Register of Professional Archaeologists, the American Anthropological Association, and the American Cultural Resources Association have all developed statements, in one form or another, regarding sharing information with the public. All agree that the profession has an obligation to share information with the public. This view is also demonstrated by the Archaeological Institute of America, which since 1948 has published *Archaeology* magazine for a broad audience that includes professional archaeologists and nonprofessionals alike. In addition, these societies have established education committees to advise them on matters dealing with archaeology and the public. They are working together to help the public better understand, appreciate, and enjoy the past.

In 1988—the same year that *The Destruction of America's Archaeological Heritage: Looting and Vandalism of Indian Archaeological Sites in the Four Corners States of the Southwest* was published (U.S. House 1988)—the SAA initiated its "Save the Past for the Future" program to understand why looting occurs and to develop legal and educational strategies to reduce it. This program was initiated at the 1989 SAA meetings in a session entitled "Our Vanishing Past: The Willful Destruction of a Nation's Heritage." As a continuation of this program, the SAA held its first "Save the Past for the Future" working conference in Taos, New Mexico. More than seventy experts addressed three major topics: understanding the problem, preventing the problem, and combating the problem. Participants developed strategies to deal with the continued loss of the remaining portion of the archaeological record and to determine ways of increasing public awareness and participation in archaeology. As a result, more than 250 recommendations were included in the SAA publication *Actions for the '90s* (1990). The spirit and direction of this program are captured in the conference mission statement, which calls for inclusion of the broader archaeological community and the public in archaeology and the protection of resources (Reinburg 1991).

The 1989 workshop was followed by a second "Save the Past for the Future" conference, held in 1994 in Breckenridge, Colorado. This time the goal was to assess progress and to focus on education, law enforcement, and integrated resource management approaches to protecting the past.

This workshop included more than 160 participants and resulted in more than one hundred recommendations to continue the work already under way (SAA 1995a, b). The "Public Benefits of Archaeology" conference, held in November 1995 in Santa Fe, New Mexico, addressed many of the same concerns and recommendations. As a result of these workshops, tremendous strides have been made in protecting the past and including the public in the process. Professional and public awareness has increased and more people and organizations than ever are cooperating in site protection. Some examples of the substantial progress made to date in protecting the past are:

- Legislation was amended to improve site protection and prosecution.
- Funding was appropriated for law enforcement and training aimed at site protection.
- Cooperation between federal agencies, state agencies, professional societies, and avocational groups has increased.
- Public education committees were formed or expanded within professional societies.
- Public outreach increased, as did the availability of teaching and resource materials.
- Information gathering and sharing has become more widespread.
- Sessions at professional meetings dealing with protecting the past and public education are more common.
- Networks have been established to collect, track, and disseminate information about site protection and public education.
- Language has been adopted by professional societies calling for site protection, public education, and ethics.
- Public archaeology and cultural resource management education and training in colleges and universities are on the rise.
- Awareness of and participation in the politics of archaeology and site protection have increased within the profession and among the public.

After all the discussions and recommendations, it is perhaps the debate about priorities, which pits established practices against the need to save a past for which time is running out, that will have the most profound impact in the longest term. This debate takes into consideration new generations of research, conservation, professional training, and changing social attitudes about the past (Fagan 1995). Debate is healthy, but make no mistake, results of this dialogue will impact not only archaeology as a profession but our perceptions of the past, social values, and our national heritage.

Regardless of how the past is perceived, all probably agree in principle that the past is worth saving. Without it we collectively stand to lose a great deal; we stand to lose humanity's lifeline, we stand to lose the future. What greater loss could there be?

Acknowledgments

We would like to thank Virginia Horak for her valuable comments, editorial prowess, and attention to detail.

References

Bielawski, E. 1994. Dual Perceptions of the Past: Archaeology and Inuit Culture. In *Conflict in the Archaeology of Living Traditions*, ed. R. Layton, 228–36. New York: Routledge. Original edition 1989, London: Unwin Hyman.

Carnett, C. L. 1995. *A Survey of State Statutes Protecting Archeological Resources*. Preservation Law Reporter Special Report, Archeological Assistance Study no. 3. Washington, D.C.: National Park Service.

Carpenter, E. S. 1956. The Timeless Present in the Mythology of the Aivilik Eskimo. *Anthropologica* 3: 1–4.

Carr, R. S. 1990. The Decline of Site Vandalism in Dade County, Florida. In *Coping with Site Looting: Southeastern Perspectives*, ed. J. E. Ehrenhard, 1–3. Atlanta: Interagency Archeological Services Division, National Park Service.

Chase, A. K. 1994. Perceptions of the Past Among North Queensland Aboriginal People: The Intrusion of Europeans and Consequent Social Change. In *Who Needs the Past? Indigenous Values and Archaeology*, ed. R. Layton, 169–79. New York: Routledge. Original edition 1989, London: Unwin Hyman.

Ehrenhard, J. E. 1993. Lost Sites, Lost Forever. In *Site Destruction in Georgia and the Carolinas*, ed. D. G. Anderson and V. Horak, 96–99. Atlanta: Interagency Archeological Services Division, National Park Service.

Fagan, B. M. 1995. Perhaps We May Hear Voices. In *Save the Past for the Future II: Report of the Working Conference*, 25–30. Special Report. Washington, D.C.: Society of American Archaeology.

Friedman, E. 1991. Antecedents to Cultural Resource Management. In *Protecting the Past*, ed. G. S. Smith and J. E. Ehrenhard, 27–31. Boca Raton, Fla.: CRC Press.

Kearns, B., and C. Kirkorian. 1991. Protecting Sites at the Local Level: The Responsibility and the Legal Authority Towns Have to Protect Their Archaeological Resources. In *Protecting the Past*, ed. G. S. Smith and J. E. Ehrenhard, 247–52. Boca Raton, Fla.: CRC Press.

Layton, R. (ed.). 1994. *Conflict in the Archaeology of Living Traditions.* New York: Routledge. Original edition 1989, London: Unwin Hyman.

Linden, E. 1991. Lost Tribes, Lost Knowledge. *Time* no. 23, September 1991, 46–56.

Mangi, J. 1994. The Role of Archaeology in Nation Building. In *Conflict in the Archaeology of Living Traditions,* ed. R. Layton, 217–27. New York: Routledge. Original edition 1989, London: Unwin Hyman.

McGimsey, C. R. III. 1972. *Public Archaeology.* New York: Seminar Press.

McManamon, F. P. 1991. The Many Publics for Archaeology. *American Antiquity* 56(1): 121–30.

———. 1994. Presenting Archaeology to the Public in the USA. In *The Presented Past: Heritage, Museums and Education,* ed. P. G. Stone and B. L. Molyneaux, 61–81. New York: Routledge.

Reinburg, K. M. 1991. Save the Past for the Future: A Partnership to Protect Our Past. In *Protecting the Past,* ed. G. S. Smith and J. E. Ehrenhard, 271–76. Boca Raton, Fla.: CRC Press.

Society for American Archaeology (SAA). 1990. *Actions for the '90s.* Final Report, Taos Working Conference on Preventing Archaeological Looting and Vandalism. Washington, D.C.: Society for American Archaeology.

———. 1995a. *Save the Past for the Future II: Report of the Working Conference.* Special Report. Washington, D.C.: Society for American Archaeology.

———. 1995b. *Save the Past for the Future II: Education Workshop Action Items and Recommendations.* Washington, D.C.: Society for American Archaeology.

Stone, P. G., and R. MacKenzie (eds.). 1994. *The Excluded Past: Archaeology in Education.* New York: Routledge. Original edition 1990, London: Unwin Hyman.

U.S. House of Representatives. 1906. *Preservation of American Antiquities.* Committee on the Public Lands. 59th Cong., 1st sess. Report no. 2224.

———. 1988. *The Destruction of America's Archaeological Heritage: Looting and Vandalism of Indian Archaeological Sites in the Four Corners States of the Southwest.* Committee on Interior and Insular Affairs. Subcommittee on General Oversight and Investigations. 100th Cong., 2d sess. Committee Print no. 6.

Willey, G. R., and J. A. Sabloff. 1974. *A History of American Archaeology.* San Francisco: W. H. Freeman.

Williams, N. M., and D. Mununggurr. 1994. Understanding Yolngu Signs of the Past. In *Who Needs the Past? Indigenous Values and Archaeology,* ed. R. Layton, 70–83. New York: Routledge. Original edition 1989, London: Unwin Hyman.

11

Roadside Ruins

Does America Still Need Archaeology Museums?

David Hurst Thomas

My views are heavily colored by a quarter century working as a museum-based archaeologist. Museums like the one where I work have been around a long time, and they still offer an important way for us to take our archaeology to the American public. Perhaps it is worth looking more deeply at the museum world to see what works and what does not.

Consider the following: "We find ourselves as a country in an emergency. . . . Those who seek to find among the American people the enthusiasm for national ends . . . find that again and again they are faced with cynicism and apathy, in people who feel they have been over-propagandized, over-sold. . . . Dishearteningly suspicious they are—except of Museums." These words sum up my own thoughts about the public benefits of archaeology fairly well. As I see it, the country is in something of a predicament (perhaps even an emergency). The American people are cynical and apathetic; there is a crisis of confidence in public institutions and a fragmentation into special-interest groups. Yet there is something about the museum world that retains great public appeal—holding the public interest and, more important, the public trust. If we substitute "world of archaeology" for "museum world," this statement might even define the baseline of archaeologists' belief in the public benefits of their discipline.

Isn't it amazing, then, that these timely words were actually written six decades ago—in 1941 by Margaret Mead, who certainly knew a thing or two about taking anthropology to an interested American public. Her advice still resonates today.

During her fifty-year career as curator of ethnology at the American Museum of Natural History, Mead pushed the museum world to do a better job of bringing the fruits of research to the public. This was not a popular view with her anthropological colleagues, and despite her international reputation, Mead's scientific career was held back to some extent by her insistence on popularizing. Although things have changed somewhat today, it remains true that scientists who popularize their science are penalized by their peers. Carl Sagan and Stephen Jay Gould are two recent examples.

In the quoted text, the emergency of which Mead speaks was World War II. I was not around at the time, and elsewhere in Mead's article, I was surprised to see her concern with "tricks of the propagandist" and "machinations of the advertiser"—way back then? We do not read much today about such attitudes during World War II; I thought cynicism and apathy came along during the Vietnam era, but obviously I was wrong. Apparently we Americans have been a suspicious lot for a long time now, even when facing such a clear-cut peril as Hitler's Nazi Germany.

Mead also wrote about a second crisis, one in the museum world within which she worked. In her 1941 article, she noted that even then, museums were accused of being old-fashioned, out of date, and out of touch—"lacking in verve and splash and modernity." But while expressing a certain sympathy with the critics, Mead urged the museum world to stick to its guns, to recognize the value of using traditional methods for presenting anthropology to the public: "Museums, almost alone among the various means of communication that have been exploited to push and prod people about, to make them feel, or want, or buy, have remained uncontaminated. Because the staffs of Museums have insisted on saying: 'Is this true?' instead of asking: 'Will this make a hit?'—they have kept the people's trust" (Mead 1941: 67).

To Mead, museums remained a place where people were not manipulated by seductive exhibition techniques and Madison Avenue–style advertising gimmicks. Museum visitors of the 1940s, Mead tells us, were "able to trust their eyes and let their minds rove over materials which have not been arranged to impress, to convert, to push them around, but merely to tell them as much of the truth as is now known, and that quietly" (1941: 67).

Why is this so? What is it about the museum exhibit that continues to fascinate without embellishment? Margaret Mead answered the question three decades later. She argued (Mead 1970) that museums—like no other institution—are about real things: the real sled that Perry used to reach the North Pole, a real dinosaur egg from the Gobi Desert, a real spear point made 10,000 years ago. For both children and adults, museums have always drawn the line between the authentic and the imitation. The museum can show you the reality of evolution, the reality of life in different cultures, the reality of our own human past. Real objects can say, as no other form can say: *this is it, itself.* To the extent that this authenticity is sacrificed to showmanship and competition with world's fairs and other fabricated exhibits, museums lose.

During her long career as a museum anthropologist, Mead continually emphasized the importance of simplicity and, above all, reality in museum exhibitions. To her, the mission of the modern anthropology museum in this country was simple: to show the American public what is real. Unembellished anthropological "things," explained clearly, anchor us culturally to the rest of the world and to our own past. This is what Mead thought museums were all about.

American Archaeology as a Museum

I take a pretty broad view of what a museum is. To me, an archaeology museum is anything that publicly presents something important from the past. America contains thousands of such museums, from the largest urban natural history museums to major archaeological sites like Cahokia and Chaco Canyon. But we cannot forget those small roadside attractions signaled by a fading roadside sign saying simply: "Point of Historical Interest, 1/2 mile ahead." These are archaeology museums as well.

This is, of course, an expansive definition of *museum*—a place where the public can see objects of import. Sometimes those objects are ancient and precious. Sometimes they are paltry and plebeian. Sometimes, the artifacts are secondary to the place itself.

America is, in effect, one immense outdoor museum, telling a story that covers 9 million square miles and 25,000 years. America is a land of hands-on historians, people who want to get out and see the real thing. And this is what museums have traditionally always offered—a chance to experience the real thing.

But the key question is this: To what extent does Margaret Mead's advice still work? Is reality still the key?

Let us look at a couple of America's premier outdoor museums, two sites with extraordinary intrinsic appeal, both to professional archaeologists and to the American public at large. Each site, I think, has something to say about our efforts to "take archaeology public."

Encountering the Medicine Wheel

Wyoming's renowned Bighorn Medicine Wheel is one of American archaeology's most celebrated sites. Standing there, you are confronted by simplicity itself: a stone circle—the "wheel"—nearly ninety feet in diameter, astride an isolated peak 9,640 feet above sea level. Inside the circle are twenty-eight unevenly spaced stone "spokes" radiating out from the central "hub," a stone cairn about fifteen feet across. Five smaller cairns dot the periphery.

For nearly a century, archaeologists have puzzled over why anybody would build this high-altitude rock alignment. Here are some of the more widely discussed ideas, none of which is universally accepted:

- Some suggest that the rock cairns were originally constructed as grave markers, each a memorial to the war deeds of a dead leader. The rock piles at the end of each rock line may represent enemies killed in battle.
- Others draw upon the rich ethnohistoric record of the Northern Plains and relate the alignment to the widespread and ancient practice of the vision quest, in which a solitary individual seeks communication with the spirit world. Although the specifics varied widely, participants were usually sequestered in remote sacred places, without food or water, praying for spiritual guidance. Some modern Indian people use the Medicine Wheel this way.
- John Eddy (1974) set out the most highly publicized hypothesis more than two decades ago, suggesting that the Medicine Wheel was an outdoor astronomical observatory. Noting that selected stone cairns might once have held wooden poles, Eddy concluded that simply by observing the sunrise over these cairns, aboriginal astronomers could have predicted the timing of the summer solstice.
- It has been suggested that the Medicine Wheel was built to aid travel, the rock piles left as directional aids to newcomers.
- To some, the plan view of the Medicine Wheel suggests a two-dimensional imitation of the twenty-eight-raftered lodge built as part of the Sun Dance ceremony.
- Other hypotheses hold that the Medicine Wheel may have been a boundary marker, a depiction of a stone turtle, or an enduring stone marker demonstrating geometrical expertise.

Here then, played out in Wyoming's windswept Bighorn Mountains, at times dramatically, are the diverse objectives of modern science, archaeoastronomy, cognitive archaeology, and traditional Native American religion (for which the Medicine Wheel continues to be an important sacred site). Like so many elements of the human past, the Medicine Wheel means many different things to many different people. Today, at least in academic America, there is an overarching sense of theoretical pluralism, a feeling that no grand synthesis is likely to emerge any time soon.

But if we agree that it is important to take our archaeology to a broader American audience, several big questions arise: Where is Mead's "truth as is now known?" Where is the consensus of scientific opinion? Who has the authority to tell the story? Can that public learn to live with mutually irreconcilable views about the past? Will our public lose respect for an archaeology that can't seem to make up its mind about the past? In short, where is reality?

Multiple Realities at the Alamo

Before exploring these important questions more deeply, let us shift our attention to another of America's sacred sites—the Alamo. In 1836, a Mexican force of perhaps 4,000 soldiers commanded by Antonio López de Santa Anna reached the outskirts of San Antonio, Texas. The Anglo-American garrison, numbering 187 men under the command of Colonel William Travis, withdrew to the Alamo. For thirteen days the Texans withstood siege before Mexican troops breached the walls and killed the Alamo defenders.

Today's textbooks pay homage to this heroic episode in the Texan war of independence against Mexico. As one late nineteenth-century historian put it, the courageous trio Travis, Bowie, and Crockett shed their blood upon "a holy altar" (quoted in Weber 1988: 138). Their dying as martyrs is commonly praised as a strategic and well-executed military move, a sacrifice that successfully delayed Mexican forces and ultimately set up a glorious victory for Texas at the subsequent Battle of San Jacinto, where Santa Anna was roundly defeated. The victorious battle cry became "Remember the Alamo!"

And remember it we have. Enshrined in dominant American folklore, the Alamo is one of America's most cherished cultural icons. According to frontier ideology, Americans arriving in Texas brought with them a culture capable of transforming the wilderness into a productive part of the

United States of America. The birth of Texas, it is written, was made possible by the death of the Alamo defenders. For many, the Alamo remains a symbolic confirmation that the spread of Anglo-Texan culture across the American Southwest had been predestined by God Almighty. Many a Texan ranks the Alamo alongside Lexington and Concord in terms of historical significance.

But for many Texans of Hispanic descent, the Alamo has become a recurring bad dream that continues to exclude the Hispanic population from any honorable role in Texas history. More than half of San Antonio's population is Hispanic, and many are challenging the traditional heroic image of the Alamo. Some voices today demand that the Hispanic people be assigned a more positive and significant role in the history of the American Southwest.

The Alamo, they point out, began as a small-scale Spanish mission long before it became an Anglo-Texan shrine. Known as Mission San Antonio de Valero, it was established in 1718 to bring Christianity to the local Indian population. By this view, a handful of brave and unarmed friars attempted to bring their own brand of civilization to the untamed Texas wilderness. They had no interest in storming sturdy fortresses. They were men of peace, whose goal was to save souls.[1]

What does all this have to do with archaeology? Plenty. Representatives of San Antonio's Hispanic community believe that additional research should be conducted at the Alamo—archaeological research emphasizing not the short-lived 1836 battle but rather the eighteenth-century mission period. Archaeologist Anne Fox of the University of Texas at San Antonio agrees. She has a deep and long-standing interest in the Spanish missions of Texas and believes that further excavations in and around the Alamo would shed important new light on this little-known chapter of San Antonio history.

But there is a problem. The Daughters of the Republic of Texas (DRT) are the state-appointed custodians of the Alamo and its archaeological record. According to Fox (personal communication), the DRT has actively stonewalled any applications for archaeological excavations targeting the Alamo-as-mission. For decades, the DRT has felt that mission period research would detract from the true historical significance of the site as "the cradle of Texas liberty" (thereby effectively denying the DRT their ancestral identity).

Fox finds the apprehensiveness of the DRT toward mission research troublesome. But she is also critical of those in the Hispanic community who are keeping alive the animosity between Anglos and Hispanics regarding the Alamo. Fox believes that archaeologists should ignore both factions and simply do their research.

Anthropologist Holly Breachley Brear (1995) has analyzed the social and political situation surrounding the modern Alamo. According to Brear, archaeologists like Fox threaten the current political structure in San Antonio. Although that attitude has softened somewhat in recent years, in the eyes of the DRT members, it is those "thirteen days to glory" that still constitute the primary significance of the Alamo.

And they are probably right. If the DRT were to recognize the historical significance of the earlier mission period, or to honor the Mexican soldiers who fought in the Battle of the Alamo, they would threaten the sociopolitical power balance in modern San Antonio. They would be empowering an ethnic group directly descended from the "enemy" at the Alamo.

In addition, any strategy for understanding the mission period would require excavations reaching far beyond the boundary of state-owned property at the Alamo. As archaeologists sought to locate and expose the foundations of the mission compound, their excavations extended well into the predominantly city-owned portion of the Alamo Plaza. Clearly, these new physical and conceptual boundaries better serve the Hispanic community's broader interest in the site and undermine the DRT's narrow focus on the Alamo-as-battlefield. Many politically active Hispanics are encouraging broad-scale archaeological research and public interpretation of the Alamo-as-mission to highlight peaceful Hispanic origins within the state of Texas and to support the Hispanic claim to owning the so-called "hallowed ground" at the Alamo.

Archaeologists digging and interpreting America's historic sites such as the Alamo likewise face considerable pressure from tourist expectations. The Alamo attracts visitors mostly because of the famous 1836 battle. When archaeologists like Anne Fox excavate there, they can expect to read about their finds in tomorrow's newspaper. The dig itself becomes a tourist attraction.

Such excavations are always in danger of threatening the prevailing ideology. During the 1988 field season at the Alamo, one reporter from an Austin newspaper complained that the archaeologists working on mission period remains outside the Alamo "seemed to be drawing as much reverent attention from the tourists as the indoor exhibits on David Crockett, William Travis and the other heroes of 1836" (Brear 1995: 146). The problem is clear: archaeologists allowed to dig at the Alamo are supposed to find the concrete evidence of the known past—that is, the 1836 past.

Similar problems plague the serious historian seeking to conduct meaningful research elsewhere in the Hispanic Southwest. As David Weber, a distinguished historian of the Spanish Borderlands, points out, some of the most cherished morsels of Alamo lore simply have no basis in historic fact: "They have moved out of the earthly realm of reality into the stratosphere of myth" (Weber 1988: 135–36). Here is what Weber thinks about some of those morsels of Alamo lore:

> Myth: William Barret Travis is supposed to have traced a line in the dirt and said something like: "Those of you who are willing to stay with me and die with me, cross this line" (quoted in Weber 1988: 136).
>
> Fact: There is no convincing evidence that Travis ever uttered this famous speech or drew such a line. In fact, many military historians have concluded that the defense of the Alamo is best characterized in terms of indecision and fatigue.
>
> Legend: The battle slogan of Colonel Travis at the Alamo was "Victory or Death."
>
> Fact: True enough, but Travis was no deliberate martyr. He said "Victory or Death" only at the beginning of the siege, when he fully expected to win and live. He firmly believed that victory was at hand so long as reinforcements arrived; they never came.
>
> Legend: The fearless Alamo defenders fought to their last breath, only to perish beneath a human tidal wave of Mexican soldiers.
>
> Fact: Davy Crockett and half a dozen other Alamo defenders were probably captured by Mexican troops and then, on orders from Santa Anna, executed. Even worse, some contemporary accounts suggest that Crockett and the others may even have—horrors!—surrendered.
>
> Legend: We'll never know exactly what happened at the Alamo; after all, nobody who fought there survived.
>
> Fact: Actually, there were lots of survivors—thousands of victorious Mexican soldiers. But their recorded observations have won scant acceptance because, after all, these are "enemy" sources.

When serious students of Texas history turn to the evidence contained in these nineteenth-century accounts, they are sometimes publicly reviled.

One Texas newspaper termed Hispanic perspectives on Alamo history "a commie plot to trash our heroes" (quoted in Weber 1988: 137). Another writer—from Crockett's home state of Tennessee—questioned the manhood of the historian involved, describing him as a "gutless wonder" (quoted in Weber 1988: 138).

Such are the tensions surrounding America's sacred sites. When archaeologists excavate and interpret their findings, they are increasingly faced with pressure and conflict from various public constituencies. The world of archaeology is only beginning to appreciate the ramifications and conflicts involved when multiple versions of ultimate reality are taken to the American public.

Touring America's Sacred Sites: Not an Easy Call

In the case of the Alamo, tourism is a given. Historic battlefields are an important element in our national identity. American pride will always motivate people to visit such places, to experience the power of the place for themselves.

As Brear has pointed out (1995: 1), these places "are still where we fight the social and political Other, but with images and words rather than with guns. Here we create boundaries between 'us' and 'them' with identities born from historic individuals, identities inherited by entire groups in current society. Our battle sites, in being the origin of these images, become our most hallowed ground and the object of patriotic pilgrimages." Closing the Alamo to tourists would be sacrilegious to Anglo-Americans; for the dominant society, such historic touchstones inform us about our national, heroic roots. The Hispanic community also wishes to see people visit the Alamo but wants to present a very different message there.

However, tourism at the Medicine Wheel raises a rather different set of concerns. To many Indian people, this remains a holy place, one of many sacred sites where important ceremonies are performed to this day. Sacred lands are considered to be vital to individual and tribal harmony. And some important sacred sites—including the Bighorn Medicine Wheel—are overrun each year by thousands of non-Indians: well-meaning tourists, scientific teams, and New Agers seeking a spiritual experience. There is great concern in Indian communities that the plants, paths, shrines, rocks, and other aspects of sacred sites are being destroyed by the curious and the insensitive.

I suspect that many North American archaeologists would agree that the Bighorn Medicine Wheel is one of America's more intriguing ancient sites. With its spectacular setting and puzzling past, the Medicine Wheel seems to be a natural for the heritage tourist. Or is it? Should tourists be encouraged to visit the Bighorn Medicine Wheel? As archaeologists, how do we balance out our dual concerns with bringing American archaeology to the interested public while respecting the wishes of the descendant populations still involved with many of those sites?

Let me sketch two different approaches to this problem, once again using the Bighorn Medicine Wheel as a concrete example. Today, there are popular guidebooks aimed at bringing North American archaeology to an interested traveling public. In *America's Ancient Treasures* (1993), Franklin and Mary Etling Folsom describe thousands of archaeological museums and sites available for tourist visits. They provide a first-rate, encyclopedic overview, aiming "to open doors to those who are curious and who want to dig metaphorically into the past" (1993: xi). My own *Exploring Ancient Native America* (Thomas 1994) is intended to do the same thing but employs a more selective, more personalized and thematic framework. Both books are designed to educate the traveler about the ancient Native American past. Both likewise acknowledge the sometimes conflicting imperatives of archaeological research and traditional American Indian religious beliefs.

The Folsoms considered this issue carefully and decided to exclude the Medicine Wheel from their fourth edition of *America's Ancient Treasures*. After consulting with representatives at the American Indian Rights Fund, they declined either to discuss the site or to provide directions for visiting it. Instead, they simply wrote (Folsom and Folsom 1993: 251) that the Bighorn Medicine Wheel "is sacred to Native Americans who worship there. They request that visitors stay away and do not invade their privacy." This position reflects a sensitivity to native interests not evident in the previous editions of *America's Ancient Treasures*. They made a good decision.

At about the same time, I struggled with precisely the same issue but came to the opposite conclusion. In *Exploring Ancient Native America*, I spent eight pages describing the Bighorn Medicine Wheel in some detail, discussing several possible explanations of its origin and use, and providing precise directions for tourists wishing to get there.

Like Folsom and Folsom, I discussed this matter with various Native American people. These conversations elicited a broad range of opinion.

Some expressed the view that sacred sites should never be visited by the non-Indian public. Other Indian people saw no particular problem with tourists visiting such sites. After all, they noted, places like the Medicine Wheel are already visited by thousands of non-Indians every year; no single author can hope to stem this flood of visitation. The key issue, they pointed out, was to educate the public about native values and to be certain that such sacred sites are protected from looting and despoliation.

I was still undecided about whether or not to include the Medicine Wheel when I discussed the matter with the late William Tallbull, a Northern Cheyenne elder with a deep and long-lasting relationship to the Medicine Wheel. Tallbull was an important part of a coalition of tribal, scientific, ecological, and government interests cooperating to assure that the Medicine Wheel would be protected, preserved, and respected. He supported the U.S. Forest Service's decision to keep the site open to the public but with the last 1.5 miles of the access road closed to vehicular traffic. Tourists would still be permitted to visit the site but would be required to cover the remaining distance on foot. In his view, this solution minimized the negative impacts of tourism while maintaining the religious freedom of the native people who worshipped there, himself included.

To Tallbull, education remained a key consideration. He also felt it important to keep the site accessible to anybody who wished to experience the power of place. People have been drawn to this isolated mountaintop for centuries, and Tallbull believed it inappropriate to exclude anyone. Not only did he encourage me to include the Bighorn Medicine Wheel in *Exploring Ancient Native America*, but he offered to write a sidebar to my own discussion. In his perspective, sacred sites offer an important opportunity for teaching tolerance and respect.

William Tallbull's comments read in part (Tallbull 1994: 238–39):

> To the Indigenous Peoples of North America, the archaeological sites found on North American soil are not "archaeological" sites. They are sites where our relatives lived and carried out their lives. Sacred Sites such as the Medicine Wheel and Medicine Mountain are no different.... When Native Peoples have been blessed by a site or area, they go back to give thanks and leave offerings whenever they get a chance. These should be left undisturbed and not handled or tampered with. Today many of our people are reconnecting with these sites after many years of being denied the privilege of practicing our own religion at these very sacred areas. In the past, trips were made in secret and hidden from curious eyes. If you go to see a Sacred Site,

remember you are walking on "holy ground," and we ask that you respect our culture and traditions. If you come to a site that is being used for a religious purpose, we hope you will understand.

In my discussion of the Medicine Wheel, I also published a lengthy poem in which Suzan Shown Harjo (Cheyenne/Hodulgee/Muscogee) speaks eloquently about the importance of respecting Indian sacred ground.

Which approach is "correct"? As we take American archaeology to the public, what should we do about sacred sites? I don't know. I certainly have no quibble with the Folsoms' decision to exclude the Medicine Wheel; they did so for exactly the right reasons. But I am also glad that I included it, juxtaposed with the personal perspectives on this site from two prominent Indian people.

Reality at the Millennium

To return to my central theme, does Margaret Mead's advice about American museums still work today? Is reality still the key?

While I suspect that the answer is probably yes, it seems clear that her recommendations on reality need some reworking. Mead was a frontline scientist in the modern world of her day. She lived in an optimistic time, when anthropologists believed that they could develop a fairly objective science of humanity, with universal standards for morality and conduct. In 1941 Mead could ask, "Is this true?" And if so, then this was what museums should serve up to the public. If it was not true, it should be left out.

With this single-minded approach, Mead would continue to argue that museum curators could—and should—address current issues of the day, including "race relations, the population explosion, the ravished environment and the concerns of the imprisoned children of the slums. . . . The museum is a perfect setting in which to represent the hazards to the environment, the devastation wrought by man and how it can be prevented or corrected, the price of overcrowding, the restoration of balance and beauty" (Mead 1970: 24–25). She wrote passionately that museum exhibits should systematically present "the truth as is now known" and that the museum is a place in which people "can renew their trust in science and in democracy" (Mead 1941: 67).

Margaret Mead died in 1978, and the world has changed since then. Today, we hear a great deal about the new postmodern world—a world that has grown distrustful of the kind of truth and reality that Mead wished to present in her museum. Postmodernist critics disparage efforts such as

hers to speak for "the other," whether they be colonized peoples, indigenous groups and minorities, religious groups, or the working class.

Postmodern anthropologists minimize the authority of the "cultural
producer." Instead the preference is to create opportunities for popular participation and democratic determination of cultural values—even at the
expense of a certain incoherence. Rather than listening to authority figures (such as the all-knowing museum curator), postmodernists argue that
each group deserves a right to speak for themselves, in their own voice, and
that each voice should be accepted as authentic and legitimate.

Today's interpretive anthropology, an offshoot of the postmodern
movement, also questions the discovery of scientific truths about other
cultures; in their place are composed interpretations about the "other." For
some interpretivist circles, the brand of ethnography pioneered by Mead
(and many others) was not really an empirical account of another culture.
It was just another species of fiction.

Deconstructionist approaches are said to be appropriate in anthropology because they get away from traditional "scientific" notions of ethnography—"what the culture was really like"—and focus instead on hidden intentions and unexpressed biases of the ethnographer/author: all
truth is relative; all perceptions are mediated by one's cultural and sexual
identity. As the influential postmodern thinker Jean-François Lyotard
notes (quoted in Harvey 1990: 52), "consensus has become an outmoded
and suspect value."

Few modern anthropologists believe in absolute value neutrality or
complete objectivity. Today, most philosophers of science recognize that
science exists as part of culture, not outside it. Values, properly factored in,
can be productive, not contaminating. In other words, many contemporary
anthropologists suggest that indeterminacy, multivocality, and relativism
have become the messages of today.

Taking Archaeology to a Postmodern Public

Many (perhaps even most) archaeologists are, I believe, sympathetic to the
multiple voices being heard in today's archaeology. Most would agree that
it is a good thing to have increased Native American participation in national archaeology meetings (even if some do not like the specific messages
being delivered). Most archaeologists are glad that female voices are increasingly included in the profession and that women's contributions are
recognized and rewarded (although some are uncomfortable with specific

views expressed by some feminists). And I also think the upsurge of interest in fields such as African-American and Hispanic-American archaeologies is widely recognized as a vital new direction in the field. These are all important new voices in Americanist archaeology.

There is, I believe, a real question about the degree to which postmodern thought has penetrated the American psyche. To be sure, there is an increased level of tolerance for other opinions within the academic world of professional archaeology, the rest of social science, and the humanities. But how much of this is strictly academic fad and fancy? As archaeology becomes increasingly inclusive, as previously disenfranchised groups are empowered and their voices are heard, as power is more broadly and more democratically distributed, what is the message for the American public?

Will we continue to hear about the "death of authority"—or the "death of your authority"? Will the new openness remain open, or will we experience the same old intolerance of different ideas, only with the power shifted from the traditional "haves" to the "have-nots"? The widespread call for multiple voices and diverse perspectives does not necessarily ensure tolerance for opinions that differ from one's own. Will the new inclusiveness turn out to be but a warmed-over version of the old exclusionism—dressed up in a different mix of racial, sexual, economic, and ideological dogma?

Here, I think, Mead's advice still resonates. Archaeologists have special responsibilities, not only to recover and interpret evidence of the human past but also to ensure that the past is not used for malevolent purposes in the present. This is not an easy task because it requires that individual archaeologists balance sometimes conflicting realities.

It is possible for multivocality to go too far, as any review of racist or chauvinist nationalistic readings of the past would demonstrate. Clearly, we must reject the extreme relativist position—that archaeological data are no more than mental constructs created by archaeologists and that interpretation is merely an individual expression of ideology or personal opinion. The problem posed by extreme relativism is that there are no viable means for deciding between multiple pasts—each is valid and equal. At its extreme, this chaotic view holds that no intellectual criteria are necessary to evaluate theories or to judge among them.

The program of extreme relativism leaves archaeology wholly at the mercy of political forces, forces that can employ censorship and domination to produce interchangeable pasts, which ultimately serve only as the bases of ideologies and not as frameworks for understanding humanity.

Accepting the position that one yarn is as good as another severs archaeology from the real world and trivializes the enterprise; we might as well be writers of pure fiction. Diversity in approach is a valuable thing— but not when taken to the extreme position of one-person's-view-of-something-old becoming the accepted archaeological standard. So viewed, archaeology becomes merely an article of faith.

Sixty years ago Mead argued that museums, unlike the mass media, insist on asking, "'Is this true?' instead of asking: 'will this make a hit?'" As she also said, this is how museums have kept the people's trust. Truth and reality continue to have an important place in the world of archaeology, but taking that message to the American public has never been more difficult—or more important.

Acknowledgments

I thank Margot Dembo, Lorann S. A. Pendleton, and Niurka Tyler for their assistance in preparing this chapter.

Note

1. We must note, of course, that alternative views exist here too. A number of contemporary native people point out the dark side of missions throughout America. Ed D. Castillo, a historian specializing in California history and a member of the Cahuilla tribe, views California's missions as "huge feudal estates ... [that] grew rich from the efforts of a mass of unpaid forced laborers. . . . No reasonable person can argue that the California Indians in any way benefited from a colonization scheme that confiscated their land and resources; uprooted entire villages; forced them to migrate to the feudalistic mendicant estates on the coast; subjected them to daily floggings, forced labor, and wholesale sexual assaults on their wives and daughters; and resulted in the deaths of thousands of innocent men, women and children" (Castillo 1989: 378, 392). Although Castillo's comments were specifically addressed toward California's mission system, many Native Americans feel that similar conditions characterized missions throughout America's Spanish Borderlands, including Mission San Antonio de Valero—the Alamo.

References

Brear, H. B. 1995. *Inherit the Alamo: Myth and Ritual at an American Shrine*. Austin: University of Texas Press.
Castillo, E. D. 1989. The Native Response to the Colonization of Alta California. In *Columbian Consequences*, vol. 1, *Archaeological and Historical Perspectives on*

the Spanish Borderlands West, ed. D. H. Thomas, 377–94. Washington, D.C.: Smithsonian Institution Press.

Eddy, J. A. 1974. Astronomical Alignment of the Big Horn Medicine Wheel. *Science* 184 (4141): 1035–43.

Folsom, F., and M. E. Folsom. 1993. *America's Ancient Treasures.* 4th ed. Albuquerque: University of New Mexico Press.

Harvey, D. 1990. *The Condition of Postmodernity: An Enquiry into the Origins of Cultural Change.* Cambridge: Blackwell.

Mead, M. 1941. Museums in the Emergency. *Natural History* 48(2): 67.

———. 1970. Museums in a Media-Saturated World. *Museum News* 49(1): 23–25.

Tallbull, W. 1994. Archaeological Sites or Sacred Places? A Native American Perspective. In *Exploring Ancient Native America: An Archaeological Guide,* by D. H. Thomas, 238–39. New York: Macmillan.

Thomas, D. H. 1994. *Exploring Ancient Native America: An Archaeological Guide.* New York: Macmillan.

Weber, D. J. 1988. *Myth and the History of the Hispanic Southwest: Essays by David J. Weber.* Albuquerque: University of New Mexico Press.

12

Archaeology and Tourism at Mount Vernon

Esther C. White

Mount Vernon, George and Martha Washington's plantation home on the Potomac River near Washington, D.C., does not employ archaeologists to promote archaeological fieldwork as a major tourist attraction. Few people come to Mount Vernon specifically for the archaeology. Instead, an archaeology program was established at this house museum in 1987, primarily to identify resources and evaluate and retrieve data about the past. However, because these archaeologists work in a public environment, their program is necessarily structured to improve and enhance the quality of the visitor's experience. Thus one of the principal goals of public archaeology at Mount Vernon, as at historic house museums across the country, is to connect with the enthusiasm that tourists have for archaeology.

Most visitors are excited to see the archaeology excavation and exhibit while they tour Mount Vernon, and many have observed or participated in public excavations elsewhere. Thanks to increased visibility in the media, and the expansion of the Internet, Mount Vernon's archaeologists find themselves interpreting the past to an increasingly educated audience. Because of the audience's increased knowledge, expectations of archaeological interpretation are more sophisticated. Worldwide, archaeologists profit from this familiarity, using fieldwork to attract visitors during the summer, providing tours, and offering opportunities to excavate (Davis 2001).

More often than not, this relegates the discipline to "tourism curiosity" rather than it being a fully integrated research tool, capable of conveying meaningful messages to various components of the community or museum with which it is affiliated (Comer 2000: 3). Slowly, archaeology and tourism are melding, and there are more and more destinations worldwide that have evolved from merely showcasing an ongoing excavation. Perhaps the most successful is the reconstructed village at Jorvik Viking Centre in York, England, where lines form early each morning.

In this country, archaeologists often struggle to convey the relevance of their work and fumble in attempts to promote and incorporate their results within established infrastructures. Mount Vernon's archaeology program, like those of other historic house museums, is an excellent illustration of how archaeologists can educate, integrate, and market their discipline and achieve success in extending archaeology's influence into heritage tourism.

Background

Public archaeology as part of the tourism industry began during the late 1970s and early 1980s with work in Alexandria, Virginia; Annapolis and Baltimore in Maryland; and Colonial Williamsburg. What set these programs apart was the emphasis on the visitor exploring the past through the medium of excavation. With the success of these community-based programs came the creation of an archaeology department at Monticello, Thomas Jefferson's home in Charlottesville, Virginia. Today there are permanent archaeology programs affiliated with six presidential homes.[1]

These presidential house museums are a good model for archaeology's role in heritage tourism because their small size and budgets are realistic for a range of institutions, communities, and historic districts. In addition, archaeological programs at many of these historic house museums are expanding and are permanent fixtures in their museums. The experience of the public archaeologists employed at these presidential homes is invaluable for others interested in marketing archaeology to a broader public as more than a curiosity.

Why have the people operating presidential house museums decided to continue and expand long-term archaeological investigations? The success of archaeologists within these organizations involves a formula, the basic recipe of which can be transported to a range of tourism sites, both historic and prehistoric. The key ingredients are education, integration, and marketing.

Structure of Archaeological Programs

Archaeology departments affiliated with historic house museums are primarily research programs, exploring the properties to learn about the diverse groups that inhabited them during the past. Although not mandated to excavate within sight of the visitors, most sites are located within the exhibition area, in high-profile locations. This central placement of the archaeological work fostered the need for public interpretation; the archaeology was not initiated as an attraction, nor did the museum administrations hire archaeologists with the intention of gaining anything other than knowledge.

The serendipitous discovery that excavations are exciting exhibits "that both teach and challenge the public" (Heath 1997: 178) is an additional benefit of an archaeological research program, a benefit that most museum professionals had not originally anticipated. Visitors to these public excavations observe the fluid and subjective nature of the research process and see that the interpreted past is constructed from fragmentary discoveries. These archaeological programs also enrich tourism sites through the tangible link with the past that archaeology provides.

To maintain the integrity of a research excavation that is also an exhibit, the archaeologists within these presidential homes have honed their interpretive skills and learned to budget the time and money that such interpretation requires. Public archaeologists have developed a variety of strategies for interacting successfully with visitors and responding to their curiosity.

Mount Vernon provides an extreme example of tourism at an archaeological site. One million people a year visit Mount Vernon, making this archaeological program quite visible. During peak periods Mount Vernon's archaeologists are challenged in attempts to field the typical visitor's many questions. At these times one person is assigned to interact with the crowd, although invariably everyone on the site works with the public. Interpretation ranges from simply answering questions to engaging in conversations about archaeological methods, research design, and how archaeology is but one of many tools used to learn about the past. While logistics and liability force the roping off of Mount Vernon's sites, when possible the archaeologists encourage participation to help excavate, screen, or process artifacts.

Other museums attract fewer visitors than Mount Vernon and therefore their archaeologists can present more interactive interpretations. For instance, excavations at the slave quarter of Thomas Jefferson's Poplar Forest were well off the beaten path for most visitors. Tourists who visited this out-of-the-way excavation yearned to learn about archaeology, which provided the opportunity for an intensive exploration of the site and for ongoing archaeological research (Heath 1997: 180).

Active excavations with engaging interpretations will probably always be the foundation of archaeology programs within the tourism industry. However, because excavations are temporary exhibits, they should be the catalyst by which archaeology is integrated into the fabric of the museum. The enthusiasm we have all experienced for archaeology is based upon the thrill of discovery. It is imperative for public archaeologists to maintain the momentum that excavations initiate. The archaeological programs at the presidential house museums have sustained and increased this energy by actively educating, integrating, and marketing their discipline both within the institution and to the public.

Education

University-accredited summer archaeological field schools remain the foremost educational program as well as a source of funding and labor for many public archaeology programs. This vestige maintains the public's perception that all archaeology is tied to the academy, rather than financed and managed by the tourist attraction. Volunteers not conforming to this stereotype vehemently defend their volunteer status when visitors suggest that they are either students or paid for their labors. Half the battle is often challenging the public's conventional wisdom, not only about what archaeology is—why and how it is done—but also about who archaeologists are.

Education is one weapon utilized to challenge these conventions. The education of both the museum's staff and the public is a primary component for the success of a public archaeology program. A legitimate mandate for these endeavors is provided by most museum mission statements, which include education. Increasingly, the presidential house archaeologists are educating a variety of constituencies. Besides serving college students, these museums have developed diverse programming for seniors, teachers, boy scouts, and summer campers as well as for elementary, middle, and high school students, deaf students, and avocationals, among others. This creative programming has expanded the scope of museum excavation to something more comprehensive than the summer field school and has fostered education and public relations skills among the archaeologists.

When archaeologists are communicating with museum colleagues, education of the public occurs as well. By educating the museum staff, the archaeologist can spend more time on archaeology, while the archaeological program gains exposure due to an increased understanding of the discipline. Teaching museum staff the benefits of archaeology and how to publicize it, obtain grants, create educational units, or conduct public relations for and with it is a key step in the acceptance of the profession as a permanent fixture within the museum.

The ways in which archaeologists educate colleagues in historic house museums are varied and creative and often serve to disseminate information to the public as well. Staff meetings, newsletters, periodic training, open houses, exhibits, technical reports, popular articles, and web sites are all means of communication that archaeologists employ. At Mount Vernon, the archaeologists are involved in all of these initiatives, constantly reinforcing the idea that archaeology is one means used to learn about the past. A key to the success of this education is the ability to disseminate information appropriate for specific audiences. The archaeological findings and process must be adapted into understandable quantities accessible for docents, public relations staff, potential donors, event planners, and of course the public. It sounds simple, but unfortunately this communication of accurate, clear, pertinent information does not happen often enough. When successful, education is the first step toward the second facet, full integration within the institution.

Integration

With the increased awareness from successful education, archaeological discoveries integrated into the tourism site contribute in a variety of ways, often through the establishment of more events than archaeologists alone could develop and implement. One potential benefit of this integrated program is to increase visitation by specific groups of visitors, most importantly people who had never felt a connection with the historic site.

At the presidential homes visitation is largely white and middle class. In general, African Americans have had little presence as consumers of these sites, although during the eighteenth and nineteenth centuries they made up the majority of the inhabitants. Archaeology is helping attract today's African-American tourists to these plantation homes by beginning a dialogue about the African-American slaves who built and maintained these sites. The integration of the archaeological discoveries within the larger museum framework has increased these visitor numbers to a greater extent than the excavations alone ever could have.

For example, at Monticello the interpretation of Mulberry Row, the home quarter of Thomas Jefferson's enslaved African Americans, incorporates archaeological research as one component of a brochure, self-guided walking tour, and interpreter-led plantation tour. Numerous house museums have used the walking tour technique, achieving a simple way to disseminate data and thereby attract new groups of visitors. Bograd and Singleton (1997: 198) suggest that the archaeological research acted as the catalyst to bring about this expanded interpretation at Monticello.

At Mount Vernon, it is clear that archaeological research has a large role in the continuing evolution of a broader interpretation of the plantation. Visitors to the plantation as recently as the early 1990s witnessed a Mount Vernon that was passive in its presentation of slavery. Burnham (1995) and Bograd and Singleton (1997) present narratives that chronicle the interpretation of slavery, or lack of such interpretation, at the plantation prior to 1995. While Mount Vernon has had an interpreted slave quarter since the early 1960s, discussion of African Americans and their contributions to the plantation was "mostly benign and, occasionally, willfully neglectful" (Bograd and Singleton 1997: 203).

During the spring of 1995, in an attempt to create a more active interpretation of slave life at Mount Vernon and to increase African-American visitation, the interpretive staff began thirty-minute walking tours focusing on the slaves who lived and worked there during the eighteenth century. This tour draws in part upon research completed by the archaeological staff and their attempt to make archaeological information accessible. The tour is immensely popular and has succeeded in increasing the numbers of African Americans visiting the first president's home. The archaeological study of Mount Vernon's slave population was one motivation for the creation of this tour, but it was not possible without the integration of the archaeological findings into the larger museum environment and the encouragement from archaeologists to expand the museum's vision (Burnham 1995).

As the Mount Vernon and Monticello examples demonstrate, archaeology does not have to be the primary component of these initiatives. It is important for archaeological findings to be incorporated into established brochures, self-guided walking tours, auto tours, historical markers, web sites, and tourism literature—in short, this is a matter of packaging archaeology with developed tourism venues and destinations. Working within the framework of an established medium increases archaeological visibility, presenting archaeological discoveries and interpretations to a larger population, thereby broadening the support for and interest in the discipline.

Mount Vernon's education department exploits this interest in archaeology and uses it as the focal point to illustrate how scholars learn about the past. This concept is a "chapter" on Mount Vernon's popular CD-ROM "Dig into George" (Hayward 1998), which covers all aspects of the plantation, including archaeology. During the summer the popular "Hands-on-History" tent includes an activity, in which the broken shards of ceramic artifacts are mended to demonstrate their differences and how these vessels enlighten us about daily life in the past. During the school year, a simulated root cellar is a primary component of a broader elementary school lesson entitled "Cultural Detective," which teaches how scholars learn about eighteenth-century African-American life (Hayward 1996).

Poplar Forest utilizes similar activities in a "Hands-on-History" tent, and Ferry Farm has comparable lessons within "archaeology kits" available for schoolchildren. These examples were not designed solely by archaeologists but rather utilize educators' talents to package archaeological methods and data as a component of a larger, integrated lesson, an important point in stressing the relevance of archaeology to a varied constituency.

One of the most enduring ways of integrating archaeological discoveries into the fabric of the historic house museum is through reconstruction. Generally, the investment necessary for an archaeological reconstruction is much higher than that required to produce a lesson or tour, which makes reconstruction a greater risk. But when successful, reconstructions hold perhaps the largest payback and create a strong bond between the archaeological discovery and the institution. While the task of interpreting archaeological sites via reconstruction is a complex topic, rife with multiple challenges beyond the scope of this chapter, a number of the presidential homes have succeeded in either complete or partial reconstructions based upon recent archaeological investigations.

Due in part to archaeological discoveries, the south lane at Mount Vernon has been transformed. Washington's orchard was replanted, his dung repository was rebuilt, and brick walls along the lane were taken down, to be replaced with replicas of Washington-era wooden fencing. These changes aid the visitor to see the plantation as it appeared to George and Martha Washington. The archaeologists lobbied for the changes, convinced that fence posts, trees, and buildings could be resurrected from postholes, planting holes, and foundations, to present a complete setting. As at Mount Vernon, Monticello has also utilized archaeological data to recreate many elements of Jefferson's landscape (Heath 1997: 185–90). Reconstruction on a smaller scale is present at Poplar Forest, where excavations of a slave quarter were the basis for a "ghost" building. This technique employs three-dimensional framing, allowing visitors to visualize location and size of the archaeologically discovered building (Heath 1999: 66).

Numerous reconstruction projects at the presidential homes are in the planning or early construction phase: Monticello is formulating a proposal to reconstruct Mulberry Row; Mount Vernon is conducting excavations to assess the potential for rebuilding Washington's whiskey distillery; and Poplar Forest is in the midst of rebuilding Jefferson's Wing of Offices. These projects have archaeological research as their foundations and illustrate a "permanent" public benefit of archaeology at the presidential homes. By integrating the archaeological discoveries and reconstructing buildings and landscape, the institution gains a broader base for interpreting the past.

And again, note that the archaeologists have not created all these lessons, walking tours, web sites, brochures, or reconstruction plans; they are merely transmitting archaeological findings and thinking of creative methods of allowing the tourist, student, museum professional, or interested patron access to their work. Archaeologists are not normally trained as educators or marketing or public relations experts; they should therefore realize their strengths and weaknesses and explore ways of allowing others within their organization to use archaeological information creatively.

Why is the integration of the archaeological program such an important component at a tourist site? The reason is that archaeology must contribute more than just an excavation if it is to prosper when the digging ceases. According to Elizabeth Anderson Comer, "the most successful and long lived of archaeology programs are those that become an integral part" of their organizations. Thus "longevity . . . has the added benefit of tapping into the tourism industry on a long-term basis" (Comer 2000: 9).

As tourism at historic sites grows, the successfully integrated archaeological program will be a means by which novel attractions, with an archaeological focus, are readily developed. Lucid interpretations that present the significance of a site or artifact assemblage will also be formed in the course of conducting professional research. Archaeologists must become adept at working with various constituencies so that non-archaeologists can utilize the archaeological record to support fund-raising, education, or media exposure. With the proper integration, these archaeological products can become an indispensable part of our world.

Marketing

Marketing reinforces the archaeological unit within the tourism site, establishing reasons for the administration to view archaeology as an integral component of the museum. The epiphany of this is involvement in events otherwise closed to the site.

Poplar Forest participates actively in Virginia Garden Weeks, a major tourism initiative in the Commonwealth, although the site boasts no extant garden. Instead its media department markets the archaeological investigations into Jefferson's landscape, attracting the garden set to lectures and tours of the archaeology. The fact that this developing site has a hook into an established tourism event makes the archaeology department invaluable. This is archaeology working within the tourist industry.

At Monticello and Ferry Farm, reproductions of artifacts recovered from the archaeological excavations on the properties are sold in the shops and via mail order. At both sites, ceramics, glass, jewelry, and other gift items have been adapted from artifacts discovered by the professional archaeological staff. The revenue from these sales supports preservation at each museum and, more important, provides a link with the site for the consumer. This interplay of archaeology and commerce is an example of creative marketing, providing another tangible motivation for these museums to employ archaeologists.

During excavations around the mansion, Mount Vernon's archaeologists developed a thirty-minute walking tour of the plantation called "Beneath Your Feet." This provided a special activity during autumn, a season when visitation is traditionally slow. Focusing on the plantation's history and development from an archaeological perspective, the walk was widely successful; the Mount Vernon Ladies' Association, which operates the museum, emphasized this program in fall media promotions. While the event is no longer given on a regular schedule, it is one of the six tours marketed to groups as part of Mount Vernon's "Walks and Talks" program.

Poplar Forest successfully markets archaeology as a development tool. The archaeologist spends a percentage of time fund-raising for the organization, a vital activity for a museum. By utilizing the archaeological findings to generate support and donations, the Poplar Forest administration achieves a positive and vibrant link with the past, harnessing the enthusiasm so many individuals hold for archaeology.

The Perfect Tool

If in the most basic sense tourism is about the bottom line—how many people visit a site, how long they stay, and how much money they spend—then archaeological successes within the heritage tourism industry are directly linked to the ability to bring in tourists, increase their length of visitation, and part them from their money. At the presidential house museums employing archaeologists, the archaeology and archaeologists alone are not going to increase visitation substantially. Instead archaeology is effective in adding to the quality of the visit, increasing the numbers of specific groups, and making the process of exploring the past—the "how do we know?"—more exciting. It is a component of creative and novel programs providing texture to the experience of touring a house museum.

I hope more small house museums, historic districts, and communities will consider archaeology as a viable investment. The interdisciplinary nature of archaeology, and its universal appeal, make it the perfect tool to be exploited by a range of sites, especially those that do not have as vibrant a central figure as Washington, Jefferson, Madison, or Jackson. Within these museums and communities, archaeology can play a major role in increasing visitation, expanding programming, and providing an important and dynamic component. Through creative education, integration, and marketing, archaeology will continue to evolve into a significant element of the heritage tourism industry in the United States, its contributions felt in a variety of ways and not merely during the excavation season.

Acknowledgments

I wish to thank the archaeologists at the presidential homes mentioned in this article: Dennis Pogue, Scott Parker, Barbara Heath, Michael Strutt, Heather Olson, Frasier Neiman, Susan Kern, and Larry McKee. Elizabeth Anderson Comer, Pamela Cressey, and Catherine Slusser graciously discussed at length their visions of public archaeology and the potential for archaeology to play a role within the tourism industry. Thanks go also to John Sprinkle and Barbara Little, who commented on drafts of this chapter.

Note

1. Archaeology can be experienced in a variety of ways at the six presidential homes that have permanent archaeology programs. The first five are all in Virginia. To learn more about these individual programs visit Monticello, <www.monticello. org>, Thomas Jefferson's home in Charlottesville; Poplar Forest, <www.poplar-forest.org>, his retreat outside Lynchburg; Ferry Farm, <www.kenmore.org>, George Washington's boyhood home at Fredericksburg; Mount Vernon, <www. mountvernon.org>, Washington's plantation along the Potomac River near Alexandria; Montpelier, <www.montpelier.org>, James and Dolly Madison's home in Orange, Virginia; and the Hermitage, <www.hermitage.org>, Andrew and Rachel Jackson's plantation near Nashville, Tennessee.

References

Bograd, M. D., and T. A. Singleton. 1997. The Interpretation of Slavery: Mount Vernon, Monticello and Colonial Williamsburg. In *Presenting Archaeology to the Public: Digging for Truths*, ed. J. H. Jameson, 193–204. Walnut Creek, Calif.: AltaMira Press.

Burnham, P. 1995. *How the Other Half Lived: A People's Guide to American Historic Sites*. Boston: Faber and Faber.

Comer, E. A. 2000. Public Archaeology as a Tool for Community Preservation and Empowerment. Elizabeth Anderson Comer Archaeology Home Page <http://www.eacarchaeology.com/publicBalto.html>

Davis, M. M. (ed.). 2001. *2001 Archaeological Fieldwork Opportunities Bulletin*. Dubuque, Iowa: Kendall-Hunt Publishing Company.

Hayward, N. 1996. Mount Vernon Hands-On History: A Discovery of 18th-Century Life at the Home of George Washington. Mount Vernon, Va.: Mount Vernon Ladies' Association.

———. 1998. *Dig into George*. CD-ROM. Mount Vernon, Va.: Mount Vernon Ladies' Association.

Heath, B. J. 1997. Archaeology and Interpretation at Monticello and Poplar Forest. In *Presenting Archaeology to the Public: Digging for Truths*, ed. J. H. Jameson, 177–92. Walnut Creek, Calif.: AltaMira Press.

———. 1999. *Hidden Lives: The Archaeology of Slave Life at Thomas Jefferson's Poplar Forest*. Charlottesville: University Press of Virginia.

Jameson, J. H., Jr. (ed.). 1997. *Presenting Archaeology to the Public: Digging for Truths*. Walnut Creek, Calif.: AltaMira Press.

13

Broadening the Interpretations of the Past at Harpers Ferry National Historical Park

Paul A. Shackel

When I first arrived at Harpers Ferry National Historical Park in 1989, I was given a tour of some buildings within a forthcoming archaeology project area. The Denver Service Center of the National Park Service had performed some archaeological work around the same buildings in the mid-1970s prior to the placement of a sewer line. In one outbuilding I found a sign caked with mud from the 1985 flood that devastated the Lower Town area. Part of a handwritten word—"archaeol"—was visible. A park ranger verified my assumption that this sign was a remnant of the 1970s archaeology project. As I flaked the rest of the encrusted mud off the sign, I was reminded of how too many archaeologists in the 1970s interacted with and interpreted their work to the public. The entire sign read:

> Yes—we are archaeologists.
> Yes—we are doing archaeology.
> Please do not disturb us.

In some ways, this artifact of the 1970s archaeology project is one of the more significant items found during my early tenure at the park because it strengthened my commitment to using archaeology to create a new public outreach program there. The sign represents an era in American archaeology when many practitioners alienated the public. Archaeologists trained in the New Archaeology tradition of the 1960s and 1970s used scientific methods to find the "true objective past." They thought they could learn little from public participation and outreach. Many believed that their work was so important and so far beyond the comprehension of most visitors that they did not have to involve visitors in their investigations, even in highly visible and accessible areas (Fagan 1996: 238–43).

The New Archaeologists introduced a new vocabulary to the field. The new technical jargon could be deciphered only by other archaeologists trained in these methods and vocabulary. The terminology found in archaeology reports perpetuated the mystification of the discipline. For the most part, if archaeological results were published, they usually found their way only into scientific journals. Little information was shared with the public. Jacquetta Hawkes (in Finn 2001: 38), a critic of the New Archaeology, wrote in 1968: "[Some discussions of archaeology] have seemed to me so esoteric, so overburdened with unhelpful jargon, so grossly inflated in relation to the significance of the matter involved, that they might emanate from a secret society, an introverted group of specialists enjoying their often rather squalid intellectual spells and rituals at the expense of an outside world to which they will contribute nothing that is enjoyable, generally interesting or of historical importance."

Much has been done since the late 1970s to include the public and to share with people many significant archaeological discoveries. Some archaeologists, like Ivor Noel Hume (e.g., Noel Hume 1991), have long known the value of public interest. Noel Hume's writings have appealed to a wide audience since he came to the United States in the 1950s. His insights created the foundations for a very successful historical archaeology program at Colonial Williamsburg in Virginia. Other archaeologists who crossed the line—from a scientific to a public audience—often met serious criticism from their peers. In particular, I recollect the negative reception Stuart Strueaver faced when he coauthored a popular book on the Koster site (Strueaver and Holton 1979).

In the early 1980s some archaeologists made pioneering efforts to design on-site public interpretation programs. For example, archaeologists associated with the Historic Annapolis Foundation and the University of Maryland made some initial and significant strides to welcome visitors on site and to create intellectually challenging tours (Leone 1983; Leone and Potter 1987; Potter 1994). Individuals who were both archaeologists and tour guides explained the methodology and theory of a particular excavation. Recently, projects that have provided intensive public interpretation on their working archaeology sites have been met with great enthusiasm by the public. Many interesting and groundbreaking enterprises are under way to share with the public the excitement of archaeology (see, e.g., Bense 1991; Lerner 1991; Smith 1993; Fagan 1984; McManamon 1994).

Challenging Consensus History

While many national parks use archaeology to tell a nationally significant story, often the discipline is used to reinforce what we already know or to bolster the story mentioned in the congressional enabling legislation that created the park. What we see as important enough to remember and set aside to memorialize is more than a romantic version of a bygone era that may be inaccurate and escapist in nature. It is apparent that people and events are commemorated to help reinforce what society sees as important (Thelen 1989: 1125).

The meaning and mission of a historic site are often very telling as regards when the site was commemorated. For instance, in the first half of the twentieth century this country commemorated great men to reinforce the national ideology of power and unity based upon white Anglo-American ideals. Glorifying industry and capitalism was also reinforced through commemorative and memorial activities. After the Civil Rights Movement, Americans experienced a growing trend to be more inclusive in our national story. New laws enabled minority groups that had once been left out of the national histories to take their place with the other histories (Kook 1998). This transition has not been smooth in some cases, and the debate about which histories should be told at national historic sites continues today.

As we move into the twenty-first century, it is apparent that a debate over interpretation and meaning is perpetual. The issue is this: Should local, state, and national parks continue to support a memory of the era in which a historic park was created, or should these sites be seen as dynamic, fluid, and changing, reflecting the attitudes of contemporary society?

Traditional meanings associated with a collective national memory have focused on elites and traditional heroes and have fostered the perception that American history is linear and straightforward. This uncomplicated story occurs only when we leave "others" out of the picture, such as African Americans, Native Americans, Asian Americans, women, the poor, and laborers. This "sacred story with strong nationalist overtones . . . derived much of its coherence from the groups it ignored or dismissed" (Leff 1995: 833; see also Nash et al. 1998: 100). Those who disagree that we should create and reinforce multiple histories of a single site claim that "it is difficult . . . to see how the subjects of the new [social] history can be accommodated in any single framework, let alone a national and political one. . . . How can all these groups, each cherishing its uniqueness and its claim to sovereign attention, be mainstreamed into a single, coherent, integrated history?" (quoted in Nash et al. 1998: 100–101). Historical events are often complex, entangling many different people and groups with varying views.

Harpers Ferry

When I first came to Harpers Ferry in the 1980s as a visitor, I was told by park interpretive staff that the town had been destroyed during the Civil War and had remained a ghost town until the National Park Service acquired it. In the 1950s, when the National Park Service acquired the town, the agency dismantled all existing Victorian structures in an attempt to freeze the landscape in its 1860s appearance (Shackel 1996). With virtually no Victorian structures remaining, interpreters used the existing landscape created by the 1950s National Park Service restoration policy to justify their interpretations. Their version of history recalled a time when industry thrived before the Civil War and highlighted the strategic role the town had played during the insurrection. Interpreters did not mention how citizens coped with the war or how they struggled to resurrect the town and recreated a viable economic center in the decades following the devastation of the war (Shackel 2000).

The official history of the United States has a long-term tradition of placing industry and capitalism on a pedestal. It is difficult to create a compromise interpretation that highlights the stories of labor and capital equally. The preservation of industrial buildings is, in itself, an expression of remembering the ideals of industry and industrial labor. A national park like the one established at Lowell, Massachusetts, claims to present a history representing a balanced view of labor and capital although the majority of buildings saved and stabilized are related to industry rather than to domestic life.

Yet while accounts of ordinary people and minority groups do not necessarily find their way into official accounts, they often do become part of the individual private memory (see, e.g., Wachtel 1986: 2–11). Many members of the working class view the preservation of old buildings and ruins as an attempt to save a degrading phase of human history. Robert Vogel of the Smithsonian Institution notes, "The dirt, noise, bad smell, hard labor and other forms of exploitation associated with these kinds of places make preservation [of industrial sites] ludicrous. 'Preserve a steel mill?' people say, 'It killed my father. Who wants to preserve that?'" (quoted in Lowenthal 1985: 403). Therefore, while there are individual dissenting views on the true benefits of industrialization, the federal government remains strong in supporting ideas of industrial progress at other national parks, such as Saugus in Massachusetts and Hopewell and Steam Town in Pennsylvania.

Finding a balance between labor and capital has also been difficult at Harpers Ferry National Historical Park. One component of the park's mission is to celebrate and interpret industry. Visitors entering the park can go to specific exhibits that highlight fragments of history. The stories of John Brown, Storer College, the Civil War, and industry can be all learned in separate buildings. There is little effort to integrate these topics, and the goal of the park is to keep the history as simple as possible.

Much of the early archaeology in Harpers Ferry was done to support this fragmentary history and to highlight the prominence of the town's industrial era. Archaeologists have worked in Harpers Ferry National Historical Park since 1959, and until recently most of the excavations have been focused on the early and mid-nineteenth-century gun manufacturing industry and supporting commerce. The earliest archaeology was performed to find parts of the U.S. Armory complex (Cotter 1959). Edward Larrabee (1960a) excavated several trenches during the summer of 1960 and found the walls of the arsenal building. He also did the initial excavations on Halls Island and found some foundations belonging to the U.S. Rifle Works (Larrabee 1960b). David H. Hannah (1969) produced the first cultural resource assessment of Virginius Island, a small private nineteenth-century industrial center in Harpers Ferry, sometimes called little Pittsburgh (Hannah 1969). In the 1970s and 1980s major excavations occurred around a set of commercial buildings in the Lower Town commercial district (Blee 1978; Pousson 1985).

From the 1960s through the 1990s many of the park's industry-related interpretive exhibits emphasized the development of industrial technology. The exhibits show the implementation of machinery and "time-saving devices" that revolutionized the manufacturing of weapons. The use of water power is presented as an important development in the progress of industry, and products are displayed and interpreted as material advancements of the new industrial developments. People are not mentioned, and the impact of the implementation of a division of labor is ignored.

Archaeology has recently made significant inroads toward producing a more class-conscious history of Harpers Ferry. As much as archaeology has served to highlight and glorify Harpers Ferry's industrial past, it has also functioned as an equally powerful tool in overturning the myth that industry and technological development are the only histories worth interpreting to the public. The recent National Park Service–sponsored excavations in Lower Town Harpers Ferry, begun in the summer of 1989, set a new goal for studying the town's industrial era. The archaeology focused on questions related to the everyday lives of residents who prospered, struggled, and worked in this commercial district. These were questions that had never before been asked in the archaeology at Harpers Ferry, and we sought to answer these questions by focusing our analyses on boardinghouses, stores, and dwellings. Our goal was to change the current interpretations of the industrial era of Harpers Ferry and to broaden the story to include working people.

In the past, if archaeologists found materials that could not help in the reconstruction of the Civil War era or the antebellum town, the materials were often ignored and thrown away (Hershey 1964; Gardner 1974). In the more recent case of the archaeology performed on a postbellum context, only sparse historical documentation exists on the Civil War, postwar, and recent habitation of a block that contained domestic dwellings, a boardinghouse, and commercial sites. A Mrs. Stipes ran a boardinghouse (1862–65) on the same property during the Civil War. The presence and contributions of the working-class boarding families to the commercial development of the town's Civil War and postbellum history became harder to ignore when the archaeology team uncovered several large deposits dating to their occupations. These deposits yielded one of the most abundant late nineteenth-century assemblages yet identified in Harpers Ferry (Shackel 1993; Burk 1993; Hull-Walski and Walski 1994; Larsen 1994; Lucas 1994). The assemblages illustrate the differences in material wealth and health conditions between classes of people in an industrial society (Shackel 2000).

This information is interpreted in a new permanent exhibit that showcases the town's history, incorporating both the antebellum and postbellum histories. The exhibit goes beyond the "great men" histories and provides an account of the living conditions among the working-class families who lived and worked in Harpers Ferry. Further, the exhibit illustrates class differences in an industrial society (see Little 1998). For instance, more than a thousand medicine bottles found in a privy indicate reliance on self-medication when working conditions were poor and capitalists were not required to be concerned about the health of their workers. A high concentration of parasites is another line of evidence that shows how workers' health was impacted by poor living conditions. The predominance of calves' heads and the finding of only a few remains of fruits and vegetables (from seed and pollen) in the privy matter show the lack of a substantial and varied diet (Shackel 2000).

A class-conscious historical archaeology of Harpers Ferry can only enrich our national heritage and increase awareness of an era that has traditionally been overlooked in the commemorative landscape. Although the Victorian era is not mentioned in the park's enabling legislation, it is now a major theme in a new permanent archaeological exhibit in Lower Town. Archaeology has contributed to overturning the myth that Harpers Ferry was not an economically viable town after the Civil War, and it allows us to tell the story of working-class families.

Putting Unseen People Back into History

Archaeology's popularity can be sustained only if archaeologists can share with people some exciting and informative results. Many interpretations in parks, like much traditional history, are derived from the writings of those who controlled the pen—that is, the powerful and the literate. Some national parks were established expressly to celebrate their deeds and to create a consensual public memory. Groups found on the periphery of the dominant culture are not always part of the story that is told of our national heritage (see, e.g., Little 1997). There are more inclusive histories to tell about our past, and archaeology can supplement the story that cannot be found through the documentary record.

Many interpreters and archaeologists agree on the great potential that archaeology can serve in supplementing our national history. There is no set recipe on how to incorporate archaeologists into park interpretation. How the story of "others" becomes included in any park's everyday interpretation has unfolded with some trial and error. However, the importance of national parks in the consciousness of the American public in creating our national identity makes the challenge worthwhile.

Public support for archaeology has increased tremendously over the past decade. We have come a long way from hanging up signs implying to the public that our work is beyond their comprehension and that we cannot spare the time to involve them in our thrill of discovery. In my seven-year tenure at Harpers Ferry National Historical Park, more than two million visitors entered the park, and some of them came to see our excavations. It gave us an opportunity to share with them the unfolding stories about working-class families. Doing archaeology in a national park was one of the most important responsibilities I have ever undertaken in my professional career. National park sites have been recognized as important by Congress and they represent some of the most significant places in America. They help establish and reinforce a public memory that supports American values and ideals.

The National Park Service is charged with delivering a message that reinforces a patriotic past. The theme is often underscored by the material culture that the agency oversees, protects, and conserves, such as buildings and artifacts. These things help create a sense of security and a feeling of stability (see Bodner 1992). The objects provide a sense that the ideals they represent are timeless and embedded in American tradition. However, these messages are continually being challenged and changed, depending upon the current social and political circumstances within the dominant culture. There is increasing public awareness that archaeology can provide histories of people who have traditionally been forgotten by the National Park Service. In the case of Harpers Ferry National Historical Park, archaeology indeed provides a history of those traditionally forgotten in the national story, such as the boarders and laborers of the Victorian era. Archaeology has made these voiceless groups part of the national consciousness.

Acknowledgments

I thank Barbara Little for inviting me to participate in this volume.

References

Bense, J. A. 1991. The Pensacola Model of Public Archeology. In *Archeology and Education: The Classroom and Beyond,* ed. K. C. Smith and F. P. McManamon, 9–12. Archeological Assistance Study no. 2. Washington, D.C.: National Park Service.

Blee, C. H. 1978. *Archaeological Investigations of the Wager Block Buildings 1977–1978: Harpers Ferry National Historical Park, West Virginia.* Denver, Colo.: Denver Service Center, National Park Service, Department of the Interior.

Bodner, J. 1992. *Remaking America: Public Memory, Commemoration, and Patriotism in the Twentieth Century.* Princeton, N.J.: Princeton University Press.

Burk, B. J. 1993. Calf's Heads on a Platter: A Late Nineteenth-Century Boardinghouse Privy Faunal Analysis. In *Interdisciplinary Investigations of Domestic Life in Government Block B: Perspectives on Harpers Ferry's Armory and Commercial District,* ed. P. A. Shackel, 15.1–15.12. Occasional Report no. 6., National

Capital Region. Washington, D.C.: National Park Service, Department of the Interior.

Cotter, J. L. 1959. Preliminary Investigations at Harpers Ferry: Harper House Garden and building 23, Arsenal Area at Shenandoah and High Streets, April 8, 1959. Harpers Ferry National Monument. Typescript, Harpers Ferry National Historical Park, W.Va.

Fagan, B. 1984. Archaeology and the Wider Audience. In *Ethics and Values in Archaeology*, ed. E. L. Green, 175–83. New York: Free Press.

———. 1996. The Arrogant Archaeologist. In *Archaeological Ethics*, ed. K. D. Vitelli, 238–43. Walnut Creek, Calif.: AltaMira Press.

Finn, C. 2001. A Rare Bird. *Archaeology* 54(1): 38–43.

Gardner, W. M. 1974. Archeological Excavations in Lower Town (Back Yards) and the Paymaster's House (Yard), 1973–1974. For the NPS, Denver Service Center. On file at Harpers Ferry NHP.

Hannah, D. H. 1969. *Archaeological Investigations of Virginius Island, Harpers Ferry, National Historical Park, 1966–1968*. Harpers Ferry, W.Va.: Harpers Ferry National Historical Park.

Hershey, W. D. 1964. Archeological Survey of the Lockwood House (Paymaster's House), Harpers Ferry, West Virginia. Manuscript, Harpers Ferry National Historical Park.

Hull-Walski, D. A., and F. L. Walski. 1994. There's Trouble a-Brewin: The Brewing and Bottling Industries at Harpers Ferry, West Virginia. In *An Archaeology of Harpers Ferry's Commercial and Residential District*, ed. P. A. Shackel and Susan E. Winter. *Historical Archaeology* 28(4): 106–21.

Kook, R. 1998. The Shifting Status of African Americans in the American Collective Identity. *Journal of Black Studies* 29(2): 154–78.

Larrabee, E. M. 1960a. Report of Archaeological Investigation of the Arsenal Square at Harpers Ferry National Monument, Harpers Ferry, West Virginia, from July 20 through September 5, 1959. Manuscript, Harpers Ferry National Historical Park.

———. 1960b. Report of Exploratory Archeological Excavations Conducted on the Lower Hall Island Rifle Factory, Harpers Ferry National Monument, Harpers Ferry, West Virginia, from August 25 through August 29, 1959. Manuscript, Harpers Ferry National Historical Park.

Larsen, E. L. 1994. A Boardinghouse Madonna: Beyond the Aesthetics of a Portrait Created through Medicine Bottles. In *An Archaeology of Harpers Ferry's Commercial and Residential District*, ed. P. A. Shackel and S. E. Winter. *Historical Archaeology* 28(4): 68–79.

Leff, M. 1995. Revisioning U.S. Political History. *American Historical Review* 100(3): 829–53.

Leone, M. P. 1983. Method as Message. *Museum News* 62(1): 35–41.

Leone, M. P., and P. B. Potter, Jr. 1987. Archaeology in Public in Annapolis: Four

Seasons, Five Sites, Seven Tours, 32,000 Visitors. *American Archaeology* 6(1): 51–61.

Lerner, S. 1991. Saving Sites: Preservation and Education. In *Protecting the Past*, ed. G. S. Smith and J. E. Ehrenhard, 103–8. Boca Raton, Fla.: CRC Press.

Little, B. J. 1997. Expressing Ideology without a Voice, or, Obfuscation and the Enlightenment. *International Journal of Historical Archaeology* 1(3): 225–41.

———. 1998. Considering the Context of Historical Archaeology for Museum Interpretation. *Public Historian* 20(4): 111–17.

Lowenthal, D. 1985. *The Past Is a Foreign Country*. Cambridge: Cambridge University Press.

Lucas, M. T. 1994. À la Russe, à la Pell-Mell, or à la Practical: Ideology and Compromise at the Late Nineteenth-Century Dinner Table. In *An Archaeology of Harpers Ferry's Commercial and Residential District*, ed. P. A. Shackel and S. E. Winter. *Historical Archaeology* 28(4): 80–93.

McManamon, F. P. 1994. Presenting Archaeology to the Public in the USA. In *The Presented Past: Heritage, Museums and Education*, ed. P. G. Stone and B. L. Molyneaux, 61–81. New York: Routledge.

Nash, G. B., C. Crabtree, and R. E. Dunn. 1998. *History on Trial: Culture Wars and the Teaching of the Past*. New York: Knopf.

Noel Hume, I. 1991. *Martin's Hundred*. Charlottesville: University Press of Virginia.

Potter, P. B., Jr. 1994. *Public Archaeology in Annapolis: A Critical Approach to History in Maryland's "Ancient City."* Washington, D.C.: Smithsonian Institution Press.

Pousson, J. F. 1985. *Archeological Investigations, Harpers Ferry National Historical Park, Package No. 110A, Wager Block Backyards*. Denver, Colo.: National Park Service, Northeastern Team, Department of the Interior.

Shackel, P. A. 1996. *Culture Change and the New Technology: An Archaeology of the Early American Industrial Era*. New York: Plenum Press.

———. 2000. *Archaeology and Created Memory: Public History in a National Park*. New York: Kluwer Academic–Plenum Publishing.

——— (ed.). 1993. *Interdisciplinary Investigations of Domestic Life in Government Block B: Perspectives on Harpers Ferry's Armory and Commercial District*, Occasional Report no. 6, National Capital Region. Washington, D.C.: National Park Service, Department of the Interior.

Smith, B. 1993. A New Goal for Academia. *Archeology and Public Education* 3(3): 1.

Strueaver, S., and F. Holton. 1979. *Koster: Americans in Search of Their Prehistoric Past*. Garden City, N.Y.: Anchor Press–Doubleday.

Thelen, D. 1989. Memory and American History. *Journal of American History* 75(4): 1117–29.

Wachtel, N. 1986. Memory and History, Introduction. *History and Anthropology* 2 (October): 2–11.

14

Myths, Lies, and Videotapes

Information as Antidote to Social Studies Classrooms and Pop Culture

Fay Metcalf

Much of today's social studies curriculum is made up of myths and lies and inaccurate videotapes. Outside sources such as television sitcoms, radio, and movies on tape or in theaters—all with their omnipresent advertisements—deliver messages that are false or laced with foggy, faulty reasoning. It is clearly understood that good intentions lie behind some of this misinformation. Moreover, we recognize that a society needs myths and other aspects of folk tradition to help interpret the culture's particular worldview, its belief systems, mores, attitudes toward natural phenomena, and the approaches used to inculcate patriotism. No one would dispute that a major goal of social studies is development of the socially aware, allegiant citizens every nation needs. But it is long past time to suggest that knowledge of the nation's past and necessary patriotism be inspired through such fantasies, illusions, or such downright falsehoods as those concocted by the infamous Parson Weems, who invented the story of Washington and the cherry tree, and his clones. We are *not* more able to grasp the sagacity of George Washington as he led the nation in its perilous early years by being told of his inability to tell a lie or of his strong pitching arm that allowed him to throw a coin across the Potomac. We recognize that Weems with his superpatriotic adulating was simply silly. And some modern myth makers are equally silly.

An interesting example of how oft-told children's tales glorifying social archetypes can be accepted as factual history was uncovered some time ago by Michael Frisch of the State University of New York at Buffalo. Curious about how we "know" what we know, Frisch began to examine the patriotic archetypes held by his entering freshman students. He asked his classes to make a list of ten historical figures who reflect American history before the Civil War. The students listed men who figured prominently in high school history textbooks—Washington, Lincoln, and other political figures. Then Frisch asked students to make another list of important ante-bellum Americans, but this time they were to exclude presidents, generals, or statesmen. For seven out of eight years, entering freshmen placed Betsy Ross at the head of that list, with Paul Revere often coming in second. What intrigued Frisch was that Ross was not an important historical fig-ure. She played no role whatsoever in the actual creation of any actual flag, and her name did not come into prominence until about 1876, when some of her descendants made the claim that she had made the first American flag. Since the story of Betsy Ross is not told in high school history courses—she was not mentioned in the various textbooks his students had used—Frisch wondered how the students had learned about her and why they would idolize her. Perhaps, he believed, they had read about her in children's storybooks or had heard about her from pageants performed in their elementary schools. What is unclear is how the common culture produced students who widely held the understanding that "Washington calls on the humble seamstress Betsy Ross in her tiny home and asks her if she will make the nation's flag to his design. And Betsy promptly brings forth—from her lap!—the nation itself, and the promise of freedom and natural rights for all mankind" (Frisch 1990: 30–47).

We recognize that adult Americans also believe that Washington be-came the Father of Our Country (the god) and Betsy Ross the Blessed Virgin (the mother) because most of us have been exposed to the same influences as those affecting our students or to similar ones. We know that glorification of social archetypes did not stop with Parson Weems. As James Loewen explains (1995: 21) in his best-selling *Lies My Teacher Told Me*, it continues to this day as historical personages are first exalted and then heroified. Heroification, he writes (1995: 9), is a "degenerative pro-cess (much like calcification) that makes people over into heroes. Through this process, our educational media [and much pop culture] turn flesh-and-blood individuals into pious, perfect creatures without conflicts, pain, cred-ibility, or human interest." He uses Helen Keller and Woodrow Wilson as informative examples.

Every schoolchild learns the inspirational story of blind and deaf Helen Keller who, helped by the uniquely qualified teacher Anne Sullivan, learned not only how to read, write, speak but managed to graduate from Radcliffe at the age of twenty-four. Some know that she supported humanitarian causes such as raising funds for the American Foundation for the Blind. That, however, is the total substance of most students' knowledge of a remarkable but controversial woman. Few know or even wish to know that she also helped found the American Civil Liberties Union, supported Eugene V. Debs in his several campaigns for the White House, and became a socialist full of praise for the USSR and its leaders.

Every schoolchild knows that Woodrow Wilson tried to keep us out of World War I but that when our involvement became necessary, he was a fervent wartime leader and an eager peacemaker. He persuaded the international community to join him in founding the League of Nations. Few students also know that he insisted on racial segregation of the federal government and he frequently ordered military intervention in foreign countries. For example, he ordered troops into Mexico in 1914 and 1916, Haiti in 1915, the Dominican Republic in 1916, Cuba in 1917, and Panama in 1918. He kept troops in Nicaragua throughout his administration, using them to assure that a pro-American president was elected and a pro-American treaty was passed.

Another historical figure who has undergone heroification is the well-known Powhatan Indian girl Pocahontas. Those who recall the blockbuster animated film (and now video) can easily figure out how heroification actually takes place. The film shows us a gorgeous black-haired, gazelle-like maiden who ran through the forests, breaking out in song every five minutes or so, apparently because she had fallen madly in love with young, blond, equally gorgeous John Smith. Many moviegoers are shocked to discover that if Pocahontas actually saved John Smith's head (it is unlikely that the "execution" was really meant to take place), she was only eleven or twelve years old at the time and Smith was a thirty-year-old dark-haired man with a heavy black beard. While there probably was a friendship between the two since Pocahontas served as emissary for her father, Powhatan, a romance would have been most unlikely. In fact, in what was probably a political alliance, Pocahontas married John Rolfe in 1614 when she was nineteen and bore him a son. She died of smallpox in 1617 in her early twenties during a visit to England, where she was presented at court and created a sensation among the English gentry. Her real life was in fact very interesting and would have made a fascinating film. But the truth of her life is apparently unimportant. The movie makers did send forth a message that it is okay for people from two different "worlds" to have a deep friendship or love affair, and they heap kudos upon the lovely Indian maiden who, one must assume, was the nation's first environmentalist.

It is clear that Keller and Wilson and Pocahontas had characteristics that might qualify them as less than perfect, but in textbooks, movies, and videotapes they are conclusively presented as if they were perfect. Heroification of the type that they underwent may be an inevitable process. All nations do need social archetypes to help the young learn the values that keep a society lubricated. Only in the past two decades have teachers and textbook writers tried to present historical persons as multidimensional personalities—good people, perhaps important people, but nonetheless humans with warts and all.

Many myths and lies about America's past, whether developed from faulty history lessons or through movies and videotapes, can be demolished or set straight through school use of information from the domain of archaeology. Likewise, many mandated skills and modes of higher order thinking can best be taught to students through the use of archaeological studies. For example, let us examine how most students learn about America's prehistory, consider why modes of problem solving used by archaeologists should occupy a larger role in the school curriculum, and suggest how workers in the field can use their sites to develop lessons that can profitably be infused into ongoing school programs.

How the Work of Archaeologists Currently Reaches Typical Classrooms

At least three times during their schooling, and with few exceptions, students start their U.S. history courses with the traditional story of the crossing of the Bering Strait. Few textbooks or teachers mention that there is any debate over the starting points of the people, their origins, the number of waves of immigration, or the time periods involved. When it is time to order new textbooks, some teachers will care enough about the opening chapter to pick up a couple of recent introduction-to-anthropology textbooks to see how much the story has changed in the seven years since they last bought books for their class or wrote new curriculum guides. Other teachers will check out the first chapter of new college-level U.S. history books, believing (often erroneously) that the authors responsible for producing these have studied the latest research and know what they are talking about. If they choose to look at books by scholars of the field of ethnohistory or those with a special interest in the multiple cultures that developed in the Americas, they may find wonderful new material to teach. If they look at the works representing the older consensus, by political historians, they may find the "same old, same old"—a golden age that never was. They need more than the "history is progressive and history is patriotic" (Schlereth 1980: 208–10) fallacies of the past.

Teachers and their students need to know that the story constantly changes with new discoveries and new hypotheses put forth by those whose business it is to explain the earliest American culture groups. Since textbooks cannot always keep up with the new scholarship, teachers need other sources of information, and for part of the story of our past, it is archaeologists who must provide the new data.

The need is urgent. What happens too often in kindergarten through twelfth grade classrooms is a hit or miss presentation of the peopling of America. It is a rare student who knows more than the vague story that "they" (those hairy beings in animal skins with raised spears) somehow came across the Bering Strait, killing mastodons and losing a few Clovis and Folsom points as they made their way to Maine or Florida or Tierro del Fuego. Some time later, some of them learned to weave and build adobe houses or birchbark canoes and longhouses; some even became skilled orators like Pontiac or Chief Joseph or became icons like Pocahontas.

Equally spongy but deeply embedded in students' knowledge of America's prehistory is the belief that Aztecs once lived in what are now America's southwestern states. Here they tore out the hearts of virgins at such a rate that the people could never have reproduced themselves. Not only is the geography wrong; the whole meaning of sacrifice is unexplained. The purpose behind the extended coverage of the Maya, Aztec, and Inca civilizations in United States history books seems to relate to the traditional American inferiority complex—if Europeans could cite the achievements of the Greeks and the Romans, Americans could brag that there were once also great civilizations in the New World.

In fact, of course, there were. Archaeologists have told us that early Americans built huge cities with thousands of mounds anchoring temples or the homes of the priests and the nobility. They built four- and five-story apartment buildings with secret passages providing access to water and stored food. They developed trade routes that spanned the North American continent. And they developed oral traditions and graphic and plastic arts that rival any generated anywhere else on the globe.

There are many wonderful teachers who know the scholarship and who present a realistic picture of our nation's beginnings. Many such teachers discuss the variety of creation myths and ways of living that are the basis for modern Native American societies. They have their students discover such complex generalizations as the one that holds that culture areas exist because the people in particular regions at given times learned to exploit their environments in particular ways. These knowledgeable teachers make it clear that earlier groups did not remain static in their lifeways, just as modern people do not, and they continue the story of Native Americans to the present time.

The archaeologists who contribute to students' opportunities to hear a more complete story help with curriculum development, review manuscripts of textbooks and other curriculum materials, serve on school committees and school boards, make presentations to classes, and offer guided tours of their projects to classes within a reasonable distance. Some conduct week-long, on-site courses for upper elementary and secondary students who come away really understanding the procedures and methods used in the field and, more important, who receive exposure to the habits of mind that archaeologists must develop if they are to interpret successfully what they have found.

Habits of Mind and Thinking Skills

Why should some aspects of archaeology and the habits of mind of archaeologists become a more important part of the school curriculum? The short answer is that historians who have more or less controlled the social studies curriculum since 1916 have not been able to influence curriculum and textbook writers to make the changes necessary for students who will need to live intelligently in a multicultural society in a multicultural world that is increasingly complex. It is not that historians themselves are necessarily less skeptical or more hidebound than some archaeologists. Rather, it is that school history is increasingly the tool of people with a particular political agenda. Moreover, it is widely believed that teaching history or social studies requires no special training—if you can read a textbook, you can teach history. No one would think this was true for a math teacher or an art teacher or a science teacher.

One of the perennial panaceas offered to improve the teaching of social studies in the schools comes from scholars who believe that if everyone were just like him or her, we would have nothing but excited, interested, and competent students in the nation's classrooms. The formula is that if one offers students the materials and opportunities of the scholar, they will metamorphose into little historians or little economists or even little archaeologists. The truth, however, is that what excites a historian, economist, or archaeologist is quite different from what interests the vast majority of Americans below the age of eighteen. While one supposes that some archaeologists are by the nature of their jobs sitters and thinkers, the majority are at once physically active and mentally engaged—not just when working in the field or the laboratory but in daily life away from work. I suppose Indiana Jones helped along the reputation of archaeologists among students; but it is not the handsome, swashbuckling Harrison Ford who makes archaeology a popular subject among the young. Rather, it is the mystery and puzzle of the work that entices.

Some archaeologists warrant applause for their efforts in developing exciting and intriguing curriculum materials that are currently being used in the schools. Even a cursory examination of a few of the new materials described elsewhere in this volume reveals that along with sound content, students will learn such skills as locating and gathering information from a variety of sources, interpreting graphic materials, developing a sense of time and chronology, organizing and presenting positions related to materials, analyzing and evaluating reasoning used in written materials and oral arguments, and synthesizing and applying knowledge gained.

The students who use these materials will be lucky indeed. For those who study a lesson or unit on archaeology or take a semester course in anthropology and archaeology, the world is changed. Perceptions of the realities of the past become so enlarged and extended that students can never again accept the status quo or believe that what is must be. Habits of mind can be changed.

Using Archaeological Sites to Infiltrate and Enhance Curriculum

Archaeologists and people in allied fields can directly influence school curriculum by providing teachers with knowledge and with lessons that can be used on Monday morning with little preparation.

As a member of many, many committees on the teaching of history over the years and as executive director of the National Commission on Social Studies in the Schools, a five-year project funded by the Rockefeller and Carnegie foundations, I became quite accustomed to haranguing college and university historians to be good citizens and to help a scholarly discipline that was in deep trouble in the nation's schools. Clearly, according to constant newspaper reports, those efforts and the endeavors of many other similar groups of education reformers have failed. Students' test scores have not improved to any significant degree. But the battle is not lost; there are ways to teach the history of humankind that are truthful and meaningful. Many teachers are doing a wonderful job.

One way concerned archaeologists can effect change without laying blame is to take part in the Teaching with Historic Places project of the National Register of Historic Places.[1] The project produces lessons on topics that in some way amplify or extend elements of the required curriculum. Among the sixty or so lessons that are available, only four directly involve Native Americans—"Knife River: Early Village Life on the Plains," "Battle of Horseshoe Bend: Collision of Culture," "Gran Quivira: A Blending of Cultures in a Pueblo Indian Village," and "San Antonio Mission: Spanish Influence in Texas." A number of other lessons— "Frederica: An 18th-Century Planned Community," "Mammoth Cave: Its Explorers, Miners, Archaeologists and Visitors," and "Saugus Iron Works: Life and Work at an Early American Industrial Site"—also utilize archaeological studies.

What all those lessons have in common is the wondrous story of real people who lived in another time and place and how they coped with the business of making a living and enjoying their lives. Besides the intriguing tale of what life held for these people of the past, the story of how we know what we know of them makes available the learning of the higher order thinking skills. All humans in a complex society need the ability to make inferences from meager clues. As Jane White (1989: 32), a former cochair of the American Anthropological Association's Task Force on Teaching Anthropology in the Schools, wrote:[2]

> Fishbones reveal dietary habits, postholes or hearths yield clues to household size and settlement patterns, differences in jewelry help to establish hierarchical social structures. Central to the study of archaeology are the interrelationships between technological development and economic, social, and ideational factors. For example, evidence of agriculture can usually be linked to population increase. In different areas of the world archaeologists find clusters of dense population linked with a differential system of labor, centralized power, social stratification, bureaucracy, literacy and monumental architecture as characterizations of early civilizations.

What seems to me to be really important about this semiofficial statement from the American Anthropological Association is both what is said and what is not. What is said is that the analysis of artifacts and disturbances of the earth can help us to understand culture and to find similarities and differences among cultures. What is not said is how we find the sites to dig, how we recover the fishbones, and how we use imaginative reconstruction to test our conclusions. Going "beyond the facts" to see contradictions and paradoxes and still coming up with generalizations is what archaeologists do every day. Archaeologists are the synthesizers, putting things together, combining and recombining. Consequently, archaeologists are great role models for students who will have to puzzle out how to make decisions in the twenty-first century.

With indebtedness to Thomas J. Schlereth, and with apologies for putting my own spin on his words, I would like to suggest that if we want our children and grandchildren to learn how to think—to inquire, to make considered judgments, to know myths for what they are—we must help them to use material that allows interpretation and practical application: the social studies should provide the field of inquiry that students personally and communally try to understand. Through developing appropriate lessons for students from the middle grades through high school, archaeologists could be the ones who can achieve what the historians have failed to do.

Notes

1. Author information and lesson plans are available through the Internet at the Teaching with Historic Places web site: <www.cr.nps.gov/nr/twhp>.

2. Schlereth makes the case that aboveground archaeology is as useful as traditional archaeology for teaching the skills of analysis and that both can refute some of the worst excesses of unimaginative, unquestioning, and hidebound historians and museum curators.

References

Frisch, M. H. 1990. *A Shared Authority.* Albany: State University of New York Press.
Loewen, J. 1995. *Lies My Teacher Told Me.* New York: New Press.
Schlereth, T. J. 1980. *Artifacts and the American Past.* Nashville: American Association of State and Local History.
White, J. J. 1989. Anthropology. In *Charting a Course: Social Studies for the 21st Century.* Joint project of the American Historical Association, Carnegie Foundation for the Advancement of Teaching, National Council for the Social Studies, and Organization for American History. Washington, D.C.: National Commission on Social Studies in the School.

15

Project Archaeology

Putting the Intrigue of the Past in Public Education

Jeanne M. Moe

The goal of public education is to teach young people to be good American citizens (Goodlad 1994). An understanding of traditional subjects such as math, science, language arts, art, and social studies is an important component of the process. Schools have the added burdens of preventing drug abuse, offering controversial classes such as sex education, and providing learning opportunities for students with special needs, to name just a few. In sum, turning youngsters into good citizens is an enormously complex task.

Archaeology education efforts are typically driven by preservation; that is, by the need to protect our cultural legacy. Federal law mandates land-managing agencies to develop programs to "increase public awareness of the significance of the archaeological resources . . . and the need to protect such resources" (16 U.S.C. 470 ii[c]). Concomitantly, archaeologists all over the United States and the world, alarmed at the destruction of archaeological sites and theft of artifacts, have launched education programs designed to teach people to cherish and preserve their cultural legacy.

Thus, producing good citizens steers public education while archaeology education is primarily aimed at protecting archaeological resources. How can archaeology and public education interface? The fit between the two is actually quite good if one does not try to teach archaeology itself in the classroom but, instead, keeps the broader goals of education in mind while delivering the stewardship message. Surprisingly, this is relatively easy to accomplish. Archaeology furnishes a good springboard for teaching many prime educational concepts (Rogge and Bell 1989; Rogge 1991; Smith 1991; Moe and Letts 1992; Moe 2000a).

Inquiry-based science instruction is currently at the educational fore-front. "Inquiry is central to science learning. When engaging in inquiry, students describe objects and events, ask questions, construct explanations, test those explanations against scientific knowledge, and communicate their ideas to others" (National Research Council 1996: 2). Archaeological questions and data can be easily adapted to an inquiry format. For example, while learning the process of overlaying a "site" with a grid, students may notice the distribution of artifacts and wonder why the flakes and pottery sherds are concentrated in certain areas (fig. 15.1.) Questions that students themselves generate provide a good opportunity to model the process of scientific inquiry.

Archaeological knowledge can be used to examine human-environ-mental relationships in the context of enormous time spans and to apply the information to current and future problems (Lippitt et al. 1993; Moe et al. n.d.). For example, the prehistoric residents of the American Southwest grew a variety of crops. Their successes and failures can be instructive for agriculture in arid regions today.

The issues and ethics of conservation in general concern educators (Matthews and Riley 1995), and archaeological examples can be adapted to teach basic concepts (Smith et al. 1996; Moe 2000b). In addition, students can apply archaeological knowledge and use problem-solving skills to pro-pose solutions for real conservation problems in their own communities. They might protect a site through a monitoring program or start an educa-tional campaign designed to prevent vandalism of the local cultural heri-tage.

Archaeological inquiry expands students' perceptions of history and the nature of historical knowledge. How do we learn about people with no written history or fill out the historical record? Educators often use ar-chaeology to address these questions (see Moe and Smith 1996).

Recognizing the historical significance of ordinary objects helps young people make a personal connection to the past. Think for moment about an object that connects you to the past. A patchwork quilt, a treasured photo-graph, or a even a cracked pitcher may remind us of our forebears or bring back childhood experiences. This seemingly insignificant exercise of seeing or touching one of these treasures from the past readily connects children to their own past and the past in general. When employed in the classroom (Smith et al. 1996: 9–10), the exercise gives youngsters the chance to ex-change and appreciate personal histories, which in turn contributes to self-esteem.

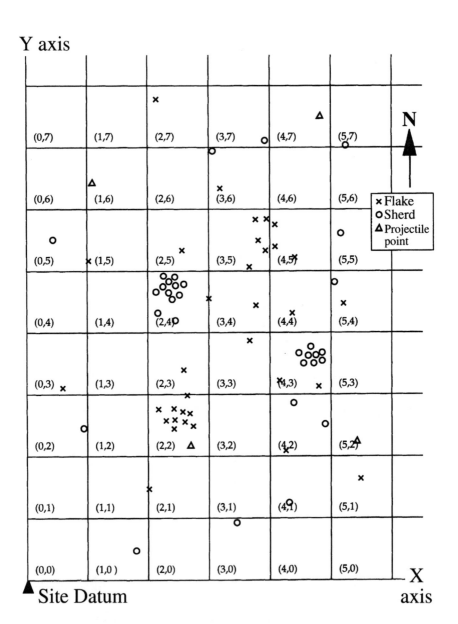

Fig. 15.1. Gridding a site as a student activity (adapted from Smith et al. 1996).

Most important, archaeology connects children to people who lived before us. And it does so in a unique way: through everyday objects that people made, used, then left behind where they lived and worked. Thus, archaeology creates a tangible link to other cultures and other times. Respect for artifacts and sites translates into respect for their owners. The same is true in reverse—respect for others fosters appreciation for these links to the past and a desire to preserve them. Once youngsters understand and value people of the past, they can more easily understand the diverse cultures of the present.

Delivering the Message

Archaeology is already finding a place within modern education (Smith 1991). Teachers have used archaeology in their classrooms for many years and some have written extensive curricula. A few statewide or regionwide programs that include curricular materials and teacher education have been established (e.g., Hawkins 1987; McNutt 1988; Willits 1997; Wheat and Whorton n.d.). Many states have embarked on education programs by establishing annual archaeology weeks or developing classroom programs (see Butler 1992). Several research and education institutions, such as Crow Canyon Archaeological Center in Cortez, Colorado, offer programs for teachers and students as well as for the general public. The list goes on, demonstrating that archaeologists and educators have not been idle. In fact, such a plethora of instructional materials has been produced that the Public Education Committee of the Society for American Archaeology recognized the need for quality control. In response, the committee established a system of criteria (SAA 1995) that can be used as an evaluative device or as a framework for developing new materials (Smith 1994).

Project Archaeology

Project Archaeology, part of the Bureau of Land Management's National Heritage Education Program, is a concrete example of an education program. The program prepares educators to teach archaeology in their instructional settings.

During the 1980s, the Utah Interagency Task Force on Cultural Resources, composed of the U.S. Forest Service, National Park Service, Bureau of Land Management (BLM), and the State of Utah, was formed to combat archaeological site destruction. The task force identified education as one of the most effective means of protecting archaeological sites over the long term. In 1990 the interagency group agreed to sponsor an education project aimed at teaching schoolchildren about Utah's archaeological heritage. BLM took the lead while the other agencies provided additional funding and assistance.

In the early 1990s this program was established in Utah as the Intrigue of the Past Archaeology Education Program. Subsequently, BLM launched a nationwide heritage education program designed to teach all young Americans to appreciate and protect the nation's historic legacy (Tisdale et al. 1991). The Intrigue program was adopted for the classroom portion of the larger program and is now known as Project Archaeology. The Anasazi Heritage Center, a public museum operated by BLM near Dolores, Colorado, houses the National Project Archaeology Program.

Project Archaeology supplies educators with the materials and training they need to teach basic archaeological concepts, to expose students to real conservation issues, and to connect young people with the past. This unique program is designed to reach elementary and secondary teachers and subsequently their students nationwide, through individualized state programs.

The program consists of three interconnected parts (Moe 1996): high-quality educational materials, professional development for teachers, and advanced workshops, field projects, newsletters, and awards for educators to sustain learning and involvement.

Intrigue of the Past: A Teacher's Activity Guide for Fourth through Seventh Grades (Smith et al. 1996) contains twenty-eight classroom-tested lessons designed to be used with existing curricula. Each lesson fulfills both archaeological and educational learning goals. For example, in the site gridding activity already mentioned, students learn the importance of recording and site preservation while they practice scientific methods. Lessons involve students in a variety of hands-on activities designed to teach concepts, processes, and content. A series of activities confronts students with conservation problems, allows them to reach their own conclusions regarding protection of sites and artifacts, and encourages them to propose solutions. Project Archaeology does not require simulated excavations, and the activity guide contains most of the materials needed.

Each state sponsoring the program develops a student handbook with the help of the national program. The handbooks contain regional culture history written for students and lessons that localize archaeological concepts and issues. Students recognize that the prehistoric residents of their state were living, breathing people. They discover that human needs have changed little over the millennia, but each culture meets those needs in different and often very creative ways.

A team consisting of an educator and an archaeologist leads teacher training workshops. Teachers know the needs and realities of the classroom and the educational system and can make archaeology teacher friendly. Archaeologists know the subject matter and relevant local and national issues. Both team members receive extensive facilitator training; archaeologists learn about education, educators learn about archaeology, and both learn how to plan and instruct workshops. Instructors demonstrate how lessons can be used in the classroom and cover scientific processes and their archaeological applications. Many Native American cultures as well as other ethnic groups have strong feelings regarding the protection of sites and the role of archaeology in learning about the past. Workshops provide an opportunity to discuss these and other issues surrounding archaeological conservation.

Sustaining the involvement and professional development of Project Archaeology educators is an important part of the program. Statewide newsletters keep teachers in touch with one another, update them on local archaeology, and provide new lessons and teaching techniques. Toll-free telephones give educators a quick way to get assistance with classroom implementation. Awards recognize excellence in archaeology education. Advanced workshops and field projects allow teachers to continue their own education and to transfer the new information to their students.

Utah Project Archaeology conducted a program evaluation in 1993 (Moe and Letts 1998). A survey of 550 educators who had attended workshops showed that 82 percent of respondents are using or planning to use the program. The majority of their students adopted positive attitudes about protection of archaeological sites as a result of instruction (fig. 15.2). Teachers who attended the Baker Village Field School in eastern Nevada in 1994 (U.S. Department of the Interior 1993) received extensive Project Archaeology instruction, then joined professional and student archaeologists to excavate a Fremont village site abandoned in the fourteenth century (Wilde and Soper 1993). Subsequent surveys show that the Baker Village participants use Project Archaeology materials extensively in their classrooms and consider it an effective teaching tool (Van Mondfrans et al. 1994; Bunderson et al. 1996). Educators and archaeologists frequently report that Project Archaeology materials and training have been used successfully in precollegiate classrooms throughout the nation and can be

Comparative Analysis of Responses

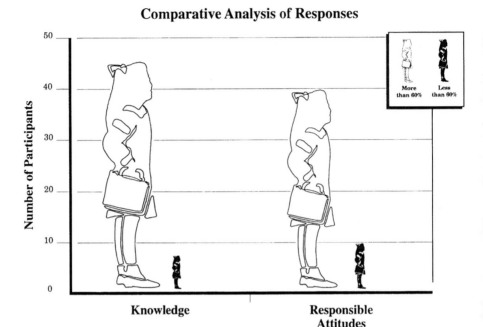

Fig. 15.2. Comparative analysis of responses in the Utah Project Archaeology evaluation survey.

adapted to other instructional settings such as museums, universities, and outdoor classes.

State Project Archaeology programs are fully operational in nine states: Utah, Oregon, Arizona, Alaska, New Mexico, Wyoming, Pennsylvania, Nevada, and Alabama (fig. 15.3). Programs are currently developing in thirteen additional states. All told, more than 4,000 educators have received training. Several additional states have recently requested sponsorship information to plan their own programs.

The national program is thriving under partnerships with federal agencies, the Society for American Archaeology, the National Science Teachers Association, Crow Canyon Archaeological Center, and Northern Arizona University. Project Archaeology states routinely involve museums, universities, school districts, state and federal agencies, state professional associations, and private consultants to establish and maintain programs.

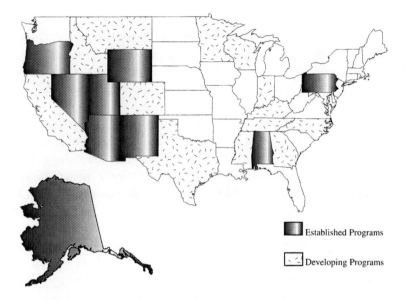

Established Programs

Developing Programs

Fig. 15.3. Project Archaeology in the United States.

Through a partnership approach, state programs are relatively inexpensive to implement and maintain.

Why Archaeology?

One can argue that everyone benefits from the accumulation of archaeological knowledge. Because archaeology encompasses enormous time spans, it is a discipline second to none in its ability to inform contemporary life and to help us make good decisions for the future (Diamond 1992: 336). However, teachers and students can benefit directly from archaeological knowledge only if it is generally available and presented in a usable format that fulfills educational goals. Project Archaeology strives to achieve these objectives. The task of educating an entire nation is enormous, and we have barely begun.

Archaeologists often feel pressured to tell "just-so" stories to satisfy public curiosity or think they must have all the answers to the mysteries of the past. While archaeologists should report as much information as possible, it is just as important to describe the data yet needed and to outline the research questions used to guide that inquiry. Although people may initially be satisfied with just-so stories, in the long run they prefer authentic information: the evidence itself, gaps in the data, and the guiding questions. Children, most of them confronted daily with unconnected abstractions, *especially* want authentic information. Presented in a palatable format, archaeology education can entice people to think about the past in a productive way and to ask their own questions.

Imagine for moment that you are a young person, out hiking for the day. The sun shines on your shoulders and the earth gives slightly under your feet. You examine the soil, rocks, and plants as you walk. Suddenly you spot a shiny rock sparkling in the sunshine. It is no ordinary rock; it is a projectile point made hundreds or perhaps even thousands of years ago. What do you do? Do you take it with you, thinking that if you don't, someone else will? Or do you leave it there, still a messenger from the past? Taking or leaving the artifact is seemingly a trivial decision. Making an informed decision, however, requires an understanding of people from different cultures and times. Laws are never enough; decisions are based on what you know and what you think is right. Project Archaeology takes the educational process beyond laws to personal ethics based on broad knowledge.

While a global culture is developing, the world still retains many distinct cultures (Anderson 1990: 16), each rich with tradition and history. The relationships among them are uneasy at best and frequently quite tense. Living harmoniously within the confines of our small planet should always be our primary goal, and when accomplished it can be our greatest achievement. Success will require an understanding of ourselves and of others, mutual respect, and tolerance. Archaeology education takes a big first step by offering children a sense of the reality of people from the past and from diverse cultures, making them seem closer.

Note

For more information about Project Archaeology contact the Anasazi Heritage Center, P. O. Box 758, Dolores, CO 81321, phone (970) 882-4811. See the web page <www.co.blm.gov/ahc/projarc.htm>.

References

Anderson, L. F. 1990. "A Rationale for Global Education." In *Global Education: From Thought to Action*, ed. K. A. Tye. Alexandria, Va.: Association for Supervision and Curriculum Development.

Bunderson, E. D., A. Van Mondfrans, and M. S. Henderson. 1996. The Baker Village Teacher's Archaeological Field School: A Case Study of Public Involvement in Archaeology. *Journal of California and Great Basin Anthropology* 18(1): 38–47.

Butler, W. B. (ed.). 1992. *State Archaeological Education Programs.* Denver, Colo.: National Park Service, Rocky Mountain Region, Division of National Preservation Programs, Interagency Archaeological Services.

Diamond, J. 1992. *The Third Chimpanzee: The Evolution and Future of the Human Animal.* New York: Harper-Collins.

Goodlad, J. 1994. *What Are Schools For?* 2nd ed. Bloomington, Ind.: Phi Kappa Delta Educational Foundation.

Hawkins, N. 1987. *Classroom Archaeology: An Archaeology Activity Guide for Teachers.* 2nd ed. Baton Rouge, La.: Division of Archaeology, Office of Cultural Development, Department of Culture, Recreation and Tourism.

Lippitt, L., T. L. Nickerson, D. Bailey, and S. L. Fosberg. 1993. Environmental Technology Is an Ancient Science: The Hupobi Heritage Project. *Science and Children* 30(8): 21–28.

Matthews, B. E., and C. K. Riley. 1995. *Teaching and Evaluating Outdoor Ethics Education Programs.* Vienna, Va.: National Wildlife Federation.

McNutt, N. 1988. *Project Archaeology: Saving Traditions.* Longmont, Colo.: Sopris West.

Moe, J. M. 1996. *Project Archaeology Primer: The Complete Guide to Creating Your Own State or Regional Program.* Dolores, Colo.: Bureau of Land Management, Anasazi Heritage Center.

———. 2000a. America's Archaeological Heritage: Protection through Education. In *Cultural Resource Management in Contemporary Society: Perspectives in Managing and Presenting the Past,* ed. F. P. McManamon and A. Hatton, 276–87. One World Archaeology no. 33. London: Routledge.

———. 2000b. Archaeology and Values: Respect and Responsibility for Our Heritage. In *The Archaeology Education Handbook: Sharing the Past with Kids,* ed. K. Smardz and S. J. Smith, 249–66. Walnut Creek, Calif.: AltaMira Press.

Moe, J. M., and K. A. Letts. 1992. Intrigue of the Past Secondary Education Project. Paper presented at the 57th annual meeting of the Society for American Archaeology, Pittsburgh, Pa.

———. 1998. Archaeology Education: Can It Make a Difference? *Common Ground: Archaeology and Ethnography in the Public Interest* 3(1): 24–29.

Moe, J. M., and S. J. Smith. 1996. Getting the Stewardship Message Across: Simulations and Other Strategies. Paper presented at the 61st Annual Meeting of the Society for American Archaeology, New Orleans, La.

Moe, J. M., L. Matis, and P. Wheat. N.d. Living on the Land: Choices and Consequences. Ms on file with the author, Bureau of Land Management, Salt Lake City, Utah.

National Research Council. 1996. *National Science Education Standards.* Washington, D.C.: National Academy Press.

Rogge, A. E. 1991. Teaching with Archaeology: An Arizona Program. In *Protecting the Past*, ed. G. S. Smith and J. E. Ehrenhard. Boca Raton, Fla.: CRC Press.

Rogge, A. E., and P. Bell. 1989. Archeology in the Classroom: A Case Study from Arizona. Archeological Assistance Program, Technical Brief no. 4, May 1989. Washington, D.C.: National Park Service, Department of the Interior.

Smith, KC. 1991. At Last a Meeting of the Minds. *Archaeology* 50(1): 36–46, 80.

———. 1994. You Can't Judge a Book by Its Cover. Paper presented at the 59th Annual Meeting of the Society for American Archaeology, Anaheim, Calif.

Smith, S. J., J. M. Moe, K. A. Letts, and D. A. Paterson. 1996. *Intrigue of the Past: A Teacher's Activity Guide for Fourth through Seventh Grades*. 2nd printing. Dolores, Colo.: Bureau of Land Management, Anasazi Heritage Center.

Society for American Archaeology (SAA). 1995. *Guidelines for the Evaluation of Archaeology Education Materials*. Washington, D.C.: Public Education Committee, Society for American Archaeology.

Tisdale, M., R. Brook, B. King, S. McFarlin, S. Smith, and G. Stumpf. 1991. *A Plan to Educate Young Americans about Their Nation's Rich Cultural Heritage*. Washington, D.C.: Bureau of Land Management, Department of the Interior.

U.S. Department of the Interior. 1993. Baker Archaeological Project: Heritage Education Proposal. Manuscript on file at the Bureau of the Land Management, Ely, Nev.

Van Mondfrans, A. P., V. Shrader, and A. NiCole Rose. 1994. Interim Report of the Evaluation of the Baker Village Archaeological Site Teacher Workshop. Manuscript on file at the Western Institute for Research and Evaluation, Logan, Utah.

Wheat, P. M., and B. Whorton (eds.). N.d. *Clues from the Past: A Resource Book on Archaeology*. Dallas: Texas Archaeological Society, Hendrick-Long Publishing Company.

Wilde, J. D., and R. A. Soper. 1993. *Baker Village: A Preliminary Report on the 1991 and 1992 Archaeological Field Seasons at 26WP63, White Pine County, Nevada*. Museum of Peoples and Cultures, Technical Series no. 93–10. Provo, Utah: Brigham Young University.

Willits, R. J. 1997. *A Place to Call Home: Anthropological Curriculum for Middle School Educators*. Archeology Popular Report no. 3. Topeka: Kansas State Historical Society.

16

Pursuing the ZiNj Strategy
Like There's No Tomorrow

Kevin T. Jones and Julie E. Maurer Longstreth

People everywhere are fascinated by archaeology. Archaeologists know it. We are all familiar with exclamations like "Oh, how interesting," or "How lucky you are," when a new acquaintance learns of our profession. We are accustomed to fielding questions like "What's the oldest (weirdest, most interesting, or most valuable) thing you've found?" Each of us has developed a set of polite responses to these questions—responses we hope are not patronizing, misleading, or didactic. If these conversations happen to involve more than just a brief exchange, we may find ourselves extemporizing, quickly trying to find a way to say something about our work that is not too arcane, while at the same time trying not to dampen curious people's interest by discounting some popular idea or recent discovery they have read about in a magazine or newspaper. Yet many of us rarely feel able to discuss the essence of our "real" work because we assume that the average citizen would probably not be interested in or even able to understand such esoterica as middle range theory, assemblage composition, close reading, spatial analysis, diet breadth models, seriation, or whatever our current obsession may be.

Some conversations can be very discomfiting, such as calls seeking appraisal of a collection of antiquities for insurance purposes; meeting an elementary teacher who takes her class out arrowhead hunting as part of their "archaeology" unit; talking to a guidebook writer looking for a "perfect" kiva to include in a forthcoming publication; or being grilled by someone about the antiquities laws, knowing that the questioner's intent is to find a loophole. Our informal interactions with non-archaeologists seem to sort people into two categories—those interested in the intrigue, romance, exotica, and curiosity of archaeology for the right reasons, and those interested for the wrong reasons. Both share a common characteristic: ignorance about what archaeology is and why it is important—indeed, almost sacred—to us. Who is to blame for this ignorance, for this lack of understanding of our field? We, the archaeologists, are to blame.

In Utah, as in much of the country, people harm archaeological sites in three primary ways: through the activities associated with development and construction, by deliberate vandalism or looting, and through inadvertent and unintentional damage caused by site visitation. The first two kinds of damage are mitigated or proscribed to some extent by a variety of laws, while the third, "loving the sites to death," is rapidly becoming a significant problem. Most would agree that public education about archaeology along with enforcement of the pertinent laws can help reduce losses from all of these sources.

In an attempt to address the growing problem of archaeological vandalism, a consortium of federal and state partners (Bureau of Land Management, U.S. Forest Service, National Park Service, and Utah Division of State History) collectively known as the Utah Task Force on Cultural Resources initiated projects to study the extent of archaeological vandalism, to improve communication with law enforcement agencies, and to create innovative public outreach programs. Task force members agreed that the best long-term solution to vandalism is education, and the partners initiated a Utah Archaeology Week, the Intrigue of the Past Education Program (now known as Project Archaeology; see Moe, this volume), and the ZiNj Education Project. ZiNj began as a children's magazine (named after the early hominid discovered at Olduvai Gorge by the Leakeys) designed to capitalize on the great interest many youngsters have in old things. We knew that we needed to capture kids' interest, because a publication must be read to be effective. We also wanted to show that science is fun and to build values about protecting heritage resources. *ZiNj* magazine became, in effect, a glossy, jazzy government brochure that looked nothing like a government brochure. For a while we also produced a kids' television program called *ZiNj TV.*

What is ZiNj?

The ZiNj Education Project is a romp through the past on a fast horse, a hands-on encounter with science in a fun, engaging, smart package. ZiNj promotes love of science, love of archaeology and paleontology, love of heritage resources; and it celebrates that love. ZiNj is subversive science literature for kids. It is undiluted science from the scientists themselves, unadulterated kidspeak from native kidspeakers, and loads of fun.

Our goal is to share with kids our love of learning, of the diversity of human culture, and of science. By inviting kids to participate in a fun learning adventure we can feed their curiosity about the old and exotic, and we can stimulate them, building values and knowledge that will lead them to develop a preservation ethic and to be better citizens, which in the long term will provide better protection for our cultural and heritage resources.

The ZiNj Education Project spun off from state government to become an independent nonprofit organization, but after several years it is now once again a program of the Utah Division of State History. It is aimed at sharing the delights of science, especially anthropology and archaeology, with children aged seven to seventeen, helping them to understand and appreciate heritage resources, which in the long run will enhance the efforts of the sponsoring agencies and others in preserving, protecting, and interpreting these fragile resources. The ZiNj project today has two major program areas: *ZiNj* magazine, which is now being published solely on the World Wide Web, and ZiNj field projects—opportunities for kids to participate in field and laboratory research.

ZiNj *Magazine*

ZiNj is a hero-sized, scholastically hip science-packed magazine aimed at kids and families. It brings three fundamental elements to informal science/heritage education: a strong commitment to solid, cutting-edge science; the integration of preservation and protection messages; and the involvement of kids in all aspects of the program. This means that scientists, resource specialists, and kids are active participants in all aspects of producing the magazine. We especially favor articles by kids about their own inquiries into a topic. The Real Advisory Board (kids only) keeps the magazine on track by assuring that there is no "talking down" to kids and that the magazine is kid-friendly. This approach has proven to be an effective means to reach kids and families with sound interdisciplinary educational material and, when combined with striking design and a sense of humor, it results in readable and entertaining presentation. *ZiNj* magazine has been the recipient of a 1994 Parents' Choice Honor, certificates of merit from the American Advertising Federation (1993) and the New York Art Directors Club (1994), National ADDY Citation of Excellence (1994), and numerous local and regional awards for excellence.

The rock art issue of *ZiNj* magazine has been placed on the World Wide

Web at <http://history.utah.org/zinj/>, and future publications will be published primarily on the web. In moving to a web-based publication, we are able to eliminate the expense of printing and distributing the magazine and concentrate instead on having current, exciting content.

A new publication, the *ZiNj Teaching Guide*, has been completed and will also soon be available on the website. The guide enables teachers to use the material in *ZiNj* magazine in a formal teaching environment to present lessons in science, geography, culture, and history.

ZiNj Field Studies

The ZiNj philosophy is predicated on brains-on involvement with scientific thinking and research. We promote, conduct, and support research by kids in partnership with scientists. As an example, in 1993 and 1994 we paired nine youngsters with adult scientist mentors to conduct original research on archaeological topics. The resulting papers were presented at a ZiNj symposium at the annual meeting of the Society for American Archaeology in April 1994. The kid researchers presented papers on topics ranging from prehistoric diet and health to lithic analysis to historic archaeology. The professional archaeologists who attended the symposium were astounded at the sophistication of the presentations. The major triumph, however, was that the kids who participated grew in many readily perceptible ways. Their enthusiasm for science increased and their self-confidence soared. We continue to involve kids in archaeological projects such as excavation of Fremont and Archaic sites in central Utah, survey and excavation of historic and prehistoric sites on Antelope Island in the Great Salt Lake, and laboratory analysis and reporting, and we have plans to expand this area of the program.

ZiNj TV

Beginning in June 1994, we worked with KSL Television in Salt Lake City (the local NBC affiliate) to produce *ZiNj TV*, a half-hour science and discovery program for kids and families. The program premiered in January 1995 and airs on Saturday and Sunday mornings throughout KSL's broadcast area. *ZiNj TV* was awarded a 1995 Rocky Mountain Regional Emmy and a 1995 national Iris award for excellence in programming by the National Association of Television Program Executives. Twenty-seven half-hour programs were produced and aired, on topics such as ecosystems, wilderness, clothing and adornment, rock art, architecture (including prehistoric architecture), garbage (featuring archaeologists William Rathje and James O'Connell), folklore and pharmacology, and extinction. The program is no longer being produced but is still being aired in Salt Lake City.

ZiNj Strategy

The basic tenets of the ZiNj program strategy are as follows:

1. *Kids are integrally involved in each segment or article.* We have kids as experts—participating in an archaeological dig, demonstrating how a packrat midden is sampled, how a dinosaur bone is jacketed, how PCR works, how lift is produced, how a ceramic vessel is reconstructed. And we have kids as kids—making mistakes, being goofy, getting excited. An audience of kids will be most receptive to other kids, to watching young experts and ZiNj kids as they experience the process of learning about a subject, interviewing scientists, and actually doing science.

2. *The focus is on how science is conducted, not on facts that are known.* This means on-site visits, discussions with scientists, and examining current studies that have not yet yielded answers. It means focusing on controversy, disagreement, things the scientist would love to learn next, and methods of investigation—how questions are asked, how data are collected, how ideas are tested.

3. *The content is varied in complexity.* Some articles or aspects of the program might be understood by six-year-old children, and some might be beyond them. Some portions might be a touch arcane for even the older kids, but these elements are intriguing and hold kids' interest and keep them paying attention. ZiNj talks up to kids, not down—they *like* to be challenged (our focus groups with kids continually reinforce this concept)—and we have the opportunity to challenge them in each program with information, humor, and oblique references.

4. *A commitment to authenticity underlies the creative process.* We do not want to show how an archaeologist works by using graphics or showing a sandbox dig; we want to go to the field with real archaeologists, involve kids, and let them learn by doing and share that experience with the viewer. The ZiNj partnership—the U.S. Forest Service, National Park Service, and Bureau of Land Management—provides access to innumerable opportunities for authentic learning experiences on some of our country's most beautiful cultural and natural sites. Working with a group of kids participating in the National Park Service's Parks as Classrooms program or in a Forest Service Passport in Time project, showing them getting dirty,

discovering things, and having a great time, is a positive way to share enthusiasm with viewers. Close contact with research scientists, universities, and especially programs that involve kids directly in research will bring many opportunities to showcase such programs as well as share authentic experiences with kids and families.

5. *Kids are brought into direct contact with the resources.* We always want to be attentive to the potential to prompt kids to experiment, explore, and learn through doing things in their own home or yard, in a museum or library, or in a national park, forest, or other public lands setting. We encourage them to read a book, to write a story, to send in a question, idea, suggestion, or criticism. We want to invite action and to encourage lifetime learning.

What's Next?

Like everything else around them, the magazine and the organization have been evolving. During the summer of 1995, the original ZiNj program made a transition from state agency to private nonprofit organization, and it has now come full circle to being a program of the Antiquities Section of the Utah Division of State History. The magazine evolved from a prototype newsletter to a full-fledged oversized magazine to a television program to a web-based publication. The partnerships with agencies that started the program remain crucial and fundamental to the core philosophy and functioning of the organization.

We are committed to continue working to share our love of history and prehistory with kids. We think that by involving kids in the program, we at once educate them and expand their appreciation of science and archaeology; and with their help, we create better educational material. The approach is best summed up in the explanation included in each *ZiNj* magazine: "Our collective goal is to share the delights of history and prehistory with kids and families because we believe that with appreciation and awareness come a sense of ownership, pride, and a desire to protect and preserve our heritage resources."

IV

Promoting the Public Benefits
of Archaeology

17

Irreplaceable Heritage

Archaeology and the National Register of Historic Places

Carol D. Shull

The National Register of Historic Places was envisioned by the framers of the 1966 National Historic Preservation Act as a list of places worthy of preservation. As such, it should help us to understand and appreciate our heritage and what specific places mean in the history of our country. Archaeological properties are underrepresented, making up only about 7 percent, or nearly 5,000, of about 73,000 listings in the National Register.[1]

Many more archaeological properties have been identified and evaluated as eligible for the National Register for their potential to yield important information about our history or prehistory.

Expanded and maintained by the National Park Service, the National Register is the most accessible source of information to many audiences about the great variety of archaeological resources, from spectacular national parks like Mesa Verde to sites of local significance. If archaeologists do not use the National Register and its power to educate Americans about the value of such places, citizens will not receive the most from our public investment in survey, registration, and protection.

Eligibility for the National Register is the threshold for identifying significant prehistoric and historical archaeological resources worthy of consideration under federal law and is the basis for determining which sites are worthy of expenditure of public money. The National Historic Preservation Act requires that federal agencies find eligible and listed sites and consider them in the planning of all federal or federally assisted projects. Agencies are directed to inventory significant sites on federal lands, to nominate to the National Register, and to manage them. Knowledge of our archaeological heritage has benefited greatly from this requirement, and numerous sites have been identified, tested, and preserved. In the last few decades, most field survey activity and recovery of archaeological data in the United States have been carried out to meet the requirements of federal law.

Many sites identified by the federal government have not been listed in the National Register. Often the results of critical research and the value of these sites are not widely known to the public beyond professional archaeologists. Some people question the costs and the public benefits of the archaeological research funded by the federal government. The archaeological community and the organizations that represent it have been diligent and effective at lobbying to protect archaeology in the United States, but recognizing and publicizing more of these fragile, irreplaceable resources through National Register listing will help garner broader support from the many audiences who benefit from archaeology.

Listing sites on federal lands and those identified in the planning of federal projects helps assure that the greatest number of our citizens benefit from the work. Twenty-four percent of properties listed for their information potential are owned or managed by federal agencies, but many more have been identified that are worthy of listing.[2] If the value of archaeological resources on federal lands is formally recognized through National Register listing, agencies have a better chance of obtaining funding to manage and preserve them for public benefit.

The National Park Service nominated Obsidian Cliff in Yellowstone Park as a National Historic Landmark in 1996, and the secretary of the interior designated it thus. While Yellowstone is known primarily for its natural wonders, Obsidian Cliff, a singularly important source of lithic materials for early prehistoric peoples over a large area of North America for 12,000 years, is also a national treasure. In 1991 archaeological excavations funded by the General Services Administration in advance of a construction project in New York City uncovered the only known eighteenth-century African burial ground in the Americas. This site was subsequently designated a National Historic Landmark by the secretary and listed in the National Register for its exceptional potential to provide information about how African Americans lived in an urban setting in the eighteenth century. The public deserves to know about this legacy.

Regardless of federal involvement, formal listing is crucial for important sites that should be preserved and for sites having values that must be accessible to a variety of audiences. For the places recognized, survey and registration are just the first steps in using the National Register. It is the most comprehensive source of information on cultural resources in the United States. Each year between 1,500 and 2,000 listings are added, including many districts with numerous resources contained within their boundaries.

The index to National Register listings is computerized in the automated National Register Information System (NRIS), which has about forty-five data elements on each National Register–listed district, site, building, structure, or object. The database may be queried on any combination of data elements. The NRIS is accessible to the public over the Internet and by calling the National Park Service. Archaeological sites can be identified by general location (county and state), cultural affiliation, areas and periods of significance, functions, and a variety of other attributes. Data from the NRIS can be downloaded into inventories maintained by federal, state, and local government agencies, colleges and universities, researchers, and others. The NRIS may be found on the National Register section of the National Park Service website at <www.cr.nps.gov/nr>.

Full documentation on archaeological sites and other listings includes a description, a statement of significance, maps, photographs, and a bibliography. This information is maintained by the National Park Service in a national repository of information on historic properties and is available to the public on request. To protect these places and their owners and users, release of information on the location, character, or ownership of historic resources may be withheld where its disclosure could result in significant invasion of privacy, could harm the historic resources, or could impede the use of a traditional religious site by practitioners.

National Register nominations summarize data from professional archaeological reports, much of which are not published or available to the broader public, to help citizens understand why sites are significant. The information needed to nominate a site is routinely collected in professional archaeological surveys. The National Register form available on paper or on various computer templates (on disk or over the Internet) can be used to record the data in the field, or, with the aid of computers, data can easily be transferred from archaeological survey reports to National Register nomination forms. National Register bulletins and other publications provide assistance in the preparation of nominations of both prehistoric and historical archaeological sites. The National Register website includes the text of the bulletins.

Listing is important in planning for the future of heritage resources.

The public needs to know about archaeological sites ahead of the planning for specific projects so that, where possible, damage to sites can be avoided. Knowing about sites and their values to the community, the states, and the nation results in better planning and prevents conflicts that occur when sites are discovered after property owners and decision makers have already formed their opinions about future development without the benefit of knowing about archaeological sites.

The variety of sites recognized, the ease of access to the information, and the cross referencing capabilities make the National Register an increasingly valuable resource for research including cross-cultural, geographic, functional, and comparative studies. In addition, the National Register encourages looking at places from an interdisciplinary perspective. Often single listings, such as historic districts, have historical, architectural, and cultural values as well as information potential. This is often true for places of traditional cultural importance to contemporary Native peoples, whose ancestors may have inhabited the sites and whose lifeways can be understood from the archaeological record.

The National Park Service also encourages states, federal agencies, and Indian tribes nominating sites to put them in context by documenting, evaluating, and nominating related sites together, giving multiple-property documentation. States including Arkansas, Kansas, Kentucky, South Dakota, Utah, and Wisconsin have studied, documented, and nominated to the National Register groups of rock art sites. Examples of the wide range of multiple-property submissions with related listings include Hohokam Platform Mound Communities of the Lower Santa Cruz River Basin, ca. A.D. 1050–1450 in Arizona; Early French-Canadian Settlement in Oregon; Indian Use of Block Island, 500 B.C.–1676 in Rhode Island; Early Ironworks of Northwestern South Carolina and the Iron Industry on the Western Rim in Tennessee; and Pueblo sites in various parts of New Mexico. As of 2001, the state of New Mexico has about twenty-five archaeological multiple-property studies on file with the National Register, with numerous sites listed under a variety of topics. Each multiple-property submission includes a cover context statement, a description of property types and evaluation criteria, and bibliographical references in addition to listing documentation for properties nominated as part of the group.

National Register Multiple Property documentation addresses one of the great needs in archaeology today—the synthesis of data on related sites, so that they can be understood better and so as to allow for more accurate conclusions and evaluations of significance. These multiple-property studies also make it easier for the public to understand the value of sites. Such studies are of interest to publishers who can bring the information to the public beyond the professional archaeological community.

Under a cooperative agreement, the National Park Service and the Society for American Archaeology completed a National Historic Landmark theme study on Contact Period sites in the Northeast. Not only was a context for evaluating such sites prepared, but eighteen sites have been designated national historic landmarks by the secretary of the interior and have been listed in the National Register. In 1995 the University of Oklahoma Press published the study as a book (Grumet 1995). The NPS and SAA are now at work on a new study of sites associated with the earliest Americans.

The National Register has developed a variety of demonstration programs and products aimed at providing information about historic places to different audiences. *African American Historic Places* was prepared as a cooperative effort between the NPS, the National Conference of State Historic Preservation Officers, and the National Trust for Historic Preservation (Savage 1994). This book includes essays and descriptions of more than 800 listed places that demonstrate the contributions of African Americans. The guide is aimed at a popular audience. The chapter by Theresa A. Singleton, "The African American Legacy Beneath Our Feet," includes sites like the Bullis' Camp Site in Texas, which served as a temporary base camp for Lieutenant John L. Bullis and his Black-Seminole Indian scouts. Here the scouts helped build a railroad to open up settlement and launched more than two dozen scoutings and engagements with Lapan, Mescalero, Comanche, and Kickapoo Indians on both sides of the Rio Grande. Investigation of the site may provide valuable information about the social interaction of the Black-Seminole scouts and their Anglo officers and about their material culture. All the places recognized by the National Register at the time because they had yielded or were likely to yield information on African Americans are described in the book. Sites on several southern plantations, the Trapp and Chandler Pottery in South Carolina, and towns with black communities are particularly important in illustrating the daily lives of African Americans because of the rarity of written records on various aspects of the African-American experience.

Educators and students need to know about archaeology. The National Register also has a Teaching with Historic Places program that produces lesson plans prepared by educators and site interpreters and provides training on using registered historic places in the classroom (see Metcalf, this volume).[3] The instructional materials can be used anywhere by teachers and students, even if they are not visiting the sites. Lesson plans are aimed at enriching the core curriculum in history, social studies, and other required subjects from the upper elementary grades to high school. Currently, five of these lesson plans help young people learn about archaeology in national parks: "Knife River: Early Village Life on the Plains"; "Gran Quivira: A Blending of Cultures in a Pueblo Indian Village"; "Saugus Iron Works: Life and Work at an Early American Industrial Site"; "Frederica: An 18th-Century Planned Community"; and "Mammoth Cave: Its Explorers, Miners, Archeologists and Visitors." Not only do the lesson plans enhance the teaching of basic skills, but they encourage young people to value sites, so that as adults they are more likely to support archaeology and be respectful stewards of valuable sites.

Tourists are another audience. Heritage tourism is a fast-growing segment of the burgeoning tourism industry. Tourism publications and tourism providers often advertise that sites are listed. Owners frequently purchase and display plaques stating that properties are listed. The National Register and the National Conference of State Historic Preservation Officers have prepared a series of travel itineraries connecting registered historic places, from national parks to local historic districts. The conference is a partner for the National Register of Historic Places travel itinerary series called Discover Our Shared Heritage because the states nominate more than 90 percent of the places listed in the National Register. State historic preservation programs, partially funded by federal Historic Preservation Fund matching grants, carry out numerous activities such as surveys, nominations, and educational offerings, and they provide tax incentives and grants that support archaeology. Some of the itineraries showcase archaeological sites listed in the National Register. For example, an itinerary for the American Southwest describes and suggests a route to visit numerous important archaeological sites that are open to the public and connects these places with interesting towns and other listed destinations. The printed itineraries have been partially funded by the American Express Company as their way of supporting the National Register. Information on the series and many of the itineraries are available on the National Register's website. The National Register helps travelers and tourism providers find authentic heritage resources for tourists to visit. Responsible heritage tourism sustains the economies of numerous communities.

The National Register of Historic Places promotes sound research and evaluation, provides a permanent record, encourages good stewardship of archaeological sites, and brings them to the attention of a variety of audiences. Registration puts the public on notice that these places and the information they contain are irreplaceable parts of our heritage. Teachers and students, visitors and researchers, planners, descendant communities, tourists, journalists, political leaders, historians, environmentalists, and others all benefit from learning about the past through archaeology. The National Register helps to illuminate the public benefits of archaeology and to assure that this legacy is not forgotten.[4]

Notes

1. The number of listings and other statistics relating to the National Register of Historic Places are current as of January 2001.

2. Listing in the National Register includes districts that contain a number of contributing sites as well as individual sites. Contributing sites on federal lands make up 53 percent of all contributing sites listed under criterion d.

3. For information on Teaching with Historic Places lesson plans, contact the National Register of Historic Places, National Park Service, NC400; 1849 C Street NW, Washington, DC 20240 or visit the web page at <www.cr.nps.gov/nr/twhp>.

4. See also Barbara Little's articles, cited among the references that follow, on the benefits of recognizing archaeological sites through the National Register of Historic Places.

References

Grumet, R. S. 1995. *Historic Contact: Indian People and Colonists in Today's Northeastern United States in the Sixteenth through the Eighteenth Centuries.* Norman: University of Oklahoma Press.

Little, B. J. 1997. Nominating Archeological Sites to the National Register of Historic Places: What's the Point? *CRM* 10(7): 3ff.

———. 1999. Nominating Archaeological Sites to the National Register of Historic Places: What's the Point? *SAA Bulletin* 17(4): 19.

Savage, B. L. (ed.). 1994. *African American Historic Places; National Register of Historic Places, National Park Service.* New York: Preservation Press, John Wiley and Sons.

18

Archaeology in Santa Fe

A Public-Private Balancing Act

Mary Grzeskowiak Ragins

Santa Fe's Archaeological Review Districts Ordinance dates from 1987 and was adopted into law after about a year-long series of steering committee meetings and public hearings. The impetus for development of the ordinance was realization of the growth that Santa Fe was going to witness, especially downtown, tangibly evidenced through the construction of such buildings as the First Interstate Building and the Eldorado Hotel. Reaction to the siting and placement of these structures (both multistoried and each having a footprint of more than 60,000 square feet), as well as the design and demolition work that occurred to ready the sites for construction, resulted in a revision to Santa Fe's Historic Districts Ordinance. Salvage archaeology was conducted during construction of these projects as schedules permitted, and we learned important information about Santa Fe's downtown area. As a result, a commitment to developing a local archaeological ordinance was born. This commitment, however, took a few years to be carried out. Through the convening of a dedicated committee of local archaeologists, members of the development community, the general public, city and county staff, and representatives of the Historic Design Review Board (HDRB)—including its city councilor representative—the language of the ordinance was developed and approved into law. Santa Fe's was the first comprehensive local archaeological ordinance in New Mexico and, with Santa Fe County's ordinance, is one of only two in the state.

The purposes of the archaeological review districts ordinance are multifaceted and include the following:

- A recognition of the value of archaeological resources from all periods of history and prehistory, including Native American settlements, Spanish colonization and settlement, and settlement and developments under Mexican and American governments.

· A means for identifying archaeological sites by requiring surveys and test excavations through the city development review and building permit processes.

· A means by which archaeological sites can be evaluated for their potential contribution to cultural, educational, historic, economic, and scientific concerns.

· The establishment of a procedure for treatment of archaeological resources on private and public land; thereby mitigating the information loss from the sometimes unavoidable destruction of archaeological resources and providing for the treatment of those resources that can be preserved.

· Provision of methods for the emergency treatment of archaeological resources found through unexpected discovery.

Enforcement of the ordinance occurs through staff in conjunction with the Archaeological Review Committee (ARC), which was established under the ordinance. The ARC is a five-member mayorally appointed volunteer committee consisting of three archaeologists; one representative from the construction, real estate, or development community; and the individual who serves as the historian on the city's HDRB. The representative from the development community is a critical member, often being the one bringing up issues not considered by the rest of the committee and, in this environment of conservative attitudes, helping keep the archaeologists from asking for more than the ordinance allows.

The ARC conducts public hearings to review and take action on the reconnaissance reports, site significance recommendations, and site treatment reports, as required by the ordinance and determined by the project location. The standards for these reports are also articulated in the ordinance. This committee has a scheduled twice-monthly meeting. Project documents are sent to the ARC through the administration staff. The issuance of an archaeological clearance permit by the ARC is an integral part of the development review and building permit approval process. That is, such approvals are "held hostage" until ARC clearance is issued. This portrayal is more extreme than the reality, however, as the ARC approval usually occurs early in the development review process.

The requirement of ARC approval as part of the development review process has been cited to explain why, in Santa Fe at least, we have been successful in achieving 100 percent compliance. This compliance has occurred after a great deal of educational outreach to the development community and to my colleagues on the development review staff at city hall. Much more is needed. Since the adoption of Santa Fe's Archaeological Review Districts Ordinance, more than 300 archaeological reports have been produced and acted upon by the ARC. These reports are maintained both at city hall and at the New Mexico State Laboratory of Anthropology for use by the profession in continued research. As part of ordinance compliance, the archaeological consultant utilized by any developer must be certified by the ARC as professionally qualified. A review by the ARC of consultants qualified to conduct this work occurs on an as-needed basis; qualifications are identified in the ordinance. The current list of qualified archaeological consultants includes more than thirty individuals.

The Archaeological Review Districts Ordinance establishes three review districts: Historic Downtown, Rivers and Trails, and Suburban. The Historic Downtown District has been the center of Santa Fe since 1610 and was occupied by Native Americans prior to that time. Land within the Historic Downtown District has a high potential of containing significant cultural remains and is part of the historic core of the city. The boundaries of this district are consistent with the boundaries for the National Register historic districts in the city, except that this one is expanded to include the rail yard and the national cemetery. The trigger for the ordinance in this district is the application for any building permit that will include work disturbing 2,500 square feet or more of surface area. Reports prepared for ARC review in this district include archival research, surface survey, and 2 percent testing of the property.

The River and Trails District is an area of prehistoric Native American occupation, later settled by early Spanish colonists, and containing the primary transportation routes important to the settlement of Santa Fe. This district has a high potential of containing significant cultural remains. It includes part of the Santa Fe River floodplain, the escarpment, ridges above the escarpment, and land adjacent to those areas, and it contains historic trails such as the Santa Fe Trail, Galisteo Road, and Agua Fria. The boundaries for this district are the thoroughfares just identified. The trigger for the ordinance in this district is the application of a development proposal that includes two acres or more and requires action by the city's Planning Commission. This type of application includes rezoning, subdivisions, and planned-unit development requests. ARC clearance is required prior to finalization of plats for such developments. Reports submitted for ARC review include archival research and surface survey. Testing of the property is not required in this district as part of the Reconnaissance Report. Land within the Suburban District has a moderate potential of containing significant cultural remains. The ordinance trigger in this district is a development proposal of ten acres or more, needing review by the Planning Commission. The procedural requirements identified for the Rivers and Trails District also apply in this district.

ARC clearance is also required for new construction of sewer mains and main lines of other utilities involving work of up to 60 linear feet in the Downtown Archaeological Review District and up to 550 linear feet in the other two districts. This component is the toughest to enforce due to the lack of tools. Permits for some forms of utility do not go through city review process, and in most cases staff are forced to scrutinize survey plats for references to proposed utilities. Increased outreach to the individual utility companies must occur to educate them better about the requirements of this ordinance.

In all cases, the ordinance makes provisions for the definition of significance and for the treatment of sites. Treatment can include the placement of a site into a cultural properties preservation easement or mitigation, the completion of a final project report that describes and documents mitigation treatment and curation of artifacts, and a cap dollar amount that a developer may be required to spend on such treatment.

Santa Fe's Archaeological Review Districts Ordinance also makes provisions for treatment of unexpected discoveries that occur during construction. This provision allows the city twenty-four hours to assess the significance of the find and to determine the appropriate action to be taken by the owner. Finally, the ordinance established an Archaeological Fund, which requires that eight dollars of every building permit fee issued by the city be placed into this fund for use by the ARC. Project types that are eligible to receive support from this fund are also identified. Such projects include analysis and/or treatment of sites located in a project area where the developer has spent the cap amount, unexpected discoveries, and archaeological surveys. In recent years, Santa Fe has used this fund to augment its annual Certified Local Government allocation from the New Mexico Historic Preservation Division to conduct archaeological and historical research at Historic Fort Marcy.

Santa Fe has seen, and continues to see, benefits as a result of its ordinance. The most obvious of these benefits have been public education and the potential for it. The Fort Marcy project, for example, produced a document that, by combining archival research with archaeological field investigation conducted over the previous two summers, tells the story of the territorial period of Fort Marcy. The city used this document in developing a master plan for on-site interpretation. Funding sources for construction of an on-site interpretive trail are being sought.

In another city-sponsored project conducted in 1993, archaeology taught us that settlement in the Santa Fe area occurred 3,000 years earlier than we had previously thought. A late Archaic period structure was identified and is believed to have been used for food processing. The find is located in the city's pet project—the Tierra Contenta Planned Community development. In this development, hundreds of detached affordable housing units have been provided through the cooperation of public and private interests. The mayor took great pride in the fact that such a sensitive development occurred in the same geographic location as our earliest settlement. It is a "centering" of sorts. In this particular development, many of the archaeology sites identified have been preserved through open space easements.

Perhaps the most visible public education activity that occurred under our ordinance was in October 1995. The city sponsored "Archaeology in Your Backyard," a symposium for the general public, at which more than a dozen archaeologists and historians presented the findings of research conducted as a result of the ordinance. Over a two-and-a-half-day period, more than a hundred members of the general public took the opportunity to learn about the history and prehistory of Santa Fe. Some even braved pretty treacherous winds to participate in tours of Fort Marcy and Pueblo Blanco near Galisteo, New Mexico. I was most proud of those archaeologists who were able to discuss their research in layman's terms so as to keep the public entertained. The results of the city's Archaeological Review Districts Ordinance, as well as its other preservation-related laws, have assisted in causing an increased awareness of the cultural heritage of the city and surrounding area. This raised consciousness has led to a pride of ownership at the grassroots level; attendance at "Archaeology in Your Backyard" was evidence of this interest. With the assistance of the New Mexico Historic Preservation Division, the city edited the papers presented at the symposium and published them in 1999 (Haecker and Ford 1999).

A 1993 visitor survey conducted by the Santa Fe Convention and Visitors Bureau revealed that the top reason people visit Santa Fe is because of the historic and cultural sites it has to offer and what they can teach. I would be remiss if I did not mention the double-edged sword of tourism as one of the benefits Santa Fe has experienced as a result of our local preservation ordinances, including the Archaeological Review Districts Ordinance. It is a double-edged sword because our economy relies upon tourism, and yet it is also somewhat of a mess because of tourism. Partly because Santa Fe is a world-class vacation destination, it has also become a place full-time residents find it difficult to afford.

I would like to close with views former Mayor Debbie Jaramillo expressed at the "Archaeology in Your Backyard" symposium in 1995, reflecting her view of the long-range benefits of archaeology and planning for Santa Fe's future: "The archaeology of this community is important because it is the tangible evidence that shows us directly both the diversity and the depth of our cultural history. By uncovering and researching this record, we save a little more of Santa Fe's essence for future generations. And with every new piece of information, we find out about our ancestors and the relationship they had with the landscape and resources of Santa Fe—and, if we use this knowledge wisely, it can help us plan for how future generations might also live and thrive here" (Haecker and Ford 1999: xiv).

Reference

Haecker, Charles M., and Nancy Ford (eds.). 1999. *Archaeology in Your Backyard: Proceedings of a City of Santa Fe Symposium.* Published by the City of Santa Fe, New Mexico.

19

Potsherds and Politics

Terry Goddard

Winning political support for archaeology is simple. Just transmit the commitment to archaeology shared by a few into something that moves the many, into an issue with political relevance. I write primarily from the local government perspective. That is the view I know best, and in the immortal words of Tip O'Neill, "All politics is local."

The challenge is great. After all, when congressional leaders talk about the evils of red tape, they are talking (in part) about archaeologists. They are criticizing section 106 of the National Historic Preservation Act and all of the extra effort needed to get these job-producing, economy-enhancing, poverty-eradicating projects going.

My own feelings about archaeology started at age thirteen. I spent a summer in northern New Mexico experiencing the wonders of the out-of-doors amid hundreds of ruins. Near the end of that summer, a fellow camper had a dream about a black-on-red pot. The next day, in a lava cave near Grants, he found that pot. It was in perfect condition, on the ledge where it had been left hundreds of years before. The magic of that summer never wore off. I hope others going into public office will experience the wonder of hands-on archaeology at interpretive sites like Crow Canyon.

I should note at the outset that in the politics of archaeology and in many other ways, New Mexico definitely is not normal. Strange and wonderful, yes; but not normal. In New Mexico, archaeology has invaded the popular culture as in no other place in North America. Most of the steps to becoming politically significant have been taken. The state is, therefore, a great place to learn the ropes. It is where we Arizonians return when we despair that the public will never understand what is so important about broken pots and fragments of wall.

Fig. 19.1. Petrogylph motifs on a freeway overpass in Phoenix, Arizona.

One morning while having breakfast at Pasquales in Santa Fe, I noticed a fellow at the next table wearing a jacket decorated with dozens of petroglyph symbols. That jacket was a political statement. More important, in New Mexico it was a *mainstream* political statement.

However trivial the form or demeaning to the trained archaeological mind, it is critical to get archaeology into the popular culture. Otherwise, how will people get even a hint of what they have and what they may be losing? In Phoenix, I was pleased to find some striking petroglyph motifs reproduced on a sidewalk, albeit outside a city museum. Similar designs were chosen to decorate a state freeway overpass nearby (fig. 19.1). But outside Santa Fe there were more and better petroglyph reproductions on the sidewalks of an outlet mall! From museum to public art to commercial culture: it is the path to political relevance.

In Arizona and most of the rest of America, private malls are not dominated by attractive archaeological symbols. Quality definitely is not prevalent. The most widely recognized archaeological item in Arizona is something called "The Thing." Anyone who has traveled across our state on Interstate 10 knows about The Thing. You can hardly help it. Scores of highway billboards are dedicated to its qualities. Although I have never stopped to view The Thing, I am told it is a mummy entombed in a service station on I-10 outside Wilcox.

The Thing proves that archaeology, even very bad archaeology, can be an attraction and a commercial success. How much better would a legitimate exhibit be? A southwestern interpretive site near the freeway where passing tourists could actually get their hands on the resource could and would really stop traffic on I-10. And it would not need billboards from Gallup to Needles.

As a lawyer, I spent almost five years fighting the federal government over the decision to locate a freeway through central Phoenix. The reasons for opposition were many, but our major cause of action was based on archaeology. We had a section 106 issue about whether the Environmental Impact Statement properly documented the incredibly rich prehistoric resources in the path of the freeway. Second, we had an issue under section 4(f) of the Department of Transportation Act about whether there were feasible and prudent alternatives to the route chosen.

I got a crisp, clear lesson on the general regard for archaeological concerns when our principal expert witness, Dr. Fred Plog, then of Arizona State University and later of New Mexico State, took the stand. Professor Plog spoke eloquently about the extraordinary cultural remains that would be destroyed if the freeway were constructed on the proposed route. As Plog put it, if a class assignment had been to devise a route that would destroy the maximum number of cultural resources in the Phoenix area, the only "A" would be for the route chosen by the federal government.

The judge leaned across the bench and asked, "Professor, we're talking about some pots, are we not?" Professor Plog said yes, that, and a great deal else. "I just want to understand what the fuss is about," said the judge. "Are these the same pots that, when I was a boy, we used to put on the canal banks and use for target practice?" It was all too clear to Plog and everyone in the courtroom that they were indeed one and the same. Our case had about as much chance as one of the pots Judge Craig had blasted into oblivion as a boy.

We lost. But we made progress in an unintended way. The case and the studies the government had to undertake to mitigate its freeway decision helped to raise popular consciousness about the rich archaeological resources beneath the city. For the first time, citizens' groups, the press, and a lot of plain folks understood that our community was literally floored in archaeological remains. Years later, before building another crosstown freeway, one house lot in the right-of-way was excavated. The archaeologists found, as I recall, more than eighty burials in that 50- by 120-foot lot!

Phoenix Begins to Get It

The name Phoenix was chosen because the first European settlers built their farmhouses on the ruins of the prehistoric houses. A poetic founder of the modern city decided that, like the mythological Phoenix bird, the city was rising from its own ashes. The canals that crisscross modern Phoenix were constructed by the original residents, the Hohokam, more than a thousand years ago. Early land developers simply scooped out those canals and started the water flowing again.

But in spite of the city's rich archaeological resources, it is safe to say that when I was elected mayor of Phoenix, archaeological issues were *not* a major part of the campaign debate. My opponent did scornfully ridicule my effort to attack the freeway; he called it an idiotic concern for some broken pots.

As mayor, I found opportunities to raise public consciousness about archaeological resources. I commend them to you. Phoenix set up an Arts Commission, which looked hard at determining what was unique about our community. And I established a Historic Commission and passed a tough preservation ordinance. The Arts Commission immediately pointed to the Hohokam canals as a key cultural theme and commissioned work by artists whose designs reflected that theme, whose works celebrated the connection with the past. The freeway I mentioned where one lot yielded eighty burials now has an overpass decorated in Hohokam motifs. It is far and away the most popular public art in the city. The designer even added a bit of modern archaeology to the mix. Residents of homes destroyed when the freeway was built helped to construct the artwork. They put their house keys and other reminders of the buildings that were demolished into the concrete of the bridge (figs. 19.2, 19.3).

We tried to make Pueblo Grande, our small city museum and interpretive site, into something that would give the visitors a window on the city's heritage. What was it like to live in the "Valley of the Sun" in the year 1000? Phoenix became, I believe, the first city in America to hire a full-time archaeologist.

The Phoenix Arts Commission collaborated with the streets department in redesigning the main street of Phoenix. Street lights across America share a remarkable similarity to dental tools. For Central Avenue

Fig. 19.2. Thomas Road overpass in Phoenix.

Fig. 19.3. Detail of Thomas Road overpass, Phoenix.

they were redesigned to showcase archaeological symbols. The medallions on the new street lights display designs based on the pottery excavated at Pueblo Grande and from the freeway rights-of-way (fig. 19.4). Of course, use of cultural symbols requires care to preserve authenticity, and it requires sensitivity to the existing cultures for whom the symbols are far more than decoration. The insensitive use of Hopi kachinas in advertising,

for example, is unfortunate. Wherever possible, the relevant tribal authority should be consulted and permission obtained.

I emphasize public display of archaeological symbols because this kind
of exposure is the critical wedge for entering public consciousness. Other
influences are more subtle. The new Phoenix central library is surrounded
by a stone wall designed to resemble the beautiful masonry at Chaco Canyon. Incrementally, these factors bring into our community some sense of
the physical reality of our heritage: how it looked and felt, why it was
beautiful. Piece by piece, these bits of awareness and appreciation create a
community mosaic, a sense of place, in which the prehistoric past is a critical element. A new pride of place grows inevitably from appreciation of our

Fig. 19.4. Cen-
tral Avenue
lighting in
Phoenix.

Fig. 19.5. Black Canyon City public art, Phoenix.

archaeological heritage. That pride is the basis for political action. People vote to protect their points of pride.

Many cities in Arizona are attempting to establish their connection with the past. Usually, public art makes that connection. Black Canyon City, a small town about thirty-five miles north of Phoenix, commissioned a sculpture decorated with petroglyph symbols outside the town library. This town, dominated by a highway and fast food joints, felt that its identity was best defined by something more timeless (fig. 19.5). In north Phoenix, a neighborhood of newly developed homes convinced the city to not only protect some petroglyphs in the area, which were rapidly being desecrated, but to establish a Rock Art Center to show them off. Like the people of Black Canyon City, these north Phoenix residents felt that their area was unique because of its archaeological connection and were proud of the distinction.

Still, archaeological symbols must struggle to gain recognition. The last time I looked, the sign outside the Pueblo Grande museum was overwhelmed by a huge billboard advertisement for Southwest Airlines vacations in San Jose. Yet we can find examples in which archaeology has moved from the province of a small, dedicated, and politically irrelevant group to public recognition with real political support. If Phoenix can get excited about decorating Central Avenue with representations of pottery designs or about saving rock art, public recognition may be possible everywhere.

Where Are the Points of Pride?

I work for the U.S. Department of Housing and Urban Development, the philosophy of which has recently been characterized as being "place based." HUD is tasked with seeking out the unique and distinctive elements of each community and helping the local government and citizens' groups strengthen these "place makers." HUD has come to recognize that community pride and ultimately community viability are rooted in a sense of heritage. To ignore—or worse, to obliterate—the record of that past deprives the community of a critical value.

Building local respect and appreciation for the unique place makers is the first step. But to be really effective, archaeology must bring economic viability to the table. We still have a long way to go before archaeological sites in Phoenix are seen not as impediments to progress but as opportunity zones. I hope to see the day, and soon, when an archaeologist comes onto a project site to test or to look at backhoe discharge, and the owner—instead of praying that nothing will be found to slow up the project—is fervently hoping that under the ground a cultural resource will be uncovered that can be integrated into the project.

Heritage tourism pays; it's that simple. At the Jorvik Viking Centre in York, England, a shopping center developer took a pretty inconsequential Viking ruin and set up an interpretive site under his shopping center. Jorvik has, I believe, over one million visitors a year, each paying two and a half pounds for the privilege of a short visit. This is a huge economic benefit, with no offsetting loss to the use of the shopping center.

Mesa Grande mound, near Phoenix, is another illustration of economic potential. The mound site was condemned by the City of Mesa for a park. The original offering price was $75,000 for approximately one acre. The

City raised the offer to $150,000 because there was talk that Mesa Grande could have archaeological importance. A presentation was made by the mound's owner based upon the earning power of a center for urban archaeology, an interpretive site. The final settlement in the late 1980s—the case never went to trial—was for $2.5 million based upon Mesa Grande's potential as a visitor draw.

In the Mesa Grande litigation, the city believed a court would have been convinced that an archaeological interpretive center for the mound would attract thousands of paying customers. Ironically, after paying a huge settlement to avoid trial on the interpretive site issue, the Mesa authorities have yet to take the next step, have not yet set up the interpretive center to recoup their payment.

Such economic arguments will convince many who question the intrinsic value of heritage. As heritage tourism becomes a more and more important economic factor, political influence will follow. The critical moment is now, before appreciation of the potential takes root and the drive to develop every square foot eradicates the means for future prosperity.

Campaigning for Heritage Resources

I would like to offer a few practical comments for advocates of archaeological resources.

Successful politics must be active, not reactive. It is critical not to be seen as always representing the forces of opposition. Fighting rearguard actions, always being the cranks with the pots and the firepits, will not win in the long run. On the other hand, educating the community, making sure that schoolchildren in particular care about the cultural resources, igniting their creative imaginations, sets up an environment for political success.

Publicize what you are doing. There has been a lot of talk about how mean the press can be; and it is true. But make no mistake about it, *the press is your most important ally.* It is probably the only mass communication tool you can afford. And every reporter loves to build up the underdog. You are definitely David against a very large development Goliath. Learn to catch reporters' imaginations. Encourage them to come out to your sites *before* there is a crisis, before the bulldozers are about to scrape everything into oblivion. Make the effort to publicize your discoveries in the popular press. Show them what gets you so excited. Television loves "visuals" and archaeology is incredibly visual. Let the news people get down in the dirt with you and share the excitement of discovery.

Politicians hate to lose. If the public thinks something has value, politicians will go to great lengths not to be seen as voting to discard that thing—or worse, to allow it to be taken away by outside force. If you establish the value of a location early, it is much less likely that anyone will cavalierly push you (or it) aside. To this end, any kind of recognition is helpful. National Register of Historic Places designation is very powerful. Lacking that, try for state or local recognition. Make up new awards and present them generously.

Coalitions are critical. Not only do you have to cultivate friends in every related academic discipline; you must also seek opportunities to help them. Someday you will need them to help you. It is the first political rule, simple but effective. Keep in touch. Your Rolodex is your weapon. You never know when you may need everyone you know to write an "uninterested" letter of support. Look for opportunities for public archaeology displays, in schools, in airports, and if you can pull it off, at city hall. Remember, schools contain the next generation of voters and politicians. Get them interested early. Obviously the local arts commissions are invaluable resources.

Find politicians who are already sympathetic. In Phoenix the Arts Commission has done more than any other entity to popularize our visual heritage. Check out politicians' education and their hobbies. Find a councilor who goes on digs or reads about them as a hobbyist. He or she will be incredibly valuable. Spread out from there. Check on family members, business associates, and inner-circle advisors with a special interest. Keep records and keep alert to interconnections. Sympathetic ears and voices on the inside mean the most when times get tough.

Use the Internet. The "Net" is the 800-pound gorilla of political communication in the next decade. Use it to find allies, to make new connections, to build coalitions, and to make sure that your stories get out.

When the politicians fail, trust the voters. Most politicians, in my experience, never warm up to historic or prehistoric preservation. Perhaps it is because dead folks don't lobby, don't make political contributions, and (except in a few parts of the country) don't vote. On the Phoenix City Council, I lost vote after vote on preserving cultural resources. Saving individual historic houses was of little consequence to the council members. In frustration, I put a measure on the ballot to fund $15 million to support the preservation and restoration of cultural artifacts, buildings, and neighborhoods. The council laughed, sure the measure would fail. The voters passed it overwhelmingly; in the same election they turned down a heavily publicized sports stadium.

Never give up. Finally, I hope that I have made it clear that becoming politically significant from a small base requires incredibly hard work, infinite attention to detail, and great creativity. But that sounds like a formula to be a successful archaeologist. You should be perfect. Don't worry about being so small in number. You have the necessary tools and a compelling cause. As Margaret Mead is reputed to have said, it is possible for a few people committed to an ideal to change the world; indeed those are the only ones who ever have.

20

Archaeology and the Tourism Train

Katherine Slick

In his opening remarks for the first White House Conference on Travel and Tourism in 1995, where more than 2,000 delegates convened, President Bill Clinton said: "A healthy travel and tourism industry is good for the economy. You are our largest business service export. You're the largest employer in the nation, providing jobs for over 6 million Americans. And of course, you employ millions more through industries that thrive when you do well" (TIA 1998).

Tourism is economic development. At the turn of the millennium tourism was predicted to be the number one industry in the world, replacing manufacturing and traditional industrial forms of economic development. In the United States alone, tourism was a $467 billion industry, according to the Travel Industry Association of America. The World Travel and Tourism Council estimated that in 2000, travel and tourism—directly and indirectly—generated 200 million jobs worldwide, accounting for 11.7 percent of gross domestic product. By 2010, these figures are expected to jump to $6.7 trillion in GDP and 253 million jobs (BEST 2001).

In looking to that future, a major objective that was unanimously supported by the White House conferees is to "preserve our natural, historic and cultural resources for future generations and expand urban and rural economic development opportunities through a national strategy fostering environmental and cultural travel and tourism." Two key recommendations were set as priorities in the new national tourism agenda: (1) hosting a series of regional natural and cultural summits to identify conservation and management strategies to meet the unique needs of each region in the country; and (2) implementing policies and programs that preserve, protect, and assure future enjoyment of our natural and cultural environments, which in turn will sustain and enhance the visitor experience. To act on some of these recommendations, the deputy secretary of the interior immediately hosted a meeting to discuss how to expand public-private partnerships; and cultural and historic preservation organizations gathered to initiate their own action plan to expand and enhance cultural heritage tourism in America today.

The White House Conference also heightened some concerns of the industry overall. First, with the demise of the United States Travel and Tourism office within the Department of Commerce, tourism development and marketing activities are to be coordinated through a new national tourism office that will embrace a "pay to play" philosophy. And second, government can no longer support initiatives alone; public-private partnerships must be financially and programmatically beneficial and mission related. Remembering that tourism is economic development, there will be a great need for sites, attractions, and service-related businesses to track their involvement in tourism: we need to know the demographic profile of current visitors, their economic impact, and motivations for travel; we need an understanding of the experience provided and our capacity for hosting and servicing travelers. Finally, as in all forms of economic development, tourism requires an investment—of people and funding—to grow. In order for the industry to capture and maintain global market share, and to protect its resources for the enjoyment of future generations, funding and partnerships must be secured. This will take some creativity in finding and maintaining relationships for appropriate corporate sponsorships.

But the prospects for those relationships are good. A survey of foundation and corporate giving executives was recently conducted by Business Enterprises for Sustainable Travel (BEST), a new initiative of the Conference Board, the world's leading business membership and research network, in association with the World Travel and Tourism Council, the industry's global business leaders' forum. The survey found that nearly 80 percent of respondents said they would be willing to add extra time to trips in order to gain a better appreciation of the unique flavors of a host community; 32 percent would be willing to spend an extra day. Two-thirds would like to see information about host communities made available in conference registration materials.

What Are the Implications for Archaeology?

Obviously, there is a need for awareness that archaeology is an important interpretive vehicle for discovering the story of a place. We must alert both our preservation partners and local tourism professionals on the importance of awareness of archaeology and its connection to the development and market potential of a site. We must consider the tourism industry our partner, rather than an adversary, if we want to increase our ability to enhance public awareness about the importance of archaeology.

In 1989 the National Trust for Historic Preservation recognized the opportunity to provide a market niche in the tourism industry and initiated the Heritage Tourism Demonstration Project. The trust's approach is based on five principles and four key steps.

Principle 1: Find the fit between your community and tourism. The community needs to be engaged in a conversation about their expectations and concerns regarding heritage tourism. What level of tourism growth will the community find comfortable? What can it support? Do people want motor coaches and recreational vehicles in particular areas or only standard automobiles? Tourism programs of any kind are about economics. Is the community getting the return it wants or expects? Santa Fe is an example of the residents questioning whether the level of tourism the city now accommodates diminishes their quality of life. Successful and sustainable programs will provide quality experiences without compromising resources or residents' quality of life, if the fit is thought through and the tourist's engagement is anticipated.

Principle 2: Collaborate. As tourism becomes an increasingly competitive business, forming partnerships with other organizations and attractions becomes even more essential for success. Too often promoters of one site see other attractions as competitors, not potential partners. Partnerships provide opportunities to get "more bang for the buck" by stretching the marketing dollar and offering more activities that encourage visitors to stay in your area longer, which gives more value to the economic development. Partnerships can be quite broad, including government agencies, state tourism offices, city or county offices, and convention and visitors' bureaus as well as public and private businesses involved in preservation, development, visitor services, and promotion.

Principle 3: Preserve and protect resources and help your partners do the same. As architect and planner Andres Duany (1995) warns, "Authentic urban experience has become such a rarity that many places have become tourist attractions simply by virtue of being real towns." Too often the tourism industry gets caught up in the need to please—to provide services and to accommodate numbers of visitors—without looking at the possible impact on the resources. In heritage tourism, as in archaeology, if you do not take care of the resources, they may not be around for the future. A historic building becomes a prime location for a parking lot for visitors, or a scenic vista may turn into a sea of billboards.

Understand what makes the experience memorable and important, and work to maintain those circumstances. The international travel writer Arthur Frommer says visitors will not travel to a community that has lost its soul. Make sure that you protect the people, buildings, and land that provide a sense of place. Be proactive against development and zoning that may have a negative impact on the resource, and communicate to the business, tourism, and civic communities why preservation and conservation are important—in language and terms they understand.

Principle 4: Focus on authenticity and quality. What separates one destination from another is its unique attributes. As more destinations latch onto the popularity of heritage tourism, it will be increasingly important to have high-quality, authentic sites. Explaining to visitors what is real, what is reconstruction, and what is rehabilitation will be important in establishing credibility. There are many communities in northern New Mexico that look at Santa Fe and fear that what they see there will be their own future; they refer to the city as Santa Fake.

Archaeologists must get the information out! If a guide shares information that is not substantiated as fact, that guide needs to tell the tourists that it is hearsay, to keep from confusing the public. As new information becomes available, the information and the process of acquiring it can clarify misconceptions about the past. While many heritage sites are nonprofits that face fiscal reductions or restraints, customers nevertheless compare each experience with that at other attractions they have seen. It is up to the heritage site to provide the best-quality experience possible if it is open to the public; otherwise, it has a negative impact for every other heritage site on the traveler's journey.

Principle 5: Make sites come alive. History is too often experienced as a string of names, events, and dates to memorize. To compete in the tourism industry, you have to look for creative ways to bring your attraction and message to life. Find ways to make connections between your attraction and the lives of the visitors—not just for wealthy, white, and powerful ancestors but also for working people, immigrants, slaves, women, families, and children. Try to engage all the visitor's senses—Pecos National

Historic Park has a wonderful outdoor bread-baking program in the summer that captures your nose and then shows how bread has been prepared in northern New Mexico for centuries. Invest the time and financial resources to develop creative interpretive strategies that are appropriate for the site and your audiences.

Entertainment is the number one reason why people visit historic sites, according to the 1994 Travelometer study conducted by the U.S. Travel Data Center for the Travel Industry Association of America (see TIA's website <www.tia.org>). It shows entertainment ahead of other motivations such as personal education, education of children, authenticity, or helping support historic preservation efforts. This is what archaeologists have been worried about—but entertainment does not need to mean fiction.

For example, one of the challenges facing the Chippewa at the Lac du Flambeau reservation in Wisconsin was meeting visitor expectations. The Native Americans at this reservation do not wear traditional dress, and their forebears did not live in teepees. Therefore they recreated a birchbark village as part of their summer powwow and used traditional songs, dance, and cuisine to help visitors understand how early Chippewa lived, worked, and played.

Steps in a Long-Range Strategy

In the same way that heritage is different from place to place, there is no single approach to tourism of any kind. Certain steps make sense for a comprehensive long-range strategy, yet the variables are different in every situation. In working with the variety of sites and communities, the National Trust for Historic Preservation has developed the following four important steps.

Step 1: Assess the potential. Certainly you will take stock of what you have in the way of natural, built, and cultural resources that can be enjoyed by the public and that will attract tourists, but assessment should also include a careful analysis of organization and protection. Isn't that the community's or the travel industry's responsibility? Yes, but if you are thinking and helping others think about the long-term viability of a site, focusing on a new marketing piece will not cut it. Creating organizations and implementing protection strategies are necessary. This is time-consuming work but important so that quick, visible projects do not put heritage resources at risk. And it is not something the archaeologist must do alone. The tourism industry, chambers of commerce, and city and county governments can help identify how many visitors are currently attracted to the area, how they spend their time and money, and what can be developed or interpreted to expand the tourist appeal.

Tourism is fluid, and few sites are "destination sites," so look to the surrounding communities as you inventory the possibilities, and think through how many visitors your site and the region can handle. Creating a well-researched inventory is critical to establishing baseline data for future comparison and evaluation. In order to provide a measuring stick to calculate the impact tourism has, and therefore the ongoing successes, the community or region must design instruments that provide answers to local questions and concerns.

Step 2: Plan and organize. Clear goals and objectives and measurable desired results should be established at the beginning so that all players understand the priorities. All the players should be involved—tourism organizations, businesses, government officials, retail merchants, city planners, preservationists, archaeologists, and representatives from local attractions. This is the time to involve residents in the process to determine their attitudes and opinions about tourism, preservation, and sacred spots they want to keep for "residents only." Find out why people want tourism—for jobs, to preserve historic sites, because someone in city government wants it? Reach agreement on what is achievable and who is responsible for turning the plan into action. Two critical elements to success are adequate funding and strong leadership. Putting together a realistic budget that provides sources of income and uses with specific dates will make for a much easier launch for such a public endeavor.

Step 3: Prepare, protect, and manage. Even though it will take time and commitment to prepare, the plan is just the beginning. Developing an ongoing relationship among protection of the resources, resident needs, and visitor wants requires continual monitoring of how that relationship is progressing. Make choices that meet the community's vision and that enhance the visitor experience. As with the inventory of physical resources, it is important to consider the needs of the human resources. Residents will serve as staff for the various visitor sites, and they will also be ambassadors and representatives for the community and the experience. If they do not regard tourism as good or beneficial—or at least neutral, a compatible economic force within the community—the visitor may feel abused by the experience. Often residents feel uninvolved in decisions that directly affect their lives, and they therefore resent the economic development that could provide their livelihood.

Step 4: Market for success. Before selling your tourism site, evaluate the market potential. Develop a good idea of what you have and who might be interested in the experience. You may say that you want to see anyone who wants to come, but we have seen that national parks need to become more user accessible as the traveling audience grows older. Indeed, group tours traveling by motor coach have very different needs and expectations than do adventure travelers, no matter what their age, or than a family on a week-long holiday.

How do you identify and then market to the appropriate audience? Local chambers of commerce and convention and visitor centers as well as the state tourism office can help determine what the tourism industry knows about market expectations and partnership opportunities. This will help prepare a base for a detailed marketing plan, which will also include the following:

- public relations strategies to get media coverage in major markets, in both trade and consumer publications;
- advertising, if the budget is large enough to provide funding for a frequent and competitive campaign;
- promotions that target travel buyers for the desired markets;
- graphic materials that provide written and visual information about the destination; and
- market research to track visitation and measure programs and trends.

With one in every ten people in the United States today employed by the travel and tourism industry, heritage tourism is an obvious addition, and it is an economic train that is moving down the track. The tourism industry needs the product we can provide to help tell the story of our country's development. With our assistance, America can offer a travel experience that is second to none. When we provide the educational and, when appropriate, experiential element, the visitor is engaged and enlightened through the discovery process and interpretation of our findings. We, in turn, benefit from a more educated public as consumers become sensitive to their responsibilities and privileges associated with travel. Without our help, understanding, and partnership to create ways to communicate responsibility and understanding, the potential negative impacts will not be defrayed. Archaeologists need to get into the tourism community and into the local communities. You cannot afford to talk only to other archaeologists. It is a challenge, and not everyone or those responsible for every site will make the choice to do so. How you make that decision is very important. To do nothing is to choose.

Note

For more information contact Manager, Heritage Tourism, National Trust for Historic Preservation, 511 16th Street, Suite 700, Denver, CO 80202, phone (303) 623-1504, fax (303) 825-8073.

References

BEST. 2001. Why Target Travel and Tourism? *Business Enterprises for Sustainable Travel (BEST) Update 2001.* New York: The Conference Board, Inc.

Duany, Andres. 1995. Presentation at National Town Meeting on Main Street, National Trust for Historic Preservation, Little Rock, Arkansas.

TIA. 1998. *From Strategy to Success, A Final Report on the White House Conference on Travel and Tourism.* Washington, D.C.: Travel Industry Association of America.

Leading Tourism Industry Associations and Organizations

ABA: American Bus Association <www.buses.org>. Trade association representing intercity, charter bus, and tour operators. Annual computerized marketplace held each December in different U.S. city. Headquarters, Washington, D.C.

ASTA: American Society of Travel Agents <www.astanet.com>. The trade association for travel agents. Sponsors educational and marketing programs, conducts advocacy programs, sponsors annual conference, and monitors industry standards. Annual conference usually held abroad. Headquarters, Washington, D.C.

NTA: National Tour Association <www.ntaonline.com>. Trade association with over 3,000 tour operators and motor coach owners specializing in inbound and outbound group travel. Annual conference includes educational seminars and computerized marketplace; held in a different U.S. city early November. Headquarters, Lexington, Kentucky.

SATW: Society of American Travel Writers <www.satw.org/index.htm>. Association by invitation/membership review of travel editors, writers, broadcasters, and photojournalists who actively cover travel news/destinations. Associate memberships include public relations and media relations representatives who work with travel trade and journalists. Annual conference held late September (10 days). Headquarters, Washington, D.C.

TIA: Travel Industry Association of America <www.tia.org>. The national travel association representing every aspect of the tourism industry. Goal is to unify the industry and increase awareness of its importance. Develops international and domestic travel marketing programs. Annual "Powwow" held each spring in a different U.S. destination matches international buyers and media with U.S. suppliers during computerized appointment sessions. Headquarters, Washington, D.C.

ITA: Tourism Industries <tinet.ita.doc.gov>. The federal office that replaces the U.S. Travel and Tourism Administration. The Tourism Industries office is within Trade Development of the International Trade Administration, U.S. Department of Commerce.

21

The Web of Archaeology

Its Many Values and Opportunities

S. Terry Childs

Archaeologists increasingly seek effective ways to captivate and communicate with a wide range of audiences who expect and demand different things from archaeology. Can our diverse information, from general interest to highly technical, be made more accessible and meaningful via a single medium? The World Wide Web, an interactive and ever-expanding mode of communication and education, can take us a long way toward meeting these challenges.

The Web has a number of features that make it particularly useful for engaging and educating a very diverse public. It offers opportunities that could hardly be imagined ten years ago, especially the ability to choose to follow a topic in great detail or to swing off into something new and unexpected. Widespread use of this relatively new medium and technology can reap rewards for archaeologists as we strive to make our discipline relevant to non-archaeologists in a modern world. One of the many communication strategies that can be used is to emphasize how archaeology informs and relates to numerous aspects of modern life. Archaeologists can and should demonstrate the numerous linkages between essential activities in the past and those common in the present. These might include business and trade, government or religious practices, communication techniques, travel, home building, obtaining medical care, and playing games. Making those connections on the Web is potentially easier than through other media, because they can be only an electronic click or two away.

I have three goals. The first is to outline the general features of the Web relevant to creating dynamic and engaging sites on archaeology. The second is to demonstrate how these and related materials are effective for promoting four values of archaeology: research, heritage, education, and economics. I use numerous examples to illustrate my points, primarily from the National Park Service (NPS) website called Links to the Past <http://www.cr.nps.gov>, which is focused on cultural resources.[1] The third goal is to identify opportunities that the Web offers to entice new people to value archaeology.

Fundamentals of the Web

The Web and the more familiar paper-based media share a few characteristics. They both use words and illustrations. To help readers or users find specific subject matter, they both require careful organization that involves navigational schemes, such as tables of content, indexes, and site maps. The similarities largely stop there.

There are four principal features of the Web that set it apart from the more traditional media of communication, such as newspapers, magazines, books, radio, and television. First, a website cannot be regarded as a standard, linear progression of information and ideas with an absolute beginning and end. It is a web of interconnected parts, hence its name. This means that a website can be entered from a host of avenues, including links from other websites, bookmarks set up by individual users, or as the result of interactive search engines.

A related and important feature of the Web for communicating the many values of archaeology is that it may accommodate a very diverse audience of visitors who have different needs and demands. One coordinated site may provide a huge array of materials to several different audiences at one time due to the Web's layered and interconnected structure as well as its navigational and search aids. General "sound bytes" of information, along with engaging graphics, may meet the needs of the lay public. Subject experts and some informed members of the public often require more detailed or specialized information, such as pertinent federal laws or a technical report about an archaeological investigation.

Third, the Web is interactive. Websites are designed to inspire choice and action. Color graphics and video serve to engage visitors visually. Other senses may also be stimulated. New software now transmits sound, such as music and voice recordings, while touch seems virtually achieved through software that presents vivid three-dimensional images. Interactive games, puzzles, tours, and tests or quizzes may also be made available.

Because the Web allows for and encourages choice, each Web user personalizes information retrieval through the use of available search engines, site indexes, and other tools. A visitor satisfied or dissatisfied with the information found can and may well comment. Well-designed websites have e-mail connection for direct communication with content providers and/or website managers.

Finally, any part of a website may be quickly and easily changed, updated, or enhanced. Website managers and developers are never locked into content, design, or an organizational scheme such as occurs once a book is published or a film is released. Web materials are often updated, and whole websites are periodically redesigned and refreshed. In fact, website managers seek to keep their audiences returning by providing new or better materials on a regular basis.

Advantages of the Web for Archaeology

It is a huge challenge to engage, communicate with, and teach diverse audiences who value and relate to archaeology in different ways or not at all. The Web, increasingly available via a personal computer in homes, schools, libraries, and offices, can meet that challenge. The wide variety of opportunities is discussed below in terms of four values that individuals place on archaeology.

Research Value

For those audiences who value the research and discovery aspects of archaeology, the Web has a number of important tools that may be used to initiate and conduct research using both primary and secondary materials, and then to communicate research results. A researcher may begin a project by using available search engines to find possible research funding sources (e.g., NPS Grants <www.cr.nps.gov/helpyou.htm>), tools, and/or primary and secondary research materials across the Web. In fact, Web-based search engines and databases encourage and help hone the investigative skills required by archaeologists.

Interactive databases allow researchers to search for and explore particular interests and topics. The Reports module of the National Archeological Database (NADB-R) <www.cr.nps.gov/aad/nadb.htm>, for example, is a partnership effort of the NPS and the Center for Advanced Spatial Technologies at the University of Arkansas to provide bibliographic information about archaeological projects conducted across the United States.

The majority of the reports are "gray literature," which is unpublished, produced in limited numbers, poorly circulated, and rarely available in public or university libraries. Users query approximately 270,000 records by author, title, date, keywords, and other terms. Another important NPS database with significant secondary research materials is the National Register Information System (NRIS) <www.nr.nps.gov/nrishome.htm>. It contains records for over 70,000 historic and prehistoric properties nominated to and registered in National Register of Historic Places. A researcher may search the database by name, location, person, or National Register status (whether or not the property is listed, removed, pending, etc.).

Increasingly, it is possible to find primary research materials on the Web. Some archives and other institutions now scan and make available archival documents. Many museums now provide summary information about the content of their collections to assist researchers, educators, and many others in determining where relevant collections are curated and where documents are archived. Such information is currently available for all NPS collections curated at park and regional center repositories <www.cr.nps.gov/csd/collections/parkprof.html>. More extensive summary information is sometimes provided on individual park pages such as Chaco Canyon National Historical Park's website <www.nps.gov/chcu/museum.htm>. Several NPS museums are populating a Web-based searchable database to provide researchers and others with information about and photographs of individual items in the near future.

Geographic Information System (GIS) maps are another means to summarize and present information with considerable research value, this time in graphic form. The Multiple Attribute Presentation System (MAPS) module of NADB <www.cr.nps.gov/aad/nadb.htm>, for example, offers a useful set of national-level GIS maps. These include an archaeological site count map and density map based on information supplied by state Historic Preservation Offices, a national map of the density of archaeological sites with fluted projectile points, and maps constructed from the frequencies of citations found in the NADB-Reports database by state and county.

It is also possible to establish via the Web communication networks to facilitate information gathering and dispersal. The "Ask an Historian" page <www.cr.nps.gov/history/ask.htm>, for example, provides e-mail access to approximately fifty NPS historians, each of whom is listed by specialty. Online discussion groups, which encourage a more dynamic interchange of information among subscribers, may be associated with a website, such as the National Historic Landmark program's <www.cr.nps.gov/nhl/list.htm>.

Once research is accomplished, the results need to be made accessible. The Web allows for the broader distribution of materials published in other media, such as the magazine *CRM* <www.cr.nps.gov/crm/>. Not only are current issues of *CRM* uploaded onto the Web as they are produced in print, but more than twenty years of back issues are now available via a searchable database. Other examples are the National Register Bulletin series <www.cr.nps.gov/nr/publications/bulletins.htm> and the Technical Brief series of the Archeology and Ethnography Program <www.cr.nps.gov/aad/aepubs.htm>. Some out-of-print books are also now made available on the Web, such as Ronald F. Lee's *The Antiquity Act of 1906* <www.cr.nps.gov/aad/pubs/>, originally published in 1970, as well as others written by archaeologists at the Southeast Archeological Center <www.cr.nps.gov/seac/onlinevolumes.htm>.

Perhaps more significant, the Web offers a publication and distribution vehicle for primary documents that might otherwise be printed in small numbers and become part of the gray literature. Increasingly, such reports, memoranda, and guidelines are available on government, university, and other websites, where their new accessibility opens many doors to further research for the archaeological profession and may add a richer understanding of archaeology by the interested wider public. A good example is the series of documents initiated from the Department of the Interior and the U.S. Army Corps of Engineers concerning the disposition of Kennewick Man <www.cr.nps.gov/aad/kennewick>. Similarly, the Web provides a medium by which researchers may make preliminary and draft reports available for comment in a very timely fashion. One example is the draft reports for the Earliest American National Historic Landmark Archeological theme study, at <www.cr.nps.gov/aad/eam/>.

Heritage Value

Some people, particularly the interested public, value archaeology for its ability to integrate the past with the present and future as well as to make meaningful connections to particular times and places in the past. While most people understand such linkages at the local level, as related to their family or community, others may also make connections between the past and the present at the regional and national levels. We may dramatically communicate these values, as well as educate new people about them, by taking advantage of the visual and audio capabilities of the Web and its nonlinear structure.

The "Ancient Architects of the Mississippi" feature <www.cr.nps.gov/aad/feature/>, for example, vividly sets the context for ways of life along the Mississippi River approximately eight hundred years ago—the same river that affects the lives of hundreds of thousands of people today. Over the last two hundred years, many people have discovered great meaning and importance in the archaeological sites found along the river. These thoughts have been effectively captured in a section of the site called "Delta Voices." Other cultural perspectives on this part of the country are provided by the Lower Mississippi River Valley Initiative. It features the Underground Railroad <www.cr.nps.gov/delta/under.htm>, one of the most dramatic quests for freedom in U.S. history, as does the Network to Freedom site <www.cr.nps.gov/ugrr/>.

Online museum exhibits are another excellent means of evoking connections between the past and the present. For example, an exhibit on Civil War camp life at Gettysburg <www.cr.nps.gov/csd/gettex/> uses stunning photographs of objects from Gettysburg's museum collections to reveal both the tedium and revelry in the daily lives of young men at war. The shapes and styles of many featured objects have changed over time, yet their functional similarities are poignant and meaningful for Web visitors today. Online exhibits on the Tuskegee Airmen, Booker T. Washington, and George Washington Carver <www.cr.nps.gov/csd/exhibits/tuskegee/> highlight the real life of past generations.

But what about all the individuals who cruise the Web yet know little or nothing about archaeology? How can they be captivated and educated about meaningful links to the past through the lens of archaeology? The interwoven structure of the Web allows the construction of such associations through seamless links between sites.

A proactive strategy that might be developed by the archaeological profession is to seek out and encourage web managers of sites focused on modern life issues, businesses, and recreation to link to appropriate archaeology-oriented sites. For this to work, archaeologists must demonstrate to undoubtedly skeptical web managers and public relations staff why and how connections made between such sites will appeal to people's cultural heritage values related to places of birth, family, work, and fun. For example, archaeologists who study ancient and historic period iron working and create web pages about that research might contact the web managers of modern steel company sites. They can argue that it is good for public relations to set the development of steel making in its historical context. Similar arguments may be made about the connections between large-scale corn farming and the rise of corn-based agriculture in the Americas or modern ship building and ancient modes of water travel. Linkages between car rental companies and studies of ancient road systems, such as at Chaco Canyon <www.nps.gov/chcu/roads.htm>, could highlight basic human needs for communication and travel.

Educational Value

Some of the examples already discussed also highlight the educational value of archaeology and the power of the Web to help teach all age groups about a host of related principles, methodologies, and perspectives. Archaeology is about investigation, research, preservation, and realistic interpretation, whether digging in the ground, surface surveying for archaeological sites, using documents in an archive, or examining artifacts in a museum. The educational value of archaeology, however, cannot be well utilized by teachers, students, and others for lifelong learning until they understand better the theoretical, methodological, and historical foundations of archaeology. These underpinnings may be taught via the Web in a variety of ways.

Web-based lesson plans are useful for teachers of grades kindergarten through twelve. The National Register of Historic Places has produced over fifty Teaching with Historic Places lesson plans <www.cr.nps.gov/nr/twhp/archeo.htm> that focus on the significance of historic and prehistoric properties. "Frederica: An 18th-Century Planned Community," for example, highlights archaeological and historical interpretation about why this British settlement was built and how it functioned as Great Britain and Spain struggled to control land between Charleston and St. Augustine. A complementary page on the Fort Frederica website <www.nps.gov/fofr/arch.html> presents a program to teach archaeology to fourth and fifth graders in both the classroom and the field. The park has also developed a curriculum guide for this program.

Online distance learning materials for "students" from kindergarten to age ninety-nine are increasingly being developed. These vary considerably in terms of breadth of content, reference materials, interactivity with professors or teachers, and level of commitment necessary for a student. Universities and continuing education programs are creating fully fledged interactive courses on the Web that require a fee and yield a grade or certificate. Other professionals are developing self-paced distance learning products that are free to the user. For example, Managing Archeological Collections <www.cr.nps.gov/aad/collections/> is a distance learning and technical assistance effort designed for students and professionals in archaeology and related disciplines, who are rarely taught this important subject matter in their formal course work. Each of the nine sections contains a breadth of content, an interactive review quiz, a bibliography, a page of related links, and access to a comprehensive glossary. In another example of distance learning, at American Defenders of Land, Sea and Sky <www2.cr.nps.gov/pad/defenders/>, children learn about National Historic Landmark historic forts, ships, battlefields, lighthouses, and other places used to defend our country during various wars. An accompanying guide for teachers, parents, and other educators is also available on the website.

The historical perspective on the development of archaeology as a discipline and its role in the preservation, protection, and interpretation of peoples and places in the past may be effectively presented through a timeline. Web-based timelines, such as Public Archeology in the United States Timeline <www.cr.nps.gov/aad/timeline/timeline.htm>, are enhanced by interesting graphics and links to a host of associated reading materials and websites.

Special features and case studies are also fruitful ways to teach people about archaeology and how archaeology relates to basic principles of mathematics and physics, chemistry, the transmission of history, cultural values, and many other concepts and practices. Virtual digs may be used to demonstrate the activities and decision making during an excavation in actual time, on a daily basis, or in a summary form to help achieve both of these educational goals. For example, survey work at two plantations along the Cumberland Island National Seashore recorded in a daily log <www.cr.nps.gov/seac/daily/daily.htm> helps demonstrate laying out a grid and artifact analysis. The Valley Forge National Historical Park web page about excavations of log cabins once used by George Washington's soldiers also summarizes the archaeological discoveries <www.cr.nps.gov/logcabin/html/rd_valleyforge.html>. On a related page for students, "Dig It: Experience an Archeological Dig at Valley Forge" <www.cr.nps.gov/logcabin/html/dig_it.html> teaches about the principles of stratigraphy. "Archeology at the Battle of the Little Big Horn" <www.mwac.nps.gov/libi/> highlights the methods used to investigate the battlefield—modern forensics, chemistry, and spatial analysis.

Similarly, the Web may be used to enliven reconstructions of past activities and events based on archaeological interpretation. For example, "Paddle into the Past" (formerly on the State Museum of Pennsylvania website <www.statemuseumpa.org>) documented the reconstruction of a prehistoric canoe and paddling it down the Susquehanna River. This project, done in partnership with the NPS, used the Web to provide daily journal entries and photos during the six-day adventure, while highlighting the many lessons learned.

Case studies also may be used to heighten awareness of issues. Site Watch <www.cr.nps.gov/aad/sitewat.htm> highlights a series of successful prosecutions against vandals of archaeological sites or illicit traders of stolen artifacts across state boundaries. Archeology at Andersonville <www.cr.nps.gov/seac/andearch.htm>, on the other hand, covers the history and archaeology of the Civil War prison camp and draws attention to the issue of fair and ethical treatment of POWs then and now.

Economic Value

The economic value of archaeology is of great interest to community leaders, tourist bureaus, newspaper reporters, and television producers. In particular, the growing heritage tourism industry can be intimately connected to archaeology through publicly accessible archaeological sites and historic buildings as well as museums. The Web provides dynamic ways to demonstrate and promote such relationships.

Travel itineraries, which encourage visits to both important and little known archaeological sites, historic buildings, and cultural landscapes, are ideal for the Web. Interactive maps are useful to help visitors visualize an area and its road networks. Visitors then click on a series of recommended places to receive useful information (written and/or audio), photographs, and perhaps video as they plan a trip. Links to related websites are also useful in the spirit of economic cooperation. In light of these benefits, the National Register of Historic Places currently offers about twenty travel itineraries that focus on themes, such as the Underground Railroad <www.cr.nps.gov/nr/travel/underground/>; regions, such as Virginia's Piedmont <www.cr.nps.gov/nr/journey/>; and cities, such as Washington, D.C. <www.cr.nps.gov/nr/travel/wash/>.

Another travel itinerary, the Golden Crescent <www.cr.nps.gov/goldcres.htm>, is focused on the south Georgia and north Florida region and on key themes. Interactive maps, photos, and text are used to highlight mounds and rings (archaeology), African-American heritage, the resort era, the clash of colonial empires, plantation agriculture, and coastal defense.

Many of the types of websites presented in the previous sections may also be used to highlight the economic value of archaeology, such as online museum exhibits and interpretive features about archaeology that stimulate a desire to visit an area for its past wonders. Information about participation in archaeological activities is helpful as well. For example, each year the State Archaeology Week or Month programs across the United States promote local and statewide understanding of and participation in archaeology through site visits and scheduled programs. Information about these opportunities is provided through an invaluable compilation of all the states with archaeology weeks or months, along with contact information and active links to related websites, at <www.cr.nps.gov/aad/statearc.htm>.

Into the Future

In the mid-1990s the Web was considered by many to be a passing fancy or a game. It is neither. The huge increase in the number of Web users over the last five years suggests that it will not go away soon. Instead, it offers archaeologists and others a "one-stop shopping" medium whereby they may communicate with and teach a large and diverse public about archaeology's multiple values. The Web also provides new avenues by which archaeologists may capture the attention of Web users who know virtually nothing about archaeology, while also sustaining the attention of interested supporters. Therefore, archaeologists need to use the Web more proactively. As noted, one tactic is to identify websites about modern activities and issues that have a history little known to average Americans. Then we must vigorously contact and convince the managers of those websites to link to archaeology sites, based on real connections between today and the past, to yield benefits for all involved. This overview provides a number of other ways to take advantage of this dynamic and interactive medium.

Note

1. There are now many excellent and comprehensive websites about archaeology. Due to space limitations, I use examples primarily from the NPS website. I recommend using search engines to find other sites. Also, there are several useful website

reviews and compilations of recommended sites in professional journals, magazines, and newsletters, such as *Archaeology*, the Society for American Archaeology's *SAA Bulletin* and the new *SAA Archaeological Record*, and *Anthropology News* of the American Association of Anthropology. Website addresses or URLs (Uniform Resource Locators) given later in the chapter do not include the standard address protocol http:// but are simply demarcated by angle brackets.

22

The Archaeologist as Storyteller

Peter A. Young

Why is it that so many people we meet wish they had become archaeologists? In an *Archaeology* article on "The Boom in Volunteer Archaeology" in this country, we quoted Florida educator KC Smith as believing that "Americans have inherited something from their elders—a congenital fascination with people, places, events, and things of the past" (Wertime 1995: 73). The author of that story, Beaver College English professor Richard A. Wertime, was more philosophical, writing that "by virtue of its mission—recovering the past and articulating it to the present—[archaeology] embodies the concept of the common good. Archaeology is a mirror held up, not to nature, but to humanity. To excavate the past is to polish that mirror, that we may better see ourselves and know more clearly who we are" (ibid.).

Archaeology's growing circulation bears out the fact that the audience for archaeological information is substantial indeed. Our paid circulation is now well over 200,000, almost double what it was a decade ago. Our weekly half-hour *Archaeology TV* series, produced by Tom Naughton of New Dominion Pictures in Virginia Beach and aired on the Discovery Network's Learning Channel, has been in worldwide syndication. According to Nielsen Home Video Index for the fourth quarter of 1994, during an average month, the program reached 2,044,000 homes and 2,590,000 adults, a testament to the fascination archaeology holds for audiences of all ages. These figures did not specify those households held in thrall by the Learning Channel's occasional weekend Archaeology marathons, hours of back-to-back installments. As those familiar with the program will realize, that was a lot of host John Rhys-Davies in one sitting.

Faced with such enthusiasm from the general public, it is only natural that we have pursued new and intriguing opportunities: a sophisticated website and a children's magazine called *Dig,* recently sold to Carus Publishing Company in Peterborough, New Hampshire.

Having said all that, I must admit to being somewhat baffled as to why, given such a ready and eager audience, so few archaeologists are interested in writing popular accounts of what they do. One reason, of course, is the traditional scholarly prejudice against popularization—writing for a journal like *Archaeology* is time-consuming and does not advance one's tenured status or enhance one's academic reputation with one's peers.

In a recent "Forum" column in the magazine, Randall McGuire (1995) of the State University of New York at Binghamton recalled a cocktail conversation with a university vice president who, upon learning that he was an archaeologist, wanted to know what he had found lately. As McGuire explained his work with competing theories of social complexity in the Hohokam Sedentary period, the vice president's eyes glazed over, causing McGuire to break out into a full-scale sweat, knowing that in all probability he was blowing his chance to impress a man who could say yea or nay to his bid for a permanent position.

Fred Hocker, then president of the Institute of Nautical Archaeology, responded in a letter to the editor that McGuire's experience only reflected "one of the worst habits developed by many research professionals and a primary reason for the difficulty in funding archaeological research in the United States. If we archaeologists," he went on, "could pay for our own work, and if it were only important to archaeologists, we could be as obtuse as we like, but we do not have that luxury. Like it or not we are in the public education business" (Hocker 1996: 12). It goes without saying that in these days of diminishing federal funds for archaeology, the public's understanding of the mission of archaeology is essential if the discipline is to survive. A classics professor colleague who made an on-camera appearance in the Time-Life Lost Civilizations series on NBC warns that those who prefer to be consigned to antiquarian isolation will wake up one day to find that Greece and Rome have really become lost civilizations.

So how do you get into the public education business? Neil Asher Silberman, author and contributing editor to *Archaeology,* has observed that the best archaeologists are invariably the most skillful storytellers and that effective presentation and compelling ideas go hand in hand. Most archaeologists, however, are not trained to be good storytellers. In fact, they are trained to be bad storytellers, which is why so many manuscripts arrive at our office bone dry and bloodless, if they arrive at all. About 50 percent of all our assigned stories never get written. With due respect to the exigencies of the profession and the need to compete and advance in the academic world, I firmly believe that the storyteller in you deserves more of your time. You are witnesses, in one way or another, to the history of humanity. The public, believe it or not, is interested in knowing what you have learned about such things. A group of subscribers, gathered recently to answer editors' questions about what they liked and disliked in the magazine, agreed that above all else they wanted information—lots of it. "I don't even care if it's well written," said one subscriber.

Anchored in sound scholarship, your stories will command reader attention to the extent that they both inform and entertain. I do not agree with our focus group subscriber that even a poorly written article will sustain the interest of our average reader. To be effective, these pieces must have style and spirit. Here are some tips.

1. Acquaint yourself with the range of stories we publish. We run profiles, adventure tales, reports of major and minor discoveries, stories about the politics and ethics of archaeology, new technologies, news briefs on just about every topic, rambling letters from far-flung excavators, and amusing commentaries.

2. Don't presuppose that your material will not be interesting; we have published riveting reports on fish bone conferences, not to mention Elvis Presley's cultic legacy and the making of Sumerian beer.

3. Keep in mind our willingness to help you build up your story. Often the vital elements in the pieces we publish are not in the first draft, and we work with an author to smoke out the good stuff. We don't expect you to be professional writers; that is what we are supposed to be good at.

Some years back I learned of the work of a Belgian archaeologist teaching in Canada. She had helped harvest scores of mint-condition icons from the wreck of a seventeenth-century Russian warship on the floor of the Mediterranean Sea off the coast of France. We wanted her text and photographs for a cover story that would appear during the Christmas season. A draft in English arrived two days before the last possible deadline. Naturally, since the woman was not at all comfortable with the English language and had never tried to write anything for the popular press, the piece was unpublishable in the form in which we received it. Altering the form—that is, getting the piece rewritten in the shortest possible time— became a matter of some urgency. I arranged for her to be interviewed by phone. Richard Wertime, a published author and for fifteen years the magazine's chief manuscript doctor, spent four hours culling critical information not contained in her written version. With those data, he was able to rewrite the piece, fax it to Canada for the author's further emendations, have it vetted by a scholar familiar with her work, and get it back to me in time to make the print run. I am happy to add that the author was delighted with the result.

4. Keep it personal without being egocentric. Readers are interested in you and your role in the story that is unfolding; they should be led through your material in a way that creates for them the same sense of awe that you have felt about your work. During my first year as editor, we published an article on a spectacular intact cache of flutes and ocarinas found in a Maya tomb. The article was flat and impersonal. Rather late in the editing process, I asked the author how he had felt when he discovered the instruments. "I was very excited," he exclaimed. "These were flutes that hadn't been played for a thousand years." I urged him to put the personal stuff into the article, which he finally did, but not before reminding me that academics are taught to avoid injecting themselves into their reports.

I used to work for *Life* magazine, which had dozens of correspondents throughout the United States and abroad. I ran bureaus in Moscow and Vienna. Today I like to think of all archaeologists as domestic and foreign correspondents for *Archaeology* magazine. Don't e-mail the *New York Times* from your prehistoric caves and mountaintop shrines; e-mail us (Peter@Archaeology.org). We too stand ready to publish your reports quickly and accurately.

Unfortunately, we have lost some wonderful stories because of a scholar's lack of interest in reaching out to the public. Some of these stories would have gone a long way toward clarifying the importance of archaeology in today's world. I am reminded of one from western Tanzania, where archaeologists had succeeded in replicating iron-smelting furnaces—a long-lost technology, the details of which only two local village men in their nineties could remember. With their help, archaeologists succeeded in building such a furnace, proving important points about the metallurgical history of Africa. What made this pioneering ethnographic story most compelling to me were the reactions of the local tribespeople, who rediscovered in the iron-making process the meaning of some images in their poetry and folklore. Initially skeptical of the archaeologists in their midst, these people ended up hugging and kissing the visitors for returning to them a lost heritage. The story of the archaeology at this site recently appeared in *American Scientist*, a bimonthly magazine of the Scientific Research Society Sigma Xi. The human angle was noticeable for its absence.

I can report a more rewarding experience with a piece about ancient birth control, first published in book form by Harvard University Press (Riddle 1992), in whose hands it languished for lack of attention, then in a scholarly version in *American Scientist*. Even in academic dress, the story was irresistible. The idea that women in antiquity had developed clever ways of averting conception was an extraordinary piece of news, deserving of a far wider audience. A popular version in *Archaeology* (Riddle et al. 1994) resulted in a nice pickup from the *New York Times*, an avalanche of mail—supportive and otherwise—and invitations to author John M. Riddle to lecture on the subject from coast to coast. I am still getting mail about the piece years later.

If Riddle was amazed at all the attention he suddenly received, it only meant he had misjudged how good the story he had chosen to tell actually was. As Richard Wertime reminds us, "While the world admires—and willingly honors—academic brilliance, it truly reveres a storyteller" (1995).

References

Hocker, Fred. 1996. The excitement of discovery. Letter to the editor. *Archaeology* 49(1): 12.

McGuire, Randall. 1995. The Dreaded Question. *Archaeology* 48(6): 96.

Riddle, John M. 1992. *Contraception and Abortion from the Ancient World to the Renaissance*. Cambridge: Harvard University Press.

Riddle, John M., J. Worth Estes, and Josiah C. Russell. 1994. Ever Since Eve . . . Birth Control in the Ancient World. *Archaeology* 47(2): 29–31, 34–35.

Wertime, Richard A. 1995. The Boom in Volunteer Archaeology. *Archaeology* 48(1): 66–69, 71–73.

23

Reaching the Hidden Audience

Ten Rules for the Archaeological Writer

Mitch Allen

Archaeology is different. As archaeologists, we all know that. And the differences go beyond our bizarre habit of digging holes in the ground under inhospitable conditions, spending countless months in laboratories carefully dissecting ancient coprolites, or torturing each other with technically impenetrable analyses of our current field projects at professional meetings.

In this case, the difference has to do with our relationship to an interested public made up of people who do not have our professional credentials but share our passion, commitment, and often expertise in the subject. Consider these questions:

- What other field has such an intensive level of lay participation in the production of specialized professional knowledge? The volunteer labor that fuels most archaeological projects is almost unique in the world of scholarship. Imagine political scientists hiring people off the street to conduct polling on political attitudes or astronomers using retired teachers to examine deep space.
- What other field has similarly significant lay interest in recent scholarly and professional developments worldwide? The general public does not read the latest interpretation of Piers Plowman or homoerotic deconstructions of *Apocalypse Now*. But they do follow in large numbers the latest reports of recent archaeological fieldwork.

• What other field harbors so many quacks producing fantastic theories that get general attention? Where else would a Piltdown scandal, Chariot of the Gods, or Kon Tiki hypothesis generate blaring newspaper headlines?

A consequence of these unique circumstances is that there is extensive and genuine popular interest in what archaeologists write. The audience for our work is larger than the few colleagues and their advanced students who want to know what we have found and what we make of it. Unlike the econometrician's models or the chemist's formulas, our work is supposed to be transparent: we are asked not to hide behind the technology and jargon of our specialized field but to make our evidence and our conclusions available to a much wider public. This has enormous implications as regards to whom we address what we write, how we write it, and how we distribute what we write. I will try to describe this public audience and offer ten simple suggestions to help improve archaeological writing intended for lay readers.

Who Are Our Readers?

We think we know how to communicate with our colleagues and our students. But who are the people in the lay audience who read our work?

The general reading public forms the vast bulk of those casually interested in archaeological information. Nine million readers (or page turners) of *National Geographic* are regularly bombarded with archaeological topics, a product of the fact that the National Geographic Society is one of the key supporters of archaeological fieldwork. Millions more are titillated by pseudo-archaeological reports of demon mummies and buried spaceships in the pages of the *Enquirer* or the *Star*. For a smaller but more serious segment of the general reading public, people's curiosity about the past is massaged by a steady flow of coffee table books about the mysterious Maya or the Dead Sea Scrolls or through programming on cable television channels.[1]

In addition to this broad constituency of marginally interested readers, there is a yet smaller, committed core of archaeological readers. Members of this hidden audience for archaeology read much more seriously than the general public and follow archaeological debates and issues much as their children follow the fortunes of the local baseball team or TV superheroes. How do we characterize these people?

First, we can say that they are organized. Many belong to one of the almost 100 local chapters of the Archaeological Institute of America (AIA).[2] Others comprise the avocational component of the state, urban, regional, or provincial archaeological societies that exist throughout North America.[3] An enormous number can be identified as subscribers to archaeological magazines, as volunteers on archaeological projects, or as members of local museums. Unlike the general public, who might read casually on archaeological topics, these people *affiliate* with archaeology.

Second, they are numerous. While there is no scientific count available, we can look to popular magazines about archaeology for the dimensions of this audience. *Archaeology* magazine, the main publication for archaeological readers, boasts more than 200,000 subscribers. Its most recent readership survey (June 2000) suggests that 600,000 people actually read each issue of the magazine. Less than 2 percent of this readership is made up of professional archaeologists. Its Near Eastern archaeology counterpart, *Biblical Archaeology Review* (BAR), has an equally large subscription base.[4] Newcomer *Scientific American Discovering Archaeology* garnered 60,000 subscribers in its first year. The several hundred local archaeological societies and AIA chapters can collectively claim combined membership in the tens of thousands. Using a rough estimate of 10,000 professional archaeologists in North America, the serious lay audience outnumbers professionals by at least fifty to one.[5]

Finally, from the standpoint of an academic author or publisher, members of the hidden audience are important because they spend money. Readership surveys of *Archaeology* magazine indicate that they are richer, better educated, more well-read, and more likely to have disposable income than the average American. BAR demographics are similar. While not all of this spending was on archaeology books, readers of both periodicals are regular purchasers and readers of books on the subject. Some other characteristics of these readers are included in table 23.1.

This audience in the hundreds of thousands offers a unique opportunity for archaeological writers to address a much wider public than is available to almost any other group of scholars. In an age of declining resources, challenges to the legitimacy of the historical enterprise, and uncertainty about public policies related to excavation, preservation, and conservation, it could not hurt to have more than half a million people on your side— and not merely to make sure your books sell well.

Table 23.1. Some characteristics of readers of *Archaeology* magazine

---

- Median household income is $70,000.
- Most heavily concentrated in northeastern and western states.
- 37 percent have a postgraduate degree.
- 58 percent work in professional/managerial jobs.
- Approximately equally divided between men and women.
- 90 percent read books as a leisure activity.
- Subscribership has increased from approximately 115,000 in 1989
  to 217,000 today.
- Twice as many computer owners and software purchasers as the U.S. average.
- 91 percent read the last four issues received and 62 percent saved them.

Writing for the Hidden Audience

Knowing that this audience exists requires some changes in the way archaeologists communicate in print. In most of our professional work, we write for our "worst nightmare critic," the one scholar (real or imagined) who will take our ideas and dismantle them sentence by sentence before our assembled colleagues. The worst nightmare critic is the person for whom we write so obscurely, tentatively, and defensively, so as to offer this monster as little ammunition as possible for dismembering our fragile ideas. For the sake of mollifying this one person—who will not be denied vituperation, no matter how cleverly we arrange our language—we tend to shut out the rest of the world. Why not ignore this person completely and focus our attention on the larger audience wanting to hear what we have to say?

What I suggest here are ten simple modifications in the way we write—ten changes that will help us include the hidden audience as part of our reading public while not sacrificing either the complexity of our ideas or the necessary ambiguity of our research findings (table 23.2). These changes apply equally to regional syntheses, site reports, cultural resource management reports, and theoretical treatises. Unlike many of the ideas proposed in this volume, the ten changes I suggest are not difficult. They can be implemented by the average archaeological writer the very next time the Mac or PC is fired up. But they will make all the difference to the serious avocational reader.

Table 23.2. Rules from AltaMira Press for archaeological writers

1. Find a hook!
2. Tell a story.
3. Include yourself.
4. Write in plain English (or Spanish or Hopi).
5. Talk to a single reader.
6. Create memorable identifiers.
7. Use only the data you need.
8. Present data visually.
9. Emphasize theory and method.
10. Always think of your audience.

1. *Find a hook!* Tell your reader what is important about your finds *before* offering the gory details. Most scholarly writing is done in the reverse way: first comes the literature review, then follow the research design, findings, and discussion, and only at the end does one learn the conclusions and their implications. For nonprofessional readers (and probably professional ones as well), it makes more sense to start with the highlights to give the reader incentive to keep reading.

2. *Tell a story.* The fact that most people organize their understanding of the world through narrative has only recently been rediscovered in the social sciences (Riessmann 1993). Whether they be horror stories told around campfires or theoretical treatises written in ivory towers, we all want to be led through engaging tales. Archaeological work fits this storytelling mode nicely. Many off-the-shelf literary conventions used by master storytellers are available to the archaeological writer—the quest, solving the mystery, the puzzling paradox, the mundane object that leads to a larger truth. Use these techniques; they work. The master of this technique is evolutionary biologist Stephen J. Gould, who uses the extinction of the .400 baseball hitter to explain to the lay reader the evolutionary pattern of marine invertebrates and quotes baseball manager Casey Stengel on why we cannot see extraterrestrials (Gould 1985).

3. *Include yourself.* Another recent discovery in social science writing is that the researcher need not be absent from the tale for the narrative to be valid (Ellis and Flaherty 1992). Include yourself in the story. Be uncertain, be perplexed, be *human.* Use the vertical pronoun. Say "We don't know." The character of the archaeologist as the Great Wizard of Oz, impressively exuding smoke and lightning while manipulating his kingdom, is a feature

of past narratives, not the player in today's archaeological writing. Honest, engaged dialogue is far more compelling than an omnipotent wizard's tricks.

4. *Write in plain English* (or Spanish or Hopi). Use of simple, active language without jargon makes reading more of a pleasure and less of a chore—not just for the lay public but for your colleagues as well. Use examples from research or from the everyday world to explain your points. Writing in the passive voice will not improve the quality of the writing, nor does it endear you to readers.

5. *Talk to a single reader.* To find the right level for your writing, imagine a specific person whom you know, part of this hidden audience, and write for him or her. Provide the contextual background this person would need to follow your argument. Use language you would use with this person. If the written word is viewed as a conversation between you and your readers, it is easier to find the right tone when you have a specific listener in mind.

6. *Create memorable identifiers.* The proper *bon mot* has often made the difference between a convincing argument and a forgotten one. It is hard for the reader to embrace the designation "Mycenean IIIC1b pottery" people. While it may not be as precise historically, calling these people the "Philistines" will certainly resonate better with your audience. Look for typesites, geographic names, other cultural names more popularly known, or even a memorable neologism to describe your sites, cultures, or classes of artifacts. Certainly try to avoid computer-babble such as AGRISYS or PRECLASC; these work well as labels for your computer runs but not for general reading.

7. *Use only the data you need.* A book is not a trash can in which to dump all of your field notes. Take heed from other social sciences—sociologists, psychologists, and political scientists do not include their raw survey responses in their books. They present relevant research highlights with summaries and analyses. Leave the bulk of the data for journal articles or for your website, or keep it on a disk to send to the few colleagues who actually want the whole story. Focus on the analysis, the synthesis, providing in the general volume only the data you need to support your arguments. With the increasing availability of online data sources, alternatives are becoming ever more readily available for the reader who truly needs more.

8. *Present data visually.* Good graphics make a difference in archaeological writing. A table is not as easily readable as a chart or graph. A de-

scription works better with a photograph. A good orienting map is worth its weight in gold. Lists can be scanned more readily than can a long paragraph. Make sure your reader has the visual context to understand your arguments. After all, archaeologists study material objects, and that materiality is what grounds our work for the average reader.

9. *Emphasize theory and method.* The difference between you and Erik Von Daniken is the use of well-argued theories developed from sound field and analytic methods. As a professional archaeologist you need to teach the reader how archaeological theories and methods differ from crackpot ideas. While explaining basic philosophy of science and research methodology in every publication may seem redundant, it does serve to distinguish your work from the sensational pyramid-power book the reader can find in the local bookstore. You cannot emphasize too often the difference between what the professional archaeologist does and what others who appropriate the term *archaeology* do.

10. *Always think of your audience.* If there is no reader, why write the book? Take the single reader you have identified as a sympathetic, interested supporter of your ideas and imagine that person multiplied into many. Imagine the new avenues of communication we open up when we decide to write for the large number of people who want to hear our ideas, who will buy our books, support our fieldwork, even write to their elected representatives on cultural resource issues. It almost seems worth a little extra effort, doesn't it?

The Publisher's Role

Publishers also have an important role in this outreach to the hidden audience for archaeology. We need to find good writers and encourage their work. We need to break the traditional boundaries that separate the popular trade publisher, the textbook house, and the specialized professional and scholarly publisher (not one of the three is geared toward servicing this audience) and find ways into the intermediate niche where the hidden audience lies. We need to work with new media and other ways of presenting archaeological information such that the medium and the message match more closely than at present. Then we need to package the information better and reach out aggressively to potential audiences, telling them we have something of interest to them.

All this means taking risks, but the alternative—ignoring the great majority of those who support our work—is even riskier.

Notes

1. On several archaeological electronic bulletin boards (such as <http://web. idirect.com/~atrium/>), David Meadows offers a weekly list of archaeological (and sometimes pseudo-archaeological) shows on cable channels. The average week's menu includes half a dozen different programs, about ten hours of weekly programming in all.

2. While the Archaeological Institute of America lists ninety-three local chapters, it does not have separate membership records on these chapters, nor does it keep records on what percentage of its national membership is professional and what percentage is avocational.

3. Data on these societies are difficult to obtain. An annual e-mail Directory of Archaeological Societies and Journals, <http://archaeology.about.com/blsmokedir. htm>, compiled by Michael A. Pfeiffer of the U.S. Forest Service from a variety of other sources lists over a hundred archaeological societies in almost all U.S. states and Canadian provinces at the regional, state or province, county, or city level. A spot check of several of these organizations indicated that they rarely know their percentage of avocational archaeologists, as opposed to academic, student, CRM, or government members.

4. Information provided by *Archaeology* magazine is based upon its Audit Bureau of Circulation statement of June 30, 2000, and upon a 2000 subscriber study by MediaMark Research; it is included here with permission of *Archaeology* magazine.

5. Combined membership in the major professional societies such as the Society for American Archaeology, Archaeological Institute of America, American Schools for Oriental Research, Society for Historical Archaeology, and American Anthropological Association Archaeology Division totals about 20,000. When one eliminates individuals who belong to more than one of these organizations and the lay membership, the total number of professionals is about 10,000.

References

Ellis, C., and M. G. Flaherty (eds.). 1992. *Investigating Subjectivity.* Thousand Oaks, Calif.: Sage.

Gould, S. J. 1985. *The Flamingo's Smile: Reflections in Natural History.* New York: W. W. Norton.

Riessmann, C. K. 1993. *Narrative Analysis.* Thousand Oaks, Calif.: Sage.

Epilogue

Brian M. Fagan

Upon the eyes of Odysseus there fell a sleep, gentle, the sweetest kind of sleep with no awakening, most like death; while the ship, as in a field four stallions drawing a chariot all break together at the stroke of the whiplash, and lifting high their feet lightly beat out their path, so the stern of this ship would lift and the creaming wave behind her boiled amain in the thunderous crash of the sea.

Lattimore 1965: 200

Long ago there were no stars, no moon, no sun. There was only darkness and water. A raft floated on the water, and on the raft sat a turtle. Then from the sky, a spirit came down and sat on the raft. . . . He took earth and mixed it with water and made two figures, a man and a woman . . . and by and by then were many people on the earth.

Garbarino 1976: 166

To those who crossed the Bering Strait for the first time, the trek into eastern Beringia would have seemed like nothing more than the opening up of another foraging territory. We know now it was a watershed in human development, a moment to pause and wonder at humanity's startling ability to adapt to the extremes of life on planet earth. *Homo sapiens sapiens* had come to the frontiers of a new continent. Soon they were to wander into the heart of the Americas and explode into a new chapter of human history.

Fagan 1987: 133–34

Come, let me tell you a tale—a tale of the remote past, of the very beginnings of humankind, ourselves. I have quoted from three tales of the past—first from Homer's *Odyssey;* second from a Maidu Indian account of the creation, from California; and third from an archaeological story I once spun about the first Americans. Only one of these three tales is the product of western science, yet all represent different and legitimate perceptions of the past.

We may not think so, for we are archaeologists, scholars and scientists, experts at archaeological survey, remote sensing, excavation, and analysis of artifacts and food remains. All too often, we are stuck in our own metaphor of the past as a reality. We have often forgotten that all cultures do not organize the world, or the past, in the same way. By denying alternative perspectives on the past, we deny the very human diversity that we study.

As archaeologists, we consider our discipline one of the greatest scientific triumphs of the past century. Contemplate for a moment some of the great discoveries of the past hundred years: the Minoan civilization of Crete, the tomb of Tutankhamun, the royal tombs at Ur, *Zinjanthropus*, *Homo habilis*, and the Ice Man; the Maya Lord Pacal, the Lords of Sipán, Head-Smashed-In, and the Basque Whalers of Red Bay. Each of these discoveries, and thousands of others, have filled in the vast blanks of 2.5 million years of the human past. They give us unique insights into the growing diversity of humanity since the earliest times. We consider archaeology alone among all sciences in its ability to chronicle changes in human society over immensely long periods of time—and to reconstruct the lives of the anonymous and nonliterate of the past.

But, for all our theoretical formulations and elaborate typologies, our fine-grained science, in the final analysis we are sophisticated storytellers. Whether we like it or not, we are performers on a public stage, in the full glare of an approving—and often disapproving—audience. Finally, after more than a century of science, we have come to realize that ours is not the only story of the past to be told. And we have begun to realize that to be a storyteller is not to be the wise person who speaks from wisdom. Our job, ultimately, is to create an atmosphere in which the wisdom inherent in the world becomes apparent. This realization gives us much food for thought.

After years of busily and successfully turning archaeology into a highly specialized academic discipline, we have reached a moment when many people are questioning the faith and asking deeply unsettling questions. A public beset with tax-cutting fervor asks: Why is archaeology important? Many Native Americans and other groups ask: What right do scientific archaeologists have to impose their version of the past on the world, while ignoring traditional histories and other perspectives on ancient times?

And we archaeologists ask disturbing questions, too. Is there a future for archaeology when the archaeological record is vanishing on every side?

Can we save the past for future generations to study, respect, and enjoy? How does archaeology as an academic discipline and an emerging profession need to change for the twenty-first-century world? Who is going to spearhead this change, developing the new training programs and academic curricula needed for the future?

And students might ask: Are there viable careers to be forged in archaeology? Is it worth spending between five and seven years acquiring a doctoral degree and then being effectively unemployable at the end of it all?

For all our triumphs and remarkable scientific achievements, we are apprehensive, pessimistic about the future. We will feel better if we think of our present confusion and self-doubt as a cycle in the unfolding history of archaeology. One of the many advantages of being what is sometimes euphemistically called a "senior archaeologist" is that one has lived through such pessimistic cycles before—and seen us emerge on the other side. We endured one when the Young Turks of the 1960s trumpeted the New Archaeology like the Divine Right of Kings. We went through another in the 1980s when the post-processualists took us into a theoretical tailspin on which we are only now acquiring some perspective. And now we are in an even more complex world, where we sense that we have failed at many of our most basic trusts—where, as a colleague recently remarked to me, we live in an archaeological world where lawyers and compliance specialists sit at our right hand.

Today's archaeology requires new skills, new sensitivities for communicating effectively with the wider audience; for working closely and sensitively with Native Americans and other nonwestern societies; and for changing academically to accommodate a different archaeological world. The symptom: dozens of North Americanists, Mayanists, and Classicists, to mention only a few specialties, are on the streets with no prospects of ever finding a job in academic archaeology. A pervasive sense of failure is abroad, which is largely unfounded.

Yes, we have failed to some degree, because of the academic climate of the past quarter century, because of our own arrogance, and also because communicating with the public and working across cultures have not been fashionable issues in the archaeological world. The "publish or perish" culture still drives most academic debate. But this is no cause for uncritical, helpless pessimism, for concern that archaeology and its finite database will vanish entirely, or that we do not have important contributions to make to the understanding of the human past.

For a start, let us be proud of the remarkable achievements of twentieth-century archaeology, which, like all academic disciplines, is a product of its times. We have nothing to be ashamed of; quite the contrary. The mistakes we have made are not fatal, nor are they errors of ill will. They rarely reflect deliberate racism but are mistakes of undue conservatism, arrogance, and scholarly myopia; of a lack of sensitivity and a provincial tendency toward studying what the great humorist P. G. Wodehouse (1929: 14) called "a mere hole in the ground, which of all sights is perhaps the least vivid and dramatic, but is enough to grip [our] attention for hours at a time."

One of these emerging achievements is the burgeoning over the past quarter century of what is loosely called public archaeology. One cannot easily define public archaeology, nor is it desirable to do so. The word *public* covers a multitude of important activities, as the essays in this volume eloquently point out—everything from writing for popular audiences to developing lesson plans for public schools and working with the provisions of Native American Graves Protection and Repatriation Act. What began as tentative experiment a generation ago has become part of the mainstream of archaeology, even if many academic archaeologists are still wrapped in the specialist time warps of the ivory tower.

Archaeology, like astronomy, is somewhat distinctive among academic disciplines in that it engages the public and feeds an unending fascination with the past—with ancient Egyptian mummies, Maya scripts, and a host of other engaging topics. On the whole, we satisfy this fascination well, with television programs, books, popular magazine articles, and radio series. Of course more can be done, but the public is much more aware of archaeological discoveries today than was the case a quarter century ago.

Fortunately, public archaeology has moved far beyond this particular popular arena into more fundamental missions, of which combating looting and destruction and working with Native American communities are but two. Just as important, public archaeologists are grappling with potentially contentious issues that will take years to resolve and that are as challenging as, if not more challenging than, the most arcane basic research.

Some of our most vigorous and urgent debates surround the telling of tales about the past and revolve around a fundamental question: Who controls and owns the past? The issue of ownership and control of the past received surprisingly little attention in archaeological circles until the emergence of post-processualism in the 1980s. Since then, more arrant and often sophomoric nonsense has been written on these topics than about almost anything else in archaeology, except perhaps the curse of the pharaohs. But one important point has come to the forefront: archaeologists are not the only people with a tale to tell, with a legitimate take on history to share with the world. Science is not omnipotent and exclusive. In truth, we *all* own and control the past, whether Australian Aborigine or Western European, Native American or Maasai from East Africa.

Thus, it follows that we all have different perceptions of the past, diverse cultural values, and highly varied expectations of the lessons that can be learned from the past. But, again whether we like it or not, the past is part of our common cultural heritage, wherever we live and whatever historical, political, and social agendas we may espouse. All of us tell stories about the human universe. Such tales help us understand what is going on within ourselves. The past is one of many tools for doing this. One of public archaeology's most important tasks is to foster tolerance and understanding of diverse cultures, diverse pasts.

We archaeologists have said this for years—but now, in a much more interconnected world, we are face to face with people as never before. Pseudo-archaeologists and others tell us our research is irrelevant, sometimes insulting, and a waste of time and money. This is nonsense. We have not sinned by doing irrelevant work. Nor is archaeology a waste of money. Nor have we erred if we refuse to espouse the ideology of Afrocentrism, the idea that Native Americans never crossed the Bering Strait, or the Christian dogma that holds chapter 1 of *Genesis* to be literal historical truth. Our sin is to have been culturally insensitive occasionally, to have been myopic about the past, and to have acted as if it *is* our exclusive property. Of course it is not, and nor is it anyone else's, even if they claim it is. Nor are archaeologists mere informants on the sidelines of history. Our expertise, like that of the historians of the Fourth World, is vital to the collective enterprise.

This book results from a conference where there were lengthy exchanges about the future of public archaeology. The chapters reflect diverse takes on archaeology and the wider audience, the public benefits of doing archaeology, and the many publics that are our constituency. There are case studies on everything from modern garbage to the problems of recreational divers and working with shipwrecks. Diverse authorities explore all manner of topics from archaeological storytelling to broad interpretations of the past at Harpers Ferry. Public archaeology offers a wonderful opportunity for creating a more diverse and sympathetic view of the human past and extraordinary chances for archaeologists to work closely with other cultures, other societies. As the case studies in this book show, we have already embarked on this challenge.

But are we ready to embrace the challenge on a much larger scale? With bewildering speed, we have entered an era when it is no longer sufficient for an archaeologist to be trained in purely academic and fieldwork skills. Now we need to retool professional archaeological training to reflect an exciting and open-ended public archaeology. Incredible though it may seem, almost no archaeology graduate programs offer training in Native American history or culture as an integrated part of their curricula. Nor do more than a handful offer both academic and professional training in archaeology. We are woefully unprepared for the challenges of an entirely new kind of archaeology. Consider the realities: archaeology is now a profession, albeit with a strong academic component. (We must never ignore research, for this is what provides the data, the vitality, new theoretical insights, and interpretations: the foundations of our enterprise.) Furthermore, future expansion in archaeology will be almost entirely in the professional sector, much of it in the private sector. Within a generation, some of these companies show signs of becoming crucibles for innovative archaeological research and theoretical insights.

The academic culture is becoming increasingly irrelevant to much of what contemporary archaeologists do. Yet we persist in training predominantly academic archaeologists. Putting it bluntly, there are too many highly specialized Ph.D. holders, Yet we persist in turning out more and more. Am I alone in arguing for some Ph.D. population control? Should we be developing alternative degree qualifications, testing and evaluating new graduate curricula that reflect the real world of archaeology outside academia? Should we be developing professional schools, as in the environmental sciences, for example? Such schools bring together the academic and outside worlds in rigorous cooperation, training the leaders of the future. Should we train archaeologists in communication skills, conservation, legal issues, heritage management, and such career tracks? We have hardly begun considering these issues, let alone implementing change.

I see little sign that the academic world of archaeology, where we were or are being trained, is grappling with these issues. Some scholars go so far as to say that it is not their business, a perspective that renders me speechless. And often, arrogantly and wrongly, the traditionally minded label communicating with the public as "mere journalism." How myopic! How old-fashioned! It is everyone's job if archaeology is to survive and flourish. Make no mistake, if we do not make specific changes soon, others will take over management of the past on our behalf. In some places they are already doing so. The issue of overexposure of archaeological sites to thousands of visitors receives little attention in the mainstream academic literature. I was told recently by someone who should know better that publishing about that kind of thing was "not original research." Nonsense! The publish-or-perish culture, our current training structure, and our myopic archaeological values are major obstacles for the archaeology of the future.

All these issues come under the general rubric of public archaeology, which has become the archaeological flavor of the day. But this burgeoning aspect of archaeology is far more than a passing fad. We are at a profound and difficult moment of truth for archaeology everywhere. Can we move beyond the increasingly burdensome shackles of an academic discipline to become a truly public archaeology, with close ties to other cultures and a wider audience, to society as a whole? The answer must be yes.

In these uncertain times, with archaeology under siege, I wonder if we have forgotten that the past can be an inspiration and is for all of us to enjoy. Perhaps I am an idealist, but thank goodness I am, for I am optimistic about a future in which we will be comfortable enjoying innovative multidisciplinary research and the rich tapestry of other cultures, other pasts. The past is such a wonderful gift for all humanity. When I get depressed, I always remember the joyful things the ancient ones left behind them.

Remember the fierce joy with which the Greek smith god Hephaistos made Achilles' shield, in the *Odyssey*: "And the crippled Smith brought all his art to bear on a dancing circle, broad as the circle Daedalus once laid out on Cnossos' spacious fields. ... Here young boys and girls, beauties courted with costly gifts of oxen, danced and danced, linking their arms, gripping each others' wrists. ... And now they would run in rings on their skilled feet, nimbly, quick as a crouching potter spins his wheel, palming it smoothly, giving it practice twirls to see it run, and now they would run in rows, in rows crisscrossing rows—rapturous dancing" (Fagles 1996: 487). Such joy, such vivid evocation of the past. Let us never forget that the past is for us to enjoy.

Thank goodness I am an archaeologist! Thank goodness I am an archaeologist at this point in time when there are so many challenges, and there is so much about the past to enjoy. Public archaeology in all its various modes reminds us just how much we have to share with the wider world, with humanity.

References

Fagan, B. M. 1987. *The Great Journey.* London: Thames and Hudson.
Fagles, R. 1996. *Homer: The Odyssey.* New York: Viking.
Garbarino, M. S. 1976. *Native American Heritage.* Boston: Little, Brown.
Lattimore, R. 1965. *The Odyssey of Homer.* New York: Harper and Row.
Wodehouse, P. G. 1929. *A Damsel in Distress.* London: Michael Joseph.

Contributors

Mitch Allen is an archaeologist and founder and publisher of AltaMira Press, a division of Rowman and Littlefield Publishers.

S. Terry Childs is an archaeologist with the National Park Service Archeology and Ethnography Program.

Thomas A. J. Crist is the director of archaeological services for Kise Straw and Kolodner and forensic anthropologist for the Philadelphia Medical Examiner's Office.

John E. Ehrenhard is the chief of the Southeast Archeological Center, National Park Service.

Brian M. Fagan is a professor of anthropology at the University of California, Santa Barbara.

Terry Goddard is a former four-term mayor of Phoenix, Arizona.

Lynn Harris is an underwater archaeologist and manager of the Charleston Field Office of the South Carolina Institute of Archaeology and Anthropology, University of South Carolina.

Kevin T. Jones is the Utah state archaeologist.

Roger G. Kennedy is the former director of the National Park Service.

Leigh Kuwanwisiwma is the Hopi tribal preservation officer.

William D. Lipe is a professor of anthropology at Washington State University and is a research associate and member of the board of directors of the Crow Canyon Archaeological Center.

Barbara J. Little is an archaeologist with the National Park Service Archeology and Ethnography Program.

Julia E. Maurer Longstreth is the former assistant editor of *ZiNj* magazine.

Francis P. McManamon is the departmental consulting archaeologist for the U.S. Department of Interior and manager of the National Park Service Archeology and Ethnography Program.

Fay Metcalf is an education consultant.

Jeanne M. Moe is an archaeologist with the Bureau of Land Management.

Adrian Praetzellis is an associate professor of anthropology at Sonoma State University, California.

Mary Grzeskowiak Ragins is the former historic preservation planner (1992–2000) for the City of Santa Fe.

W. L. Rathje is professor emeritus and director of the Garbage Project at the University of Arizona and research professor at the Stanford Archaeology Center.

Paul A. Shackel is an associate professor of anthropology, University of Maryland at College Park, and director of the Center for Heritage Resource Studies.

Carol D. Shull is the keeper of the National Register of Historic Places and chief of the National Landmarks Program for the National Park Service.

Katherine Slick is president of Slick and Associates.

George S. Smith is chief of the Investigation and Evaluation Section, Southeast Archeological Center, National Park Service.

David Hurst Thomas is the curator of anthropology at the American Museum of Natural History, New York City.

Esther C. White is the director of archaeology for the Mount Vernon Ladies Association.

James P. Whittenburg is an associate professor of history at the College of
William and Mary, Williamsburg, Virginia.

Peter A. Young is the editor in chief of *Archaeology* magazine.

Index

Page references in *italics* indicate a figure or table.

ology in modern education, 179; protecting archaeological resources, 176, 177; Public Education Committee of SAA, 179; recognizing significance of ordinary objects, 177; student response, 181–82, 182; understanding diversity, 179

Protecting the past to benefit the public: Antiquities Act (1906), 122, 124; Archaeological Resources Protection Act of 1979, 124; *Archaeology* magazine, 126; cultural differences in perceptions of the past, 122; *Destruction of America's Archaeological Heritage, The: Looting and Vandalism of Indian Archaeological Sites in the Four Corners States of the Southwest* (U.S. House of Representatives), 126; diverse public interest, 123–28; historical background, 123–24; Inuit, 122; Jefferson, Thomas, 123–24; laws and legislation, 124; library of Alexandria, 121; National Archaeological Program, 125; past in perspective, 122; private response, 126–28; professionals and non-professionals sharing information, 126; public and local interest and response, 124–26; public education and anti-looting measures, 125; "Save the Past for the Future," 126. *See also* Laws and legislation protecting historic and prehistoric archaeological resources

Psota, Sunshine, 54

Public archaeology, 23; and academic responsibilities, 255–59; background of, 147, 157–58; Public Archaeology in the United States Timeline website, 235; transition from esoteric to public involvement, 157–58

Public education: adapting archaeological findings for public education, 150; anti-looting measures, 125; antiquities legislation, 60, 61, 69; archaeological vandalism, 188; artifact collecting, 35, 60, 61, 66, 69, 125; combining research with, 71–72; diving communities and archaeological certification, 60, 61; eliminating ignorance about archaeology, 187–88; interfacing archaeology with education, 176–

84; Project Archaeology, 179–82, 182, 183, 183, 184; tourism and archaeology, 140, 149–50, 154–55, 215; true-crime mysteries, 107; visiting America's sacred sites, 140; ZiNj Education project, 187–92. *See also* Laws and legislation protecting historic and prehistoric archaeological resources

Public Education Committee of the Society for American Archaeology, 25

Pueblo Bonito, 48

Pueblo Grande City Park, 33

Pueblo of Acoma, 33

Putnum, F. W., 124

Ragins, Mary Grzeskowiak, 14

Ramos, M., 10

Rathje, William, 9, 190

Register of Professional Archaeologists, 126

Revere, Paul, myth of, 168

Rhode Island, 198

Richmond Hill, 64

Richneck, 80

Riddle, John M., 243

Riverine archaeology, 65, 66–68

Roanoke Island, 77

Rock art, 198, 214–15

Rolfe, John, 169

Ross, Betsy, myth of, 168

Rowlands, Michael, 8

Rubbish! 94

Ruddy, Drew, 66

Sacramento, California, 52–54, 57

Sagan, Carl, 131

San Antonio Mission, 174

Santa Anna, Antonio López de, 134

Santa Fe, archaeology in, 14; Archaeological Fund, 205; Archaeological Review Committee (ARC), 203, 204, 205; "Archaeology in Your Backyard," 206, 207; Archaic period site, 206; education outreach of development community, 203–4; effects of tourism, 206–7, 221, 222; Fort Marcy project, 205–6; Historic Design Review Board (HDRB), 202, 203; Historic Districts Ordinance, 202; Historic Down-